Fighting
for
Paradise

To Stu Rideaut,

We Travelled many of
these Trails Together!

Kurt Nelson

Fighting
for
Paradise

A Military History of the Pacific Northwest

Kurt R. Nelson

WESTHOLME
Yardley

Title Page: Paul Kane, *Chinook Indians in front of Mount Hood* c. 1851–56. (National Gallery of Canada, Ottawa. Photo © National Gallery of Canada.)

Westholme Publishing, LLC
Eight Harvey Avenue
Yardley, Pennsylvania 19067
Visit our Web site at www.westholmepublishing.com

First Edition
First Printing: May 2007
10 9 8 7 6 5 4 3 2 1

ISBN: 978-1-59416-045-5
ISBN 10: 1-59416-045-7

Printed in United States of America

*T*o five generations of women who have supported and sustained me, and to those who are still putting up with me,
thank you. I dedicate this book to Mary Mills, my wife Sandi, and my
daughter, Emily.

Contents

List of Maps

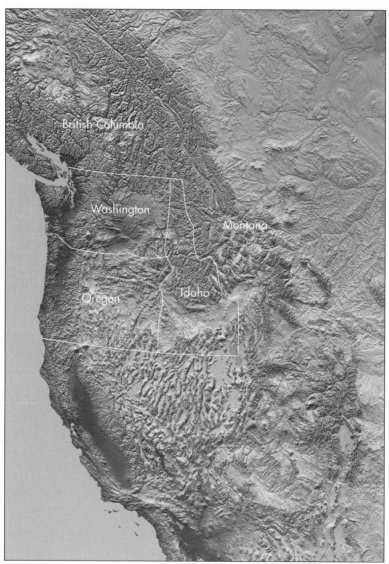

Oregon Country physical relief and present-day political boundaries. (JPL)

Introduction

When the topic of American military history arises and the discussion turns to battles on American soil, the first locations recalled are those of the Civil War. If further thought is given to the topic, perhaps American Revolution locales come to mind, and it is usually in the eastern half of our country where most Americans identify our military history. If directed to think of Indian battles, the collective thought moves west to Montana and the Battle of Little Big Horn, as well as other battles on the High Plains; and it is there where our reflections on the topic usually end.

Yet our collective thought should include the military history of the Oregon Country, a historical area encompassing more than 650,000 square miles over the present-day states of Washington, Oregon, Idaho, northern California, northwestern Wyoming, and western Montana and British Columbia in Canada. While most of the Pacific Northwest's battles were small scale, particularly when contrasted with epic engagements such as Gettysburg, the wars fought here were as real and the regional battles were just as important to nationbuilding. The Oregon Territory, carved out of Oregon Country in 1846, experienced total war in the 1850s, with nearly thirty percent of the white and American Indian populations directly engaged in periodic combat. As Western civilization overwhelmed the Pacific Northwest, the balance of both populations felt the effects of warfare and feared invasion and attack. The fate of many different peoples rested on many of the battles fought within the Oregon Country.

This book is not about the forces that created the wars, nor is this book a history of the injustice done to the American Indians. It is true many of the Indians who lived throughout the Oregon Country suffered great loss and poor treatment at the hands of the whites, but they too inflicted unjust acts on unsuspecting populations. Viewed by many Indians as invaders, the conflict with the settlers was inevitable. The whites were not willing to coexist with the native populations, and the pressure to eliminate the competition for the land was great. Equally true, is the fact that many of the Indian nations had a history of warfare that would have led to conflict with any large population moving into or through their homelands, white or American Indian.

The first U.S. Army fort was not intended as a permanent establishment. Fort Clatsop was constructed by Lewis and Clark's Corps of Discovery in 1805. It helped to establish the American claim to the Oregon Country.

The first real attempt at establishing a military base and settlement belongs to the Spanish. On May 29, 1792, the Spanish frigate *Princesa* anchored in Neah Bay at the northwestern tip of Washington state. They named the bay Bahía de Nuñez Gaona. There, they constructed a bakery, blacksmith's shop, and a fortification with six guns, among other structures. Their intention was to make Neah Bay a permanent Spanish colony. However, after discovering the limitations of the harbor, the Spanish gave up their efforts by the fall of 1792. Not until 1809 would the effort to establish a permanent settlement start.

What this book does is record the rich detail of the conflicts to seize the paradise of the Pacific Northwest. The first settlers were in the Oregon Country to exploit and to gain wealth from it. Fur was the source of new riches. It is often believed that it was almost mutually beneficial for the Indians and the traders to exist together, particularly under the rule of the British.

What is clear in examining the history is that the gain made was strictly by the Western powers encroaching on the American Indians; the British were often little better than the Americans in their treatment of the native populations.

When angered, the British lion roared with naval artillery and the complete obliteration of native populations. They never intended to establish large permanent populations. They were seen as less destructive because they were not creating permanent settlements and so there were fewer of them to interact with the Indians.

After the fur trade started to subside in the 1840s, war threatened as two nations, one great and one seeing the Manifest Destiny of its greatness, exerted their claims to paradise. The presidential election of 1844 resulted in Manifest Destiny having a rallying cry of "Fifty-four forty or fight!" It was nothing short of an American declaration to possess the entire paradise of the Oregon Country and extend itself as a great nation from one ocean to another. Both powers gathered their forces and threatened war. Fortunately, the tensions between the British and the Americans resulted in nothing more than militant posturing and a dead pig.

The Anglo-American Pig War was in stark contrast to the bloody conflicts between the white and American Indian population. This book also deals with that portion of the Oregon Country's history, with glory and shame on both sides.

If a roll call of famous Indian leaders were to be read, only one Indian from the Oregon Country might make the list: Chief Joseph of the Nez Perce. It is unfortunate that history has not recognized the leadership and vision of other Indians, such as Kamiakin of the Yakimas.[1] Equally true, if a list were made of great Indian battles, probably none would be listed from the Pacific Northwest. But the scale of Steptoe's battle was equal to that of Little Big Horn. Colonel George Wright's summer campaign of 1858 against the Spokane Indian coalition was grisly and destructive to Indian hopes. Only one American Army Indian fighter exceeded the success of Colonel Wright, George Crook, in his important defeat of the Apache in the 1870s–80s, yet his skills were forged in the crucible of the 1850s–60s Oregon Country Indian wars.

Finally, this book tells how the Pacific Northwest evolved militarily and the final battles fought in defense of Paradise. The history ends with a brief review of the Japanese attacks on the Pacific Northwest during World War II.

To understand the cultural conflict of white-American Indian wars, it helps to have a greater understanding of the Indians who lived in the Pacific Northwest. The perception of great tribes, such as the Sioux and Cheyenne, uniting to resist the western encroachment of whites does not hold for the Pacific Northwest. While we use the term "tribe" to

---

1. The tribe spells its name as Yakama. However, historically and geographically, the Indian nation's name is spelled with the "i," as in Yakima. In order to make it easier to find the geographic places associated with the tribe, the old spelling is used while acknowledging that the Indians prefer Yakama.

help organize and understand American Indians with similar languages, life styles, and beliefs, it does not accurately describe the Indians of the Pacific Northwest.

In the most general terms, starting on the Pacific Coast and moving east toward the Rocky Mountains, the social structure of the Indians became more complex. Often on the coast, the identifying social structure for the natives was the village. One village, despite sharing a common language with another nearby village, might be removed from much social interaction with their neighbors, and certainly feel that they shared little identity with the other community as a people.

Further east, the village gave way to a slightly larger social structure known as the band. The band might be in one village, or several nearby villages, often joined through extended family connections. However, more distant bands, although speaking the same language and with the same social beliefs, would not be of direct political or military concern.

It was in the arid reaches between the Cascades and the Rocky Mountains that the social structure was the most tribal. Although not reaching the social identity of the Plains, these people could be described as proto-tribal with varying degrees of tribal identity.

The failure of whites, particularly Americans, to comprehend these different cultures contributed to the difficulties between the two cultures. Because they wanted and needed someone to be an identifiable voice for the Indians, they often ascribed chief status on men of one band who, while speaking the same language, had no political or military influence on a nearby band or village. When the band, which had not signed any treaty, or even those of the band who had signed, but not understood what they had signed, transgressed against the whites, then all of the Indians of that language group might have been punished.

Indians are generally classified ethnologically by linguistic groups. Within the Oregon Country, fourteen language groups have been identified: Shastan, Takelman, Chinookan, Chimakuan, Wakashan, Yakonan, Weitspekan, Kalapuyan, Waiilatpuan, Shoshonian, Salishan, Lutuamin, Kitunahan, and Sahaptian. Of these, eight figure prominently in the history of Indian affairs of the Pacific Northwest. Shastan include tribes such as the Shastas of Northern California, and the Rogue River Indians, a catchall for a variety of tribes living in the greater Rogue River Basin.

The Cayuse are a tribe of the Waiilatpuan language group, which helps to explain how the Whitman Mission arrived at its Indian name.

Three language groups are very closely identified with one tribe: Chinookan with the Chinook Indians, Kalapuyan with the Kalapooia Indians, and Shoshoian with the Shoshonis. Each had other well known tribes using a language within the language group. For example, other tribes of the Shoshoian language group included the Bannock and Paiute Indian tribes.

Lutuamin was the language group of the Klamaths and Modoc Indians, which explains their close relationships. Sahaptian was the language group of such tribes as the Yakima, Umatilla, and Walla Walla—all allies and trade partners.

The language group with the greatest geographic distribution was the Salishan linguistic group. It had a range extending from the Kalispels and Flatheads in the far northeast part of the region, to Lummi and Nisqually Indians of Puget Sound. The range of similar languages often added to the confusion of whites, giving them a perception of greater harmony and cooperation between tribes than might actually exist.

Another feature of the natives of the Pacific Northwest was the impact of disease. The impact was felt, at least initially, again from the west to the east. As traders arrived, first on ships, they brought smallpox, measles, and venereal diseases. One source estimated the western regions of the Oregon Country as having more than 75,000 Indians in 1780, and fewer than 20,000 by 1830.[2]

The Hudson's Bay Company at Fort Vancouver reported malaria each summer in the early 1830s, probably introduced inadvertently by Hudson's Bay ships, which literally decimated the tribes of the Willamette Valley. Additional outbreaks of smallpox, measles, and tuberculosis ravaged the Indians who had not developed any immunity to Western diseases.[3] One epidemic directly contributed to the outbreak of the Cayuse Indian War.

2. L.M. Scott, "Indian Diseases as Aids to Pacific Northwest Settlements," *Oregon Historical Quarterly*, 1928.

3. The Hudson's Bay Fort Umpqua was attacked by Indians in the summer of 1840 as a result of a smallpox epidemic. The Umpqua Indians correctly blamed the European fur-trading posts as the source of their illness. Chief Trader Jean Baptiste Gagnier reported no loss to the fort's defenders, and an undetermined number of injured Indians.

W hile history can be interesting in itself, most histories are written with a goal in mind. What I have attempted to do is two-fold. First, I hope I provide an easy-to–read, one-volume history of the Pacific Northwest for those interested in military history. Second, and equally important, this book seeks through raised awareness to preserve some of the sites mentioned in the text before they are completely destroyed. The people of the Northwest, American Indian and immigrants alike, must preserve the numerous sites before they disappear to the pressures of development.

Each chapter closes with a brief second section which provides information for today's explorer to visit the sights where the events occurred, though very few have been preserved. Some have been reconstructed, while others have been at least noted with a road sign. Most have been lost.

The Oregon Country has a wealth of compelling military history for study. All sides—British, American, and American Indian—fought over the Oregon Country with the knowledge that they were fighting and dying for an earthly paradise. But what they really desired was not just to live within the greatness of the Pacific Northwest, but to secure paradise for their children. This is the story of the fight for paradise.

Chapter 1

Paradise Lost

Conflict in the Pacific Northwest Prior to the Arrival of Europeans

Paradise—Eden

American Indians of the Pacific Northwest believed that the land was a gift from the Great Spirit to his chosen people. Each tribe recognized itself as unique—the chosen people of the Great Spirit, whose blessing was seen through the abundance of everything needed for living in paradise.

Geographically distinct, Indian people viewed their paradise and its gifts differently. For those on the coast, the tidal waters supplied them with fish, crustaceans, and gifts from the Great Spirit, such as a whale washed ashore; from the lush forests came animals, berries, roots; and from select trees, clothing and magnificent cedar homes. Such abundance allowed coastal peoples to develop some of the densest populations of any Indians in the Pacific Northwest.

But, the ocean provided for more than riches for the coastal Indians. Swarming up all the rivers, most notably the Great River of the West, the Columbia, brought food and wealth in salmon. The three annual runs up the Columbia alone are estimated to have numbered between eight and twenty-five million salmon.

American Indians have caught salmon at The Dalles since 5800 B.C. Using harpoons, weirs, and specially designed traps, the Indians could gather vast numbers of fish to sustain them throughout the year, and even trade with other tribes. The fish became the focus of religious and social activities for many tribes. Once dried and smoked, the fish lasted until the next bountiful run came, as it did every spring, summer, and fall.

1

While the fish came from the west, another gift came from the east. When the last Ice Age retreated from the land, the animal that prospered the most was the bison, more commonly called the buffalo. From Georgia in the southeast to the Yukon in the north, as far south as Chihuahua, into the far west of Oregon and Washington, and clear across the continent, buffalo roamed in herds of millions.

At first the Indians were on foot using their traditional weapons of spears and bow-fired arrows to drive the animals over "jumps," or trapping them in dead-end canyons, killing the huge animals directly with their weapons. One researcher has asserted that,

> In just one day around 8500 B.C., Indians killed almost 200 animals at this arroyo, fully butchering 150 of them, and obtained about 55,000 pounds of usable meat plus 10,000 pounds of tallow, marrow, and other meat enough to sustain 100 people for a month. An estimated 150-200 people participated in the harvest. (Calloway, 40)

With abundance from both the east and the west, swollen by the gathering of food sources such as berries, nuts, bulbs—most notably the camas root, the Indians sustained their bands and tribes throughout the year. What they did not have, they could trade for with other tribes.

One focal point for trade was The Dalles, Oregon. Archeologists have found evidence of extensive trade centered on the falls of The Dalles where goods were traded from the coast to points as far east as Yellowstone, and from there, all the way to the East coast. The Dalles was one of the great North American trading centers for thousands of years.

From this nexus, many tribes spread out to their traditional lands. Each was different. In the rich, but often isolated environs of the coast, peoples centered their lives on the village with limited daily contact beyond. Some coastal tribes being mobile, such as the Chinook near the mouth of the Columbia River, looked beyond the village and had interaction between bands and other elements of the tribe. While still speaking the same language, such tribes did not always identify themselves with other similar speaking peoples, or only remotely if they did.

The interior natives expanded their group identity because they had to for survival. They had to expand their economic area of interest to gather the more dispersed gifts of the Great Spirit. As the Indians moved, they could identify with their own band or village, but they also saw other similar villages or bands as being of the same people of the Great Spirit. Such kindred tribes included the Paiutes, Cayuse, and Klickitat.

Pacific Northwest native people did not have the sense of tribal identity of the plains Indians, such as the Sioux or Cheyenne, but those that came the closest were those tribes that lived west of the Continental divide. They often traveled back and forth to the plains for hunts and trade, then returned to the Northwest. Representative of these peoples were the Nez Perce, Bannock, and Shoshoni.

Just as each American Indian group saw themselves as being chosen, their view of others was usually of being inferior. That perspective dictated their interaction between groups. Some groups lived in virtual isolation from others, distrustful of any outsider. This suspicion was characteristic of the more remote Indians of the rugged coast, from California to Alaska. Others would be wary of, but more open to, contact with neighboring bands, especially if they had a common language.

In the interior, while having more interaction between peoples, the keys to relations rested largely on how the tribes lived. Being gatherers of the plenty, if they moved little, their interaction was usually limited and rested on mutually beneficial trade. However, if the tribes were hunters, often moving, while capable of having friendly relations with tribes they viewed as being related or allied, these hunting tribes were often the most war-like.

War

Prior to the introduction of the horse by the Spanish, wars were fought between tribes on foot and on water. The instruments of war were clubs and weapons based on the Clovis point. Clovis points were made from fine-grained, easily worked stones. Chipping rocks such as chert, jasper, and obsidian, a man could flake each side of the rock to a sharpened edge meeting at a central point. He could also chisel an indentation for the secure fastening of the point to a shaft of wood. Raiders made large points into spears, while securing smaller Clovis points to arrows. Professor Emeritus George Frison from the University of Wyoming, Department of Anthropology noted from testing that the points were "a model of efficiency in terms of inflicting lethal wounds on large animals." (Calloway, 34) As with any technology, the Clovis point gave way to slightly different but effective arrow points.

The traditional Indian war method varied. Coastal natives sometimes fought canoe to canoe, firing arrows at each other, while protecting themselves with leather shields. Harpoons fashioned for use on whales by such tribes as the Makahs were effective as weapons of war.

In 1788, Captain John Meares sailed the ship *Nootka* into the harbor owned by the war-inclined Makahs.

> Twenty or thirty Makahs with painted faces, dressed in sea otter cloaks, and well armed with spears and bows and arrows paddled out in canoes to meet the ship. Their chief, Tatooche, a "surly and forbidding" character, his face painted black and glittering with sand or powdered mica, informed Meares that the power of Wickannish [chief of the neighboring Clayoquot of Vancouver Island] ended here and that his territory stretched to the south and east. He would not allow his people to trade. (Calloway, 404)

The Makahs had used such commercial interdiction for centuries to protect their territory.[1]

Inland, the method of defense and conquest was different. A Cree Indian nearly eighty years old, living with the very war-inclined Blackfeet, recalled fights of his youth, before the horse. Speaking to North West Company agent David Thompson in 1787, Saukamappee described a battle he fought as a young man when both sides "lined up in ranks

---

1. Many other ships reported attacks by coastal Indians. The Spanish ship *Sonora* was attacked by Quinalt Indians in July 1775. After suffering seven killed on each side, the Spanish used the ship's cannons to repel the Indian war canoes. The British reported another attack by the Quinalt in July 1787 when the Indians attacked the ship *Imperial Eagle*. The American captain Robert Gray noted three different attacks. While in command of the *Lady Washington*, Gray used his ship's cannons to shell a village after a landing party was attacked in Tillamook Bay in August 1788. During his 1792 cruise on the *Columbia Rediviva*, Gray was attacked on May 8 by canoes while anchored for the night in the bay now named for him on the Washington Coast. Later that same month, on the 29th, Gray fired his cannon to sink canoes attacking him on the west coast of Vancouver Island. He reported killing or wounding twenty-five Indians. As late as November 1808, whites were being attacked by coastal Indians. The Russian ship *Saint Nicholas* had a shore party attacked, and twenty-two sailors were taken captive and held for ransom. It would not be until 1811 that the survivors were finally freed by paying the demanded ransom.

behind large rawhide shields, fired arrows at each other, and sustained and inflicted few casualties." (Calloway, 295) This symbolic or ritualistic war would soon give way to blood and grief.

Wars were more infrequent and of a limited scale when the tribes were scattered and the only means of travel was by foot or canoe. They were more ritualistic rather than being wars of conquest and plunder. But, the horse would stamp war with lethal changes.

Horses

The horse was the first major innovation to Indian life introduced by Europeans. Most historians date the introduction of horses to the Indians from the New Mexican Pueblo Revolt of 1680. However, with feral herds of Spanish-descended horses and trading among Indian groups, many American Indians discovered the horse without any contact with whites. The culture of the horse quickly spread, to reach the Pacific Northwest in the early 1700s. The horse changed much of the Indian life in the interior, including war, while never entering into the culture of the coastal Indians.

Many tribes have oral history accounts of their first encounter with the horse, almost always when they met another tribe which had obtained the horse first. A member of one of the great horse-culture tribes recalls the first encounter:

> According to Cayuse tradition, sometime before 1750 a war party of Cayuses and their neighbors the Umatillas was encamped on the Malheur River... Spies were dispatched to bluffs overlooking the river to watch for the enemy Snakes. What they saw threw them into great consternation: the Snakes appeared to be riding either elk or deer. The spies hurriedly returned to their war chief, Ococtuin, with this intelligence. Perhaps disbelieving their story, the chief sent other warriors to ascertain the reason for what he thought must surely be an illusion. They, too, saw what appeared to be Snakes riding elk or deer. Dumbfounded, the group inched closer to discover that the hoofprints were not split but solid and round. Thoroughly upset by this discovery, Ococtuin abandoned his war plan for one of peace... After arranging a truce with the Snakes, the erstwhile war party returned home with a pair of horses, descendants of the Spanish ponies. (Ruby and Brown, 1972, 7)

The Cayuse quickly fell in love with their horse, and used war to steal more. Other tribes were equally overwhelmed by their first encounter with the horse:

> [The] Shoshone cavalry brought a new kind of warfare to the north-western plains. Piegans long remembered their first encounter with horses: "The Snake Indians and their allies had Misstutin (Big Dogs, that is horses), on which they rode, swift as Deer, on which they dashed at the Peegans, and with their stone Pukamoggan knocked them on their head, and they thus lost several of their best men." (Calloway, 295)

Mounted warriors completely changed the culture of the American Indians and their war-making.

The Culture of War

The largest mistake by whites in dealing with Indians was the assumption that Indians had a monolithic culture—that, if you knew one tribe, you were an expert on all tribes. Nothing could be further from the truth. The diversity of Indian culture was extreme throughout North America, and these extremes were true in the Pacific Northwest as well. Thus, it is impossible to give a complete account of each American Indian culture in any respect, let alone of war.

Generally speaking, horse-dominant tribes tended to be more war-like than tribes without horses. In coastal tribes where the horse played no significant role, this observation cannot be applied. But, there were horse-center cultures that were not war-like, usually fighting in self-defense.

Equally true, an interior tribe that came to accept the horse later on was still noted as a very aggressive tribe. "[T]he Modocs acquired their reputation as fearsome and merciless raiders, preying on their neighbors." (Murray, 12) They fought with wide wooden bow and arrows tipped with obsidian points, knives fashioned from the same volcanic glass, and basalt bladed axes. For transportation on their home territory, Tule Lake and its feeder streams, reed rafts and canoes were used. Until they acquired horses, they walked when away from home waters.

The Modocs came to accept the horse as critical to combat success sometime in the 1830s. For most warring tribes, the horse came much earlier. Evidence suggests the Shoshones came into horses by about

Spokane men on horseback probaby near a Spokane River tributary in 1909. (*Edward S. Curtis, Library of Congress*)

1700. As noted above, the Cayuse acquired horses prior to 1750. The Blackfeet (Piegans, Bloods, and Siksikas) were mounted by 1725. This rapid incorporation of the horse into Indian culture is remarkable, spreading from the Southwest, across the Plains, and into the far Pacific Northwest in fewer than fifty years.

The first tribes to get horses thoroughly integrated the animal into their culture. If it was a fighting culture, the horse quickly was an added weapon of war. The Shoshoni used their horse as transportation, crossing the continental divide repeatedly, with some of that nation primarily residing on the eastern slopes of the Rockies (referred to as the buffalo-eating Shoshonis) and some establishing their home areas to the west (referred to as the fish-eating Shoshoni, or also known as Shoshokos, or walker or digger Indians). As each crossed and joined their brethren, they brought their own trade goods and a cross-fertilization of ideas.

The horse's speed and mobility allowed all Indians to hunt beyond the methods of buffalo jumps or dead-end canyons. Now, the men could gallop among the buffalo, increasing the kill. This dramatic change in effectiveness wrought changes in social organization, as well. "Increased buffalo hunting required collective organization and greater mobility and generated changes in . . . society. Chieftainship developed to a new level as leaders emerged to coordinate the hunts, maintain order, and organize military responses." (Calloway, 294)

But the horse was not merely the means to social change; it came to be an end as well. Affluence quickly came to be measured with horses. "Horses indicated wealth and status, denoted rank. . . and constituted the principal form of property. . .They were essential. . . as the gift price for a bride. They featured prominently in. . . pictographic art, and pictographic prayers." (Calloway, 270) In short, the horse stimulated the speed of life, the measure of success, and the means to acquire all that was necessary to Indian culture.

Some tribes quickly made the horse the center of their existence, and if their existence was already war-like, it merely made the tribe more fearsome.

> "Blackfeet males embraced the equestrian warrior-hunter culture wholeheartedly: 'War, women, horses and buffalo are all their delights,' said [fur trader Alexander] Henry, 'and all of these they have at their command.' They emerged as the most formidable power of the northern plains. War, said Henry, was their 'principal occupation,' and horse stealing, said trader Edward Umfreville, was their principal inducement to going to war." (Calloway, 297)

Many tribes, plains and trans-Rockies feared the Blackfeet as their worst enemy. With the horse-forced change in tribal organization, war and defense mandated an increase in the importance of leadership. For example, the Bannocks evolved as a result of horse-driven changes. "The greater efficiency of communal hunting, plus the fear of the Blackfeet, compelled the Bannock to travel as a tribal unit under the direction of their chiefs during the trek to Montana and back." (Madsen, 23)

Other tribes made similar modifications to their culture to reflect the new way of life brought by the mounted man. Traditionally, many Indian tribes did not have a rigid hierarchical structure, relying on experience and persuasion for tribal guidance. If any individual had the largest influence, it would probably have been the shaman, or medicine chief. But, as the need to control seasonal movements and direct combat operations grew, so did the need for overall leadership.

The Cayuse provide an excellent example of this power shift. By the early 1800s, there were three distinct bands of people who identified themselves as Cayuse. Each had political autonomy within the bands, led by a chief.

When the Cayuse met as a tribe, the three chiefs acted as a tribal council, whose decision was binding on the tribe. These men were selected for their wisdom, usually associated with age and experience, but they would not be the leader(s) who led the tribe into war. Instead, a single war chief would be selected. The criteria was one (again) of experience (in combat), courage, and ability. The war chief (or chiefs, if more than one war party was being readied) had no greater voice within the council than any other experienced and wise tribal member; but within the raiding party, the war chief's control was total. Men knew the war chief's authority by his costume of a feather-adorned wolf's headdress and a bear-claw scepter.

Many other tribes had similar leadership arrangements. The Bannocks usually chose their chiefs from the descendants of previous chiefs, but would deviate when a forceful and successful leader would emerge. This chief lead the Bannocks into battle and was distinguished by the classic eagle feather war bonnet and his spear.

Similarly, the Nez Perce selected their war leaders based on skill and experience. "A young man who distinguished himself in war would have more volunteers to follow him on each succeeding raid until he gained a high rating as a fighting man. If his record proved exceptional, he might even be considered a war chief who earned the support of all the men of his tribe; but there are only two or three such instances known in Nez Perce history." (Haines, F., 16)

Whoever was the war leader, great preparation went into readying an attack. Many tribes ranging back and forth across the Rockies were influenced by the Plains Indians and their war-ceremonies. The Cayuse warrior societies, secret from the rest of the tribe, took such preparatory steps as fasting, purging (by drinking fish oil and induced vomiting), sweat lodges, and pipe smoking. The Bannock used sweat lodges and similar ceremonies, too, but also prepared their horse for the upcoming ordeal. The war horses would have feathers woven into the mane, and white clay was used to paint the horse in a variety of significant patterns, either religious, or commemorating past glories.

Tribes did war dances. Some danced to encourage brave deeds by recalling past valorous actions. Other tribes moved to the scalp dance. For the Bannocks, the scalp dance was held after the war, as a victory dance, with the display of their success giving the dance its name. All of this effort was directed to prepare the young men for combat.

Combat was an expected part of many tribes' experiences. It was both desired and unavoidable.

Contrary to popular thought, scalping was not a practice introduced by whites. "Scalping was an act of humiliation, as the Indians believed it affected their spirit life." (Aderkas, 35) The freshly taken scalps were shown as the warriors danced, highlighting their prowess. Other victim trophies were taken as well. Lewis and Clark wrote of meeting Chinooks, returning from a victorious fight against (most probably) the Paiutes. One warrior showed fourteen index fingers, taken from dead enemies; the fingers were kept in the warrior's medicine bag. Many tribes practiced mutilation as a trophy of war, including nations such as the Nez Perce. The Lekwiltok Indians, a coastal nation "were highly aggressive headhunters." (Adekerkas, 24) A warrior would sever and take a head to honor their own tribe's dead.

> Risks were great. When they located the enemy, the Cayuse regrouped to plan the attack, usually scheduling it for early morning. At the appointed time, they stealthily approached the unsuspecting camp. Then, with a rush, they shattered the stillness with shrieks. Before the enemy was alive to what was happening, the Cayuse charged, creating bedlam by peppering the camp with serviceberry shafts from their bows. At this point young men who wished to prove themselves on their first raid trailed off to steal horses. (Ruby and Brown, 1972, 14)

Many tribes took special care to defend against such an attack. Acting as lookouts, men stood guard, but it was not uncommon (nor frowned on) for the sentries to be asleep by morning. When war threatened, the Bannock set up camp in a circle, and between each tipi placed tree branches to create a continuous enclosure. This was not constructed so much to create a palisade, but rather as a corral for the horses, the tribe's wealth, which were moved inside for safeguarding.

Horses were not merely the means for combat, but they measured success in any war. Stealing horses increased personal wealth and marked a warrior's prowess. But horses were not the only desired war booty. Chief among any designs of war was slave taking.

Slaves

Capturing slaves generally involved women and children; male captives were killed.

The only direct account of such a raid came from a survivor among the Shastas who hid during the affair. As a child he witnessed a sudden, vicious Modoc attack. The adults of his own village had gone into a sweathouse near their rock-shelter dwelling when the Modocs struck. The children of the village were unharmed, but their parents were ruthlessly slaughtered as they dashed out of their bath. The youngsters and young women were seized, tied to the back of horses and taken north. The male children brought a price of about one pony each. Small girls commanded a somewhat higher price, while adolescent girls or mature young women could be traded for as much as five ponies, depending on their personal attractiveness. (Murray, 12)

Every war-inclined tribe practiced slavery by either keeping the captives within the tribe or selling them. "Slaves gave the Cayuse increased status. More practically, however, they gathered fuel, helped with the harvest and in the preparation of food, and performed many of the chores assigned to Cayuse women." (Ruby and Brown, 1972, 15)

Probably the most famous captive was Sacagawea. She was a Shoshone who had been captured by a Hidatas raiding party in 1800 at the age of eleven while her tribe was hunting on the east side of the continental divide. As a slave, she was used as a wager and lost as a gambling debt to her "husband," Toussaint Charbonneau. In turn, Charbonneau signed on with the Lewis and Clark Corp of Discovery (in 1804), taking just one of his wives, Sacagawea, whose language skills would prove to be invaluable to the expedition. But her experience was far from unusual.

One of the leading tribes in the slave trade was the Shoshones. They ranged to the south, tapping into the Spanish flesh market, obtaining horses and European trade goods, all the while being in danger of being taken captive by others, notably their enemies the Utes. Finding the trade lucrative, the Shoshones raided far and wide, to the west and onto the plains.

Being victim of a Shoshone attack gave reason for retaliation and vengeance for many tribes to strike back, thus repeating the cycle. Such may have been the case when Sacagawea was captured. War became a way of life for many tribes of the Pacific Northwest. This was true even of the coastal tribes. A war party might consist of several canoes, each carrying twenty to forty warriors armed with bows, arrows, spears, and clubs. To fend off attacking canoes, paddles were sharpened to stabbing points.

While canoe-to-canoe combat did take place, the ideal attack was for the raiding party to land near the enemy village in the predawn night. Stealthily approaching the sleeping village, the warriors prepared to attack at first light. Surprise was a critical element as many coastal tribes lived in fortified villages, complete with a log stockade and surrounding ditches, sometimes filled as a moat. One tribe, the Kitwanga, placed fallen trees on top of the walls, prepared to roll the trunks on to their attackers. To add to the defense, the branches were trimmed and the limbs sharpened to impale the invaders when the logs were released.

Once inside, each warrior had an assigned enemy, usually someone of equal stature. The preferred attack was to grab the sleeping enemy by the hair, shriek and then club the victim to death. The objectives were to plunder and take slaves.[2]

Fighting in Paradise

Indian wars were numerous, and sometimes continuous. However, except in a few cases, we do not have records of exact dates or locations of battles. The American Indians did not have the same historical sense or methodology that was true of the Europeans. The Indians' strong tradition of oral history, while rich, is not as specific as that of Western civilizations.

Indian wars can be divided into three broad historical periods: pre-horse, pre-gun, and post-white contact. We know from oral history that wars were fought on foot with many of the same objectives. Some of the richest oral histories are of the transition of Indian society from a foot to a horse-dominated culture. This event in war and in peace was so eventful that Indian oral histories passed on the stories of horses coming to the tribe.

With the introduction of guns, many of the oral histories are augmented by white history. The first debut of guns to Indian society was through fur traders, most prominently the British Northwest Company. The guns were a strong trade item for furs, but many Indian nations acquired guns without white contact, acquiring them from other Indian tribes by alliance or conquest.

---

2. Gough documents slave trading among British Columbian Indians well into the 1860s.

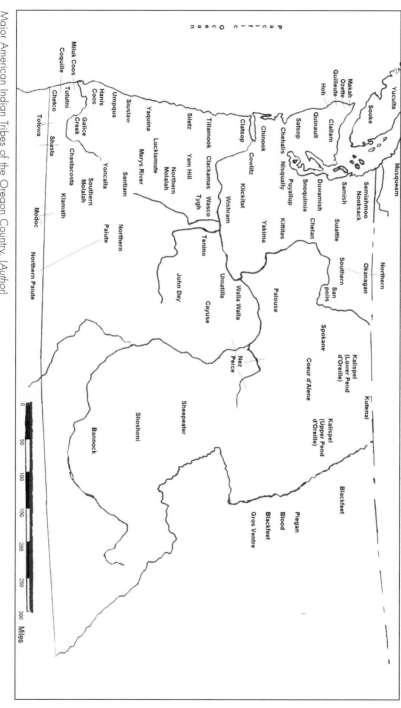

Major American Indian Tribes of the Oregon Country. (Author)

In retelling Indian wars, it is best to describe general patterns of hostilities with particular dates recalled as they are noted, starting with the coast and moving inland.

Coastal Indian Wars

Many of the war dominated coastal tribes were located in present day British Columbia. Three notable war cultures were the Haida, Tsimshian, and the Tlingist. These canoe-based cultures were noted for attacking their neighbors.

Inside the United States, a State of Washington tribal confederation dominated the coast. The Quinaults, Queets, Hohs, and Quileutes formed a powerful alliance that ranged over western Washington. This confederation attacked the Ozettes and Makahs to the north, and the Clallams located on the Strait of Juan de Fuca. To the south, they fought the Satsops and the domineering Chinooks of the Columbia River. The Spanish met this latter confederation as they explored the Northeastern Pacific coastal waters circa 1775.

Hoh oral tribal history records one battle, described as shortly before the arrival of the whites, in which a slave raid against the Chinooks and Satsops took place at Grays Harbor. As the Quileutes pursued their enemies' canoes, their own canoe became trapped on a mud flat where they were subject to repeated attacks. An unrecorded number of deaths took place on both sides, as the Satsops and Chinooks were able to repel the slave-raiders.

The Chinooks were not always the victim. Using canoes on the Pacific Ocean and the rivers that flowed into it, they raided up and down the coast and well into the interior. Lewis and Clark recorded the Chinooks returning victorious in 1806 from raiding as far inland as The Dalles, having attacked the Deschutes and Teninos for plunder. The Astorian fur traders noted the Chinooks attacking their traditional enemies the Clatsops repeatedly, until disease reduced both tribes' numbers to insignificance.

Another aggressive coastal tribe was the Cowlitz. One battle recorded by whites was an April 1814 fight with the Multnomahs. Three hundred Cowlitzs (possibly with Chinook allies) paddled forty canoes into the Willamette River near present-day Portland, Oregon. Although greatly out-numbered, what tipped the balance was that the Multnomahs had guns and were able to keep the bow-and-arrow armed attackers from pressing their numerical advantage.

The Near Interior

Just east of the Cascade Mountains were several significant militaristic tribes. The Yakima and the Klickitat in Washington were noted for their warrior prowess. South of the Columbia, the dominant tribes, until the mid-1700s, were the Molalahs and the Cayuse. The Molalahs were originally centered on the Deschutes River and the Cayuse on the John Day River, tributaries of the mighty Columbia River. Prior to their acquisition of horses, the two tribes were not only culturally close, but physically as well. But soon, they fell victim to a stronger tribe, the Paiutes.

The Paiutes ranged throughout the arid country of Oregon, Idaho, and Nevada. Able warriors, they would fight many wars, continuing until the last wars fought in the Pacific Northwest. As they attacked north toward the rich fish harvesting wealth of the Columbia, the Paiutes encountered the Molalahs and Cayuse, thus driving the two tribes apart.

The Cayuse moved east into the Blue Mountains of Oregon and Washington. The Molalahs moved west of the Cascades; one branch moved as far south as the upper Umpqua River, while another branch settled north of the upper Santiam River. The Molalah revenged their loss of homeland by raiding the Paiutes east of the Cascades well into the 1820s.

The warrior culture of the Paiutes impacted many other tribes, and not merely the people they attacked. Chiloquin, a Klamath chief, recalled the impetus the Paiutes created for war:

> When the Snakes [Northern Paiute] made war on us that made us keen to fight other Indians and we made war without provocation on the Pitt Rivers, Shastas and Rogue Rivers, but they never made willing war on us. Those wars lasted a great many years. We found we could make money by war, for we sold the provisions and property captured for horses and other things we needed. (Stern, 23)

As late as the 1850s, the Klamath were raiding into the western region of Oregon, attacking such tribes as the Umpqua.

The Eastern Tribes

The first warrior tribe to the east was the displaced Cayuse. With the acquisition of the horse, the Cayuse moved from being the victim of aggression to a dominant war society. Evidence suggests that the Cayuse raided well into the upper reaches of the Willamette Valley, and even into Northern California. The Astorians heard of a Cayuse raid in March

1814, where the mounted warriors attacked a Clackamas Indian village at Willamette Falls (present day Oregon City). Reports told of the men who were killed, and the women and children taken captive as the marauders plundered the settlement.

But the Cayuse did not limit their attacks to the west alone. Their enemies included the Snakes (a generic term often applied to Paiutes, Shoshonis, and Bannocks). War was often coup for coup, counterattack for attack.

In 1814, the Nez Perce had killed some Snakes (probably Shoshoni), who replied by attacking a Walla Walla village, killing one warrior, four women, and five children, taking scalps, plus capturing numerous slaves. After this attack by the Snakes, they sought the protection of whites at Fort Nez Perce. The Cayuse, Nez Perce, and Walla Wallas tracked the raiders as they withdrew with their captives. Four hundred aggrieved Indians confronted the whites, accusing them of giving guns to the Snakes. Additional casualties were had, but the whites intervened to restore peace. Their efforts to stop the Indian war was not based on motives of brotherly love, but on profits. If war raged between tribes, trappers were endangered as they sought the valuable furs of the Northwest.

But, peace did not last. Cayuse raiders attacked the Snakes again in 1818 and 1825 (as recorded by British fur brigades traveling through the region).

The Nez Perce were the reigning tribe of the Snake-Salmon River of Northeast Oregon, Southeastern Washington, and central Idaho. Their allies were predominately the Yakima and the Cayuse. With the Cayuse, the Nez Perce raided as far west as The Dalles, as one war raged along the Columbia in late winter-early spring of 1814.

Another war, noted by white trappers, occurred between the Nez Perce and the Shoshoni in 1819. Trappers related how five separate Nez Perce war parties raided throughout the Shoshoni villages, killing many, and capturing more as slaves. But the Nez Perce did not escape without casualties as seen through "Neeshnepahkeook, or Cut-Nose, so called because of a lance stroke he had received in a fight with the Shoshonis." (Ruby and Brown, 1981, 16-17)

When raiding with western allies such as the Yakima, the Nez Perce ranged wide. The tribes would attack the San Polis and Colvilles of north-central Washington, or to the northeast, the Blackfeet, and to the southeast, the Shoshoni. One difference practiced by the Nez Perce was having achieved victory where they would offer peace. An 1803 war with the Shoshoni was resolved by sending peace ambassadors; but this technique failed with the aggressive Blackfeet.

One of few Bannock-Nez Perce wars occurred in 1820. Usually the Bannock kept armed neutrality with the warriors of the west and the Flatheads of the north. Their more traditional enemies were with the Utes to the south, and the Crow and Blackfeet of the upper plains.

One tribe, the Blackfeet, struck fear into the Indians of the Pacific Northwest as well as the upper plains. The Blackfeet were made up of three tribes: The Piegans, the Bloods, and the Siksikas. So unrelentingly hostile was this tribe, many tribes organized their defense and culture based on their fear of the Blackfeet.

Of the tribes in the Northwest, the Bannock, Kutenais, Flathead, Nez Perce, Shoshoni, Coeur d'Alene, and Sheepeaters all suffered from chronic wars with the Blackfeet. Two Shoshoni-Blackfeet wars are known from the eighteenth century (1730 and 1787). The 1730 war was noted by the introduction of the horse as the Shoshoni were mounted, while the Blackfeet were still afoot. What offset the Shoshoni advantage was that the Blackfeet were one of the first tribes to have firearms from British fur traders:

> After some maneuvering, the Indians lined up as usual, and the Piegan [Blackfeet] chief ordered his warriors to advance. The Cree and Assiniboin [allies of the Piegans] gunmen concealed their weapons behind their shields, while each held two balls in his mouth for reloading. The unsuspecting Shoshonis were mowed down as fast as the enemy could fire. Terrified by this new magic, the survivors fled. (Trenholm and Carley, 20)

This added greatly to the legitimate fear many tribes had of the aggressive Blackfeet. The only solution the Nez Perce found to fend off the vicious Blackfeet attackers was to obtain firearms themselves.

> Another important matter discussed by the council that year [1805] was the ever-present problem of defense against the encroaching Blackfeet. Their war parties, numbering as many as 1,000 and armed with guns, were pushing farther to the south and west each year until even the Bitterroot Valley was a place of danger. The Nez Perces needed guns to meet this menace. (Hanies, F. P., 25)

The Nez Perce sent warriors to exchange their superior horses for guns from friendly tribes.

The Flathead suffered greatly for their nearness to the traditional Piegan homelands. Wars were noted by whites between the Piegans and the Flatheads in 1810 and 1811.

Of particular note was the 1810 conflict. Wishing to support his Flathead trapping allies, British fur trader Finan McDonald used his firearms to fight alongside the Flatheads in a battle with the Blackfeet. He helped to even the sides with at least seven Piegans killed (to five Flatheads) and thirteen wounded (to the Flatheads' nine).

Not so equal was a Blackfeet war against the Kutenais in 1811. Fur trader David Thompson visited a Kutenais village to trade for fur, only to find every inhabitant had been killed, victims of a Blackfeet raid. Thompson soon learned of other Blackfeet battles with the Spokanes and Coeur d'Alenes, that summer.

It is worth noting that the only clash with Indians that happened during the Lewis and Clark expedition occurred with Blackfeet. On July 27, 1806, to the east of the continental divide, Meriwether Lewis and his party battled with the aggressive Blackfeet. The attack was prompted by the Blackfeet's desire to steal guns and horses. As Lewis wrote in his journal,

> This morning at daylight the indians got up and crouded around the fire, J. Fields who was on post had carelessly laid his gun down. . .when one of the indians. . . sliped behind him and took his gun and that of his brother unperceived by him, at the same instant two others advanced and seized the guns of Drewyer [Drouilliard] and myself.

This had become a fight for life and death, not mere thievery. Lewis went on to describe the combat:

> [Joseph Fields and his brother, Reubin] jumped up and pursued the indian with whom they overtook at the distance of 50 or 60 paces from the camp s[e]ized their guns and rested them from him and R. Fields as he seized his gun stabbed the indian to the heart with his knife. (DeVoto, 437-438)

Drouilliard was able to wrestle his gun back, while Lewis threatened to shoot one Blackfeet with his pistol, and retook his rifle. But now the soldiers were concerned for their horses.

I now hollowed to the men and told them to fire on them if they attempted to drive off our horses, they accordingly pursued the main party who were dr[i]ving the horses up the river. . . .being nearly out of breath I could pursue no further, I called to them as I had done several times before that I would shoot them if they did not give me my horse and raised my gun. . .at the distance of 30 steps from me and I shot him through the belly. . . he fell to his knees and on his wright elbow from which position he partly raised himself up and fired at me. (DeVoto, 437-438)

While no whites were killed, the Blackfeet suffered due to the skill of the U.S. Army members. On the other hand, fearing Blackfeet retaliation, Lewis had his troops force-march all that day and night to flee the Indian warriors.

Wars between the Indians decreased with the arrival of the whites. This was partly due to the whites becoming a greater challenge to Indian survival, and therefore assuming the role of arch-enemy for many tribes. It was also because of white efforts to restore peaceful relations between tribes. This was not for utopian, but for pure mercantile reasons. If the Indians were at war, whites could become victims of raiding parties, resulting in a drop in fur profits.

While war was not introduced by Western civilization, its technological innovations increased the carnage of combat. The fight for paradise now became a conflict between cultures.

~

It is impossible to direct the inquisitive traveler to Indian war battle sites or monuments. Besides the obvious limitation of oral history, no effort was made by the encroaching white culture to preserve native cultural or historical sites. However, that is not to say that the traveler cannot learn more. Many museums and parks provide insight into Indian culture, as well as document the Indian history of war.

The Royal British Columbia Museum in Victoria, British Columbia, repays an informed or curious visitor. While the museum is devoted to telling the whole story of British Columbia, its section on Indian history and culture, entitled First Peoples Gallery is a premier introduction to the native peoples of British Columbia and the northern half of the Oregon Country.

Coastal Indians are represented well by the Makah Indians. Located at the most northwestern tip of Washington State, the Makah Museum tells the history of these sea-faring people.

The Indians of the Pacific Northwest interior have their story told by many tribal cultures. The Museum at Warm Springs, Oregon, tells the saga of the Confederated Tribes of the Warm Springs and includes information on the Paiutes.

The Yakama Nation Cultural Heritage Center in Toppenish, Washington, relates the chronicle of the Yakama and Klickitat Indians. To the east is the Umatilla Indian Reservation. The Tamastslikt Cultural Institute in Pendleton, Oregon, guards the history of the Umatilla, Walla Walla, and Cayuse Indians.

The National Park Service maintains the Nez Perce National Historical Park, with its main museum in Spalding, Idaho. This excellent exhibition and park has elements not only in Idaho, but also in Oregon, Washington, and Montana.

Shoshoni culture is explained at the Shoshone Tribal Cultural Center in Fort Washakie, Wyoming. While focused mainly on the eastern branch of the tribe, the center does shed light on the Shoshoni culture as a whole.

Chapter 2

Paradise Contested

The Game of Great Nations

The age of exploration was also the age of empire. European powers had long sought to extend their control into new lands to gather more wealth. The Pacific Northwest had not been neglected in the search for treasure and opportunity. Because of its distance from Europe, however, it had been sought as a source of wealth extraction as opposed to a location for colonization.

The first European nation to lay claim to Oregon was Great Britain when Sir Francis Drake sailed the *Golden Hind* to the remote coast of the northeastern Pacific in 1578. The British would not strengthen their claim for another two hundred years when, in 1778, Captain James Cook came upon the region.

Spain was the other nation with a strong claim of interest. Several Spanish explorers had sailed the Oregon coast, with some reaching as far north as 54 degrees, 40 minutes north, the northern most boundary of the Oregon Country. The latitude of "Fifty-four, forty" would figure prominently in the dispute over ownership of the Oregon Country.

While other nations such as Russia could lay title to the Oregon Country, the third major contender for ownership was the United States. Its claim dated from May 11, 1792, when Captain Robert Gray on the ship *Columbia Rediviva* crossed the Columbia River bar, thus being the first to establish the true identity and location of the Great River of the West. With the establishment of this claim, the United States became one of the contestants in the "game of great nations."

By the close of the eighteenth century, global power had ebbed and flowed, leaving the contest to just two nations: Great Britain and the United States. Each had a solid basis for establishing its respective claims.

Great Britain's assertion had the precedents of the Drake and Cook voyages and the naval explorations by Captain George Vancouver and Lieutenant Broughton, who explored the Oregon Country in 1791-92 and the Columbia River in the Fall of 1792, respectively.

By land, England would claim the Oregon Country in 1793, by the achievement of Alexander Mackenzie, who became the first European to reach the North Pacific via an overland expedition. Mackenzie's expedition reached salt water near the mouth of the Bella Coola River in present-day British Columbia, Canada.

Another explorer, David Thompson, crossed the Canadian Rockies and eventually became the first white man to navigate the entire length of the Columbia. His establishment of trading houses for the North West Company also strengthened the British hand in the Oregon Country.

Robert Gray had provided the United States with a strong basis for possession of the Oregon Country, although it was not the exclusive foundation of the American claim. The Lewis and Clark expedition (1804-06) gave great credence to the American assertion that the Pacific Northwest was a rightful extension of American territory beyond the newly acquired Louisiana Purchase. This claim was buttressed by creation of a permanent commercial endeavor, Fort Astoria, in 1811, at the mouth of the Columbia.

In 1819, the Americans raised a strong legal argument through a treaty with Spain in which that nation relinquished all claims north of the 42nd parallel to the United States. Russia augmented the legal case, when it signed an 1824 treaty with the United States relinquishing all claims south of the magical fifty-four-forty parallel. Here then were the two nations, one great and the other aspiring to greatness, posturing for possession of paradise.

Great Britain and the United States each contested ownership of the Oregon Country, from the 42nd parallel in the south to fifty-four-forty in the north, and from the Pacific Ocean in the west to the crest of the Rocky Mountains.

The Game Begun

The interaction between the natives of the Oregon Country and the entry of Western civilization had three general phases. The first phase was the Indian interaction with coastal visitors aboard ships. White traders made brief visits to exchange trinkets for sea otter furs. While occasional conflicts arose that resulted in casualties on both sides, the contacts were mutually beneficial and largely peaceful.

The second phase saw the penetration of fur traders who established permanent posts, and who were mainly tolerant of native cultures. Their objective was to use the natives to help extract natural resources, primarily beaver pelts. The Hudson's Bay Company dominated this era.

The last phase saw settlers arrive intending to build a replica of the civilization they just left. The alteration of the wilderness would ultimately result not only in the establishment of cities and farms, but in the removal of forests, the damming of rivers, and the displacement of natives.

While the first two phases had left the Indians intact, the third phase transformed native lives. And it was during the transition from the second to the third phase that the backdrop of the national gamesmanship was fought. But even as Great Britain and the United States played their games, the Indians were losing.

In 1808, the contest began when word reached Canada that the Americans were to establish a permanent outpost at the mouth of the Columbia River. In July 1809, the American ship, *Albatross*, under the command of Captain Nathan Winship, set sail intending to set up a permanent post on the Columbia River. Upon arrival in May 1810, it crossed the Columbia bar and moved up-river. Winship built a fort, but high water and hostile Indians compelled him to give up and sail away. However, this early effort gave a morale boost to another American, John Jacob Astor, for commercial empire and his dreams of greater wealth.

Astor was an American icon—a self-made man. Born in Germany in 1763, he arrived in New York City in 1784. Starting with a single fur shop, he swiftly expanded his business into all aspects of the fur trade. His opportunity to be a major player came in 1794, with the Jay Treaty between the United States and Great Britain. The treaty allowed Astor to expand his markets into previously exclusive British markets, as well as to search out new sources of his wealth: furs. Under the provisions of the treaty, Astor expanded his companies into Canada and the Great Lakes of the American west.

Created in 1808, Astor's American Fur Company was a direct competitor to Britain's Hudson Bay and North West Companies, and he would create additional rival companies to the giant British firms. The Southwest Fur Company was Astor's attack on the previous British monopoly in the Great Lakes area. But his dreams of grandeur took his vision further west where he dreamed of beating the British on the shores of the Pacific Ocean.

Astor created the Pacific Fur Company so that he could establish a permanent post on the Columbia River. Word reached Canada that the Americans were prepared to depart in 1810 for the long voyage around the Horn, and the North West Company viewed the enterprise as a direct threat.

Nor'Wester[1] David Thompson, in response to the Americans, was directed west over the Canadian Rockies. He had already pioneered the temporary Kullyspell House in 1809. However, to counter the American threat, in 1810, Thompson built Spokane House shortly before the Americans created Fort Astoria in March of 1811.

Thompson paddled the length of the Columbia and reached the mouth to find Fort Astoria an on-going enterprise. It was larger, better supplied and better supported than anything the Nor'Westers had west of the Rockies. It menaced the British fur monopoly and empire. Consequently, the Nor'Westers urged the British government to use force to eject the Americans. The Crown rejected any show of force as being a precipitant to full scale war. War fever was already high between the two countries over Britain's conduct toward American commercial interaction with Napoleon's Europe.

What made the threat manageable to the Nor'Westers was the outbreak of war in 1812. Great Britain and the United States each had official players as well as commercial players. For the first British player, this meant that the Nor'Westers viewed war as a business opportunity.

The fur company immediately dispatched officers overland to buy the fort at the mouth of the Columbia for pennies on the dollar (or pence on the pound). The sole reason that the Astorians would even consider the sale was because of the second British player, the Royal Navy.

Prior to the outbreak of war, the North West Company had planned to answer the Astorians with an armed ship. When war came, the Nor'Westers requested a convoy to escort their ship, the *Isaac Todd*, and three warships were dispatched to do so. The *Isaac Todd* missed the rendezvous, so the Royal Navy's ships proceeded to the Pacific Ocean. Told that the frigate U.S.S. *Essex* was at sea, the naval squadron divided.

---

1. The name by which members of the North West Company were known.

Fort Astoria pictured soon after its completion. (*Detail from an original at the Oregon Historical Society*)

Two of the ships were assigned to find and destroy the American, which was sinking British merchant vessels. The frigate *Phoebe* and the sloop of war *Cherub* clashed with the *Essex* off of Valparaiso, Chile, capturing her after a fierce gun battle on March 14, 1814. The third British warship, *Raccoon*, had Admiralty orders to seize Fort Astoria.

The three-ship flotilla had been under the command of a very senior officer, Commodore Hillyer, however, now that the *Raccoon* was the sole ship en route to Astoria, its young captain had an opportunity to come to the attention of his superiors.

The twenty-six gun sloop of war was under the command of William Black, and glory would be his if he successfully stormed the fort for God, King, and Country. Crossing the Columbia bar, Captain Black envisioned a bastion festooned with gun embrasures and dotted with cannon. Instead, upon his arrival, Captain Black discovered that Fort Astoria was a meager wooden fort that the Nor'Westers had already purchased. Neither glory nor prize money could be had if the fort had been sold. In order to strain some honor and glory for himself and for empire, on December 12, 1813, Captain Black ordered the Union Jack lowered and the Stars and Stripes run up the flag pole. As one Astorian wrote of the historic event,

> On the 12th day of December, the death-warrant of the short-lived Astoria was signed. On that day, Captain Black went through the customary ceremony of taking possession, not only of Astoria, but of the whole country. (Ross, 258-269)

With his lieutenant of marines and four sailors and marines present, Black ordered the American flag lowered and the British flag raised, claiming possession for King George III. Taking a bottle of Madeira, Captain Black smashed it against the flag pole and rechristened the ramshackle structure Fort George, a prize of war by right of seizure. The captain's seizure of the fort as a "prize of war" guaranteed it would be returned to the Americans with the signing of the Treaty of Ghent in 1814.

American sovereignty was restored in August 1818, when the frigate U.S.S. *Ontario* sailed across the Columbia bar. In doing so, the *Ontario* became the first American naval vessel to enter the Columbia River and her captain, James Biddle, raised the American flag over the former Fort Astoria. Shortly thereafter, the British frigate *Blossom* arrived, carrying as a courtesy American special commissioner J.B. Prevost. Prevost completed the paperwork for the transfer with the British representative, H.M.S. *Blossom's* Captain Hickey.

The first game of the set had gone to the British by gaining Fort Astoria. Although the score had been settled with a tied set once the fort was returned to the Americans, the match had yet to be decided.

The year 1818 also saw the opening set of the second game. Unable to settle the ownership of the Oregon Country, Great Britain and the United States agreed to a treaty of joint occupation, deferring the decision for ten years. Still unable to decide where to draw a dividing line, the tenants renewed the joint occupancy treaty in 1827. Each nation could make a claim for the whole territory, but it was more logical that the claim would be divided.

The Americans wanted to extend the forty-ninth parallel which had divided the Louisiana Purchase from Canada. The British wished for an actual physical boundary, such as the Columbia River. This impasse was to last for nearly twenty years.

While each side countenanced private efforts to use the Oregon Country, each government would use military and naval units to extend and strengthen its position.

Although Fort Clatsop, established by Captains Lewis and Clark during the winter of 1805-06, was a temporary army post, it allowed the Americans to claim the first military occupation of the Oregon Country. By 1824, the British were wary of a renewed American military intent. A chance encounter in the eastern portion of the Oregon Country clearly personified British fears. Alexander Ross of the Hudson's Bay Company, who had started as an Astorian with the Pacific Fur Company, came across a party led by Jedediah Smith. Ross noted in his journal, Smith's party "arrived. . . from the Big Horn River but whom I rather take to be spies than trappers." With this isolated incident as a start, the tempo picked up in 1827, after the renewal of the joint occupancy.

The British Fur Trade

The era of fur trader established posts was the period of transition for the Indians. The total independence of the natives to their eventual subordination was marked by the generation who traded furs with the whites.

The trading post period is often depicted as one of peaceful interaction between Indians and British authority, sharply contrasting with the inept and hostile actions of the Americans. While there are distinct elements of truth to this dichotomy, it is also unfair. The purposes of the two nations, at least in the Oregon Country, were different.

The British wanted limited penetration and temporary colonies. Their goal was to use the Indians, living largely unchanged, as a means to extract natural wealth. The Americans invaded to colonize, dominate, and overwhelm the existing social structure. These objectives made conflict certain. What is less well known and appreciated is that despite the British restrained goals, they had conflicts. Some were inadvertent, merely a result of competing actions between cultures. However, some were deliberate attacks as a result of policy decisions, such as punishing a tribe for profiting at the loss of a company's ship.

But combat was often premeditated. In 1818, the Cowlitz Indians killed an Iroquois trapper employed by the North West Company. Consequently, Fort George's Chief Trader James Keith ordered a retaliation to prevent further attacks. Keith gave command of the raiding party to Peter Skene Ogden. The Cowlitz passage was a crucial portage for travel to the Puget Sound from the Columbia River, and it was imperative that its employees travel unmolested.

With a party of Iroquois Indians employed by the North West Company (which was the sole British company operating in the Oregon Country at that time), Ogden surrounded the Cowlitz village. While not having proof, Ogden suspected the village as the group that had killed the trapper. With total tactical surprise, the Nor'Westers attacked the village; thirteen villagers were killed and many others were wounded. It was of no concern to the fur traders that the majority of those they killed and

injured were women and children. King George men were not to be inter-
fered with when on company business.

The fur companies sought civil relations with Indians not merely with
the stick, but also with the carrot. Rewards were given for King George
men protected or supplies returned. Intermarriage was common, not only
because of the frequent contact but also as a method of ensuring trapper
safety and as a contact point for friendly relations with the Indians. But,
this policy occasionally went awry.

To strengthen the message that the King George men must be allowed
free passage on the Cowlitz River portage, the Nor'Westers arranged a
marriage between one of its officers and the daughter of Chief How How
of the Cowlitz. In April 1819, the Cowlitz nation arrived at Fort George
for the nuptials. After the ceremony and a wedding feast rich with food
and drink, the Cowlitz's decided to leave the fort to return home, despite
it being night. After exiting the fort, as they neared their canoes, they
were attacked by their historical enemy, the Chinook. In the pandemoni-
um, the Fort George men believed that the Cowlitz had attacked. As the
men garrisoned the fort's defenses, they witnessed the Cowlitz swarm
toward the fort's walls. Instead of recognizing the Cowlitz's frantic need
for refuge, the Nor'Westers opened fire on the hapless Cowlitz creating
a wicked crossfire of muskets and cannon. Upon realization that the
Cowlitz had not been the ones to attack, the defenders of the fort lifted
their fire and then gave shelter to the Cowlitz.

But, the damage had already been done. For many years, there was no
hope for free passage through the Cowlitz Indians area. Either the
portage was avoided or traversed only with a large armed party.

Individuals within the British fur companies had minor skirmishes
with natives and used their authority in self-defense or to enforce their
right of passage. In one spontaneous combat, in the spring of 1818, Peter
Skene Ogden recorded an attack as his party made its way down the
Columbia River. Upon descent, Ogden's voyageurs camped near the
mouth of the Walla Walla River. There, the fur men were attacked by the
Walla Walla Indians. Using guns obtained from the fur traders, Indians
repeatedly hit the camp with musket fire. While they did not take any
casualties, the voyageurs struck camp and moved down river to a small
island; the Indians pursued in their canoes. Ahead, the trappers laid an
ambush. As the Indian canoes neared the head of the island, the
voyageurs opened fire, killing many Walla Wallas. This action deterred
further Walla Walla hostility for many years.

Another early conflict also occurred in 1818. A brigade of sixty men explored the southern Oregon coast and ventured up-river on the banks of the Umpqua. Finding a valley rich with beaver and natives reluctant to trade or trap for the intruders, the North West men attempted to coerce the Indians by seizing their horses. In protest, the Indians resisted and a fire-fight against the inadequately armed Umpquas resulted in the death of fourteen natives.

As the fur trappers retired to Fort George, they were ambushed by Cathlanahquiah Indians, a mere twenty miles from the post. Chief Trader

Peter Skene Ogden. (*Library of Congress*)

Alexander Ross immediately order the killers captured. Four Indians were hung as punishment for killing trappers of the company.

In 1819, Nor'Wester Donald Mackenzie led a brigade into the Snake River country. Mackenzie and his group were venturing along the Snake River near the mouth of an unnamed tributary when they were attacked. They were surprised by an Indian war party and three members of Mackenzie's group were killed. A brief fire-fight resulted in an Indian repulse. All of the fur trapper party members killed were Kanakas from the Sandwich Islands, now called the Hawaiian Islands. Another spelling from that era for Hawaii was Owyhee and the river was named the Owyhee River by Mackenzie to honor the slain Kanakans.[2]

The permanent American presence in the Oregon Country had been eliminated by the sale of Fort Astoria to the North West Company in 1812, and now Americans were limited to the occasional visiting ship or adventurous mountain men barely crossing the continental divide.

2. An even earlier incident had occurred with the Astorians. John Reed was dispatched from Fort Astoria to create a trapping post on the Snake River. In January 1813, the Snake (probably Bannock) Indians attacked the outpost, killing nine men. The Indian wife of one of the trappers escaped with her two small children, bringing word of the elimination of the post by murder.

But the contest continued, not only British against American, but British against British. The Hudson's Bay Company engaged in a hostile take-over of its British rival, the North West Company. Actual gun battles took place throughout the two company's empires until in 1821, the Crown ordered the consolidation of the two companies under the older company's charter, the Hudson's Bay, making the company the Crown's sole representative in the Oregon Country.

Thus, the North West outpost Fort George, also known as Fort Astoria, became the Hudson's Bay Company's primary depot in the Oregon Country with the take-over in 1821. In 1824, the "Most Honorable Company" shifted its primary base to Fort Vancouver, and it was from here that the Hudson's Bay Company established itself throughout the Oregon Country, eventually building twenty-nine subsidiary posts, all supplied by ships from England through its main depot, Fort Vancouver.

The Royal Charter of the Hudson's Bay Company gave it extensive governmental authority and powers. The Most Honorable Company could make and enforce laws for its area of operations and enforce those laws, including raising armies to wage war against any non-Christian people. The company was free to "make war" as long as it did not cause England to enter into a European or American war. This forced the British government to support company activities with its full power and authority. In the Oregon Country, Hudson's Bay became the British government and, except for those rare occasions when the area was visited by imperial authority, such as the Royal Navy, the British government was the Hudson's Bay Company. Until the arrival of significant numbers of American emigrants in the 1840s, the Hudson's Bay Company was the supreme power throughout the Oregon Country.

With this nearly unlimited grant of power, the Hudson's Bay Company continued to use military force as a threat as well as a retaliatory tool to guarantee the free passage of their agents throughout the Columbia Department, the Hudson's Bay name for much of the Oregon Country. As Governor George Simpson explained in a letter in 1822:

> I have made it my study to examine the nature and character of the Indians and however repugnant it may be to our feelings, I am convinced they must be ruled with a rod of iron, to bring and keep them in a proper state of subordination. (Newman, 226)

The majority of its exercises in martial power were small engagements, occurring spontaneously, although some were deliberate acts
intended to use the Hudson's Bay Company's war making authority. In
1823, for example, Blackfoot Indians attacked Finan McDonald's
Hudson's Bay brigade as it worked the Snake River country. In keeping
with company policy, McDonald sought to punish the Indians for the
attack despite his not having had any casualties. He doggedly followed
them, but was led into several traps, which cost him six dead. Despite
these traps and losses, McDonald continued pursuit and finally cornered
the Indians in a cluster of trees where he killed them all by lighting the
timber afire, and burning the Indians to death while pining them down
with musket shot volleys. Throughout the running battles, McDonald
killed sixty-eight Indians; he firmly felt the company's policy of retaliation
warranted his pursuit, attack, and casualties.

Interior Indians were not the only source of hostile contacts. The
coastal Indians of Vancouver Island had a noted warrior culture and had
preyed upon other Indians for centuries.

In September 1827, the Hudson's Bay ship *Cadboro* was trading along
the island, near present day Comox, British Columbia. The *Cadboro*, a
71-ton sailing vessel manned by twelve men and armed with four cannons, was under the command of Aemilius Simpson, formerly of the
Royal Navy. He was the cousin of the most powerful and influential man
in the Hudson's Bay Company, Governor George Simpson. Neither the
family connections nor his being a former classmate of the most powerful man in the company's North American operations hurt Aemilius
Simpson's chances when a selection was made for the captaincy, where
he retained his command through his splendid performances for the
Most Honorable Company.

Captain Simpson anchored the *Cadboro*, sending boats ashore to
replenish the ship's water supply. The Indians gathered in apparent
friendship and then attacked the water party, killing one of the crew and
wounding another. The party was saved by the ship's crew who went
ashore to drive the Indians away.

Intermittent attacks continued that year. On December 8, 1827,
Chief Trader Alexander McKenzie had arrived from Fort Vancouver with
others to spend Christmas at Fort Langley on the Fraser River. After
entering the Fraser, ice forced the party ashore where they were threatened by the Musqueam Indians who succeeded in stealing valuable

stores. The fort, receiving word of their troubles, sent out an armed escort that finally assured their safe arrival. In order to maintain the prestige and security of the King George men, a heavily armed party went to the Musqueam village on December 26 and recovered the stolen items. Thus, for the company and its policies, the old year ended on a note of profit.

With the arrival of 1828, McKenzie needed to return to Fort Vancouver. On January 3rd, the party started south. James McMillan, a Fort Langley man, accompanied them. His job was taking the fort's first year's furs. On January 13, McMillan returned after a fierce snow storm had stranded the party of five. After waiting out the snow storm, they pushed south.

Word soon got to Fort Langley that while the McKenzie party was camped for the night on Puget Sound, the Clallam had attacked the party and killed everyone. Not knowing exactly where the attack took place nor if the reports were credible, it was decided to postpone action until further news could be received.

On February 15, another dispatch courier was sent south. As the fort awaited word, rumors spread among the Indians that King George men had been killed with apparent impunity. Many local Indian tribes became bolder in their challenge of the fort's existence. Trappers spotted war parties and suffered minor attacks. Other Indian tribes, which had become allies of the Hudson's Bay Company, endured attacks from Indians made bold by word of a successful attack against the King George men. By April 15, the *Cadboro* arrived with word confirming the fort's worst fears of the overdue men being killed. Additional attacks on native allies, including the killing of a loyal chief en route to Fort Vancouver with messages from Fort Langley, made urgent the need for a plan to stop the emboldened Indians.

With additional men from the interior posts freshly arrived with the winter take, a two-pronged attack was planned for summer. From Fort Vancouver, sixty men commanded by Alexander Roderic McLeod rode north through the Cowlitz country and then by canoe. A clerk at Fort Vancouver recorded Dr. McLoughlin's words to the war party prior to their departure on July 14, 1828:

> [They]. . . were told by Chief Factor McLoughlin of the necessity
> of going in search of the murderous tribe, and if possible, to make

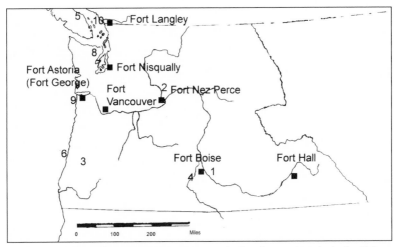

Early Forts and Incidents in Oregon Country. 1. Reed's post attacked; 2. Odgen attacked; 3. Umpquas attacked; 4. Kanakas killed; 5. Cadboro attacked; 6. J. Smith attacked; 7. Clallam Indians attacked; 8. Cadboro bombards village; 9. Naval bombardment; 10. Fort Langley attacked. (*Author*)

a salutary example of them, that the honour of the whites was at stake, and that if we did not succeed in the undertaking, it would be dangerous to be seen by the natives any distance from the fort thereafter. (F. Ermantinger, 16-17)

The armed party found a Clallam village near Liplip Point on Marrow Stone Island, by the Port Townsend portage, on Puget Sound. Timing their assault for dawn, the Fort Vancouver contingent surrounded the village. As the men crept near, an Indian sentry's call of alarm revealed that they had been detected. Indiscriminate musket balls poured into the village as the King George men opened fire. After initial resistance faded, the Clallams fled with many wounded and dying. Left in the village were eight dead, women and children amongst the casualties.

But, this surprise attack was not sufficient to insure that the "personal safety" of the Hudson's Bay men would be honored by the Indians. The armed party rendezvoused with the *Cadboro* and together the two parties proceeded to another village near present day Port Townsend, Washington. Upon arrival, they discovered an empty village, where it was put to flame in retaliation, destroying much of the Clallam Indians' wealth. Intelligence from other Indians discovered that the Clallams had retired to a large village on the New Dungeness Spit, between Port Angeles and Port Townsend.

Arriving off the spit, the *Cadboro* anchored. The Hudson's Bay men presented their demands; when these demands were not met, negotiations were continued.

But, all patience and forbearance was lost when the Clallams attempted to trap Chief Trader McLeod and Captain Simpson ashore during a parley. Returning to the *Cadboro*, Simpson trained the ship's guns on the village and commenced a fierce bombardment. McLeod and an armed party, under the cover of the naval gunfire, loaded in the ship's boats and canoes to go ashore. The cedar houses quickly caught fire and the Indians fled into the forest. Native sources said that at least seventeen Clallams died in the action.

This coordinated attack, inflicting heavy casualties as well as destroying valuable supplies, broke Indian resistance in the immediate area. "The doctor [John McLoughlin] was a firm believer in exemplary punishment for crime, especially in territories where such punishment only would act as a deterrent on savages who might at any time be tempted to outrage." (F. Ermantinger, 196)

At the same time the *Cadboro* was engaging the Clallams, Indians on the southern Oregon coast planned an attack on a group of American trappers. On July 14, a party led by the intrepid Jedediah Smith, were camped on the Umpqua River. Two days earlier, an Umpqua Indian had stolen an axe from the party and the Americans had threatened the use of force to compel its return. The Indians had taken the demand as an insult. Biding their time for two days, the Indians got their revenge.

Smith and two others left the camp early in the morning to reconnoiter a passage across the Coast Mountain Range. Shortly after his departure, nearly one hundred Indians entered the camp and attacked the fur party, killing all save one. When Smith returned to the camp, he too was attacked, but he and his companions escaped.

Smith reached Fort Vancouver on the 10th of August. Doctor John McLoughlin ordered a punitive party be sent to recover Smith's property and to reestablish the Company's authority. A brigade had been preparing to move through that area and if the King George men were to travel in safety, their authority had to be sustained.

Prior to the brigade's departure, McLoughlin sent Michael Laframboise down to the Umpqua River in a hunt for survivors; none were found. McLoughlin then ordered the brigade's leader, Alexander Roderic McLeod, to go to the scene of the attack.

McLeod set out with thirty-six men as well as Smith and his three companions. McLoughlin's instructions to McLeod included the observation that if they did not "make war" on the Indians, "will not our personal security be endangered?" (Morgan, 275-6)[3] While arrival of McLeod's brigade resulted in the return of much of what was taken, the need for the Hudson's Bay Company to protect its own interests through force continued.

The following spring, the traders of Fort Vancouver were expecting the ship *William and Ann*. The ship was bringing much needed supplies,

3. The entire letter to McLeod is worth reproducing:
Dear Sir,

I received yours of the 8th per Michael Laframboise and I am extremely sorry to find by his Statement that Mr. Smith's affair has a more gloomy appearance than I expected and it seems to be in that state, either we must make War on the Murders of his people to make them restore his property or drop the business entirely.

I know many people will argue that we have no right to make war on the Natives, on the other hand if the business is droped, will not our personal security be endangered wherever this report reaches. Again suppose that by accident a Vessel was wrecked on the Coast, to possess themselves of the property would not the Natives, seeing these Murders escape with impunity, kill all the crew that fell in their power and say as these now do. We did not take them to be the same people as you have not the natives of Cape Look-out not many years since killed a vessel wrecked opposite their village, and is it not our duty as Christians to endeavor as much as possible to prevent the perpetration of such atrocious crimes and is their any measures so likely to accomplish so effectually this object as to make these Murderers restore at least their ill-gotten booty now in their possession. But it is unnecessary after the various conversations we have had for me to say any thing further on this subject. You know those Indians you know our means, as a failure in undertaking too much, would make this unfortunate affair worse and as you are on the spot you therefore will decide on what is best to be done and depend that whatever that decision may be at least as far as I am concerned every allowance will be made for the situation you are placed in.

N.B. Laframboise and Cournoyer will go to the Umqua or return immediately as you think proper. Mr. Smith offers himself and party to accompany you to War on the Murders. I refer him to you for an answer.
I am Sir
Yours truly
Jon McLoughlin

since it was Hudson's Bay Company policy to maintain one year's worth of trading supplies to support its fur trading posts throughout the Columbia Department. After making landfall, on March 10, 1829, the ship attempted to enter the Columbia River, but ran into trouble on the constantly shifting sand bars at the mouth causing the *William and Ann* to go aground on Peacock Spit. While it was probable that the crew of twenty-six had perished in the ship wreck, much of the cargo became flotsam and washed ashore on the south bank of the Great River of the West.

Soon the Clatsop Indians would reap a harvest of trade goods from the wreck. Rumors reached Fort Vancouver that the Clatsops had slain the survivors as they had come ashore. No evidence supported this report, which could have been started by the Clatsops' enemies. Nevertheless, it appeared that the authority of the Hudson's Bay Company had been challenged. It was the very fear that Dr. John McLoughlin, Chief Factor at Fort Vancouver and the man responsible for the entire Columbia Department, had written about the previous year: the possibility of ship-wrecked survivors being killed by Indians upon reaching the shore. Dr. McLoughlin quickly acted as he had said he would when he had written what had been the implied policy until 1828: The Hudson's Bay Company would "make war" to protect its interest throughout the Columbia Department.

Chief Trader William Connolly assembled a war party. Escorted by the *Cadboro*, they proceeded to the Clatsop village closest to the wreck. The party discovered that the villagers were flush with the ship's wealth. Connolly made demands, without any apparent hope that they would be met, and when not met, the ship's cannons opened fire on the village, destroying it. Casualties, from the white's perspective were reportedly light. Three Clatsops were killed, among them, the chief.

The cannon fire sent home the point that Hudson's Bay men would be safe in the Oregon Country or the Most Honorable Company would make war. In fact, a year later, another Hudson's Bay ship was wrecked near the same area wherein all of the crew were saved by the Indians, convinced of the strength of the King George Men.

About the same time as Chief Trader Connolly was engaging the Clatsops, the last recorded Indian attack on men from Fort Langley occurred. On March 21, 1829, as a party of ten men headed up the Fraser River, a war party of over a hundred Yucultas from Vancouver

Island blocked the river with armed canoes. Instead of fleeing as other enemies of the Yucultas had always done, the Fort Langley men charged ahead with their boats, dodging bullets and arrows and breaking the blockade. Soon, the Langley crew made it to shore to good fighting ground and opened fire on the pursuing Indians. A fire-fight ensued, and after nearly a half hour, the Indians fled with heavy casualties.

Fort Vancouver in 1845. Note the Hudson's Bay Company flag. (*from Sketches in North America and the Oregon Territory by Sir Henry James Warre, 1848*)

Throughout the Oregon Country, whether north or south of 49 degrees of latitude, the Hudson's Bay Company would use force or the threat of force to further the company's objectives. That force, while reduced in scale, was as violent and indiscriminate in its application as any ever employed later by American forces, as witnessed by the naval bombardment of villages and the killing of women and children. What would ultimately push the Hudson's Bay Company out of the "American" portion of the Oregon Country was a huge influx of American citizens. The swelling of the American population in the Oregon Country started innocently with people the Americans called explorers. The British had another name for them.

Spies and Explorers

The next game opened with a mission to reconnoiter the country done under the guise of a civilian scientific exploration party. In 1832, Benjamin Louis Eulalie de Bonneville took a twenty-six month leave of absence from his commission as a United States Army captain "for the purpose of. . . exploring the country to the Rocky Mountains and beyond, with a view to ascertaining the nature and character of the several tribes inhabiting those regions; the trade which might be profitably carried on with them; the quality of the soil; the productions, the minerals, the natural history, the climate, the geography and topography, as well as the geology of the various parts of the country." (Carey 269) From this description, the exploration seemed an innocent scientific exploration effort, without overt military intent.

On May 1, 1832, Bonneville's party of 110 set off from Fort Osage, Missouri. Crossing the continental divide, his force entered Pierre's Hole, just west of the Teton Range, where they met hostile Indians. On July 18, Bonneville's force camped to trap and trade. Instead, they were attacked by nearly five hundred Indians. In one day of fierce fighting, the Indians were repulsed by the superior fire-power of Bonneville's men.

After his one battle, Bonneville explored well into the Columbia River basin, visited the Hudson's Bay Fort Nez Perce, also known as Fort Walla Walla,[4] and returned to American settlements by August 1835. From his reports, the true nature of his assignment becomes clearer. His first report to Major General Macomb, General in Chief of the Army, was written in 1833, "the language of which indicates that he understood that he was to collect information as to the practicability of military occupation." (Carey 271) His reports detailed the strength of the British and the size of the military force needed to effect American control. In recognition of his service to the United States, Bonneville was restored to the Army and eventually reached the rank of general.[5]

The next army exploration was commanded in 1843, by Second Lieutenant John C. Fremont of the Army's Corps of Engineers. His travels extended throughout the Oregon Country including a stop at Britain's Fort Vancouver. While the intent of his expedition was exploration, the British could not help but note that the U.S. Army was traveling throughout the region. Further, whatever the declared purpose of the expedition, it would have been prudent for the British to believe that its true purpose was to obtain military intelligence.[6]

In addition to these overland deployments, the United States military periodically sent the U.S. Navy to show the flag. As noted above, in 1818, the first ship to do so was the frigate U.S.S. *Ontario*. But, as the tensions over the division of the Oregon Country increased, so did naval visits.

President Andrew Jackson personally dispatched the region's next

4. Although its official name was Fort Walla Walla, most trappers referred to it as Fort Nez Perce. Nez Perce is used here for the fort's name to avoid confusion with the much later U.S. Army Fort Walla Walla.

5. As lieutenant colonel of the 4th U.S. Infantry, Bonneville was in command of the U.S. Army post, Vancouver Barracks from 1852-1855.

naval visitor, Lieutenant William A. Slacum. The lieutenant had acted as Jackson's confidential agent previously and was known to be discreet, resourceful, and effective. Ordered by the State Department to avoid any overt spying, his mission's goal was to gain information on matters "political, physical, statistical, and geographical, as may prove useful or interesting to this government." (Carey, 262)

On December 22, 1836, Slacum arrived on the Columbia River from the Sandwich Islands, prepared to change from his gentleman's attire and into the clothes of an explorer of the unending wilderness. His analytical roaming of the vast territory included a welcome trip to American missionary Jason Lee's outpost in the Willamette Valley. Afterwards, as historian Charles Carey noted, "Lieutenant Slacum was received at Fort Vancouver with some suspicion." The suspicion was conveyed by Chief Factor John McLoughlin in a letter to the Hudson's Bay Company. He summed up his assessment of Slacum by writing, "I suppose Mr. Slacum was an agent of the American Government." Justified though that suspicion may have been, the British did not act upon it and Slacum returned to Jackson with the information he had been sent to obtain.

Two years later, one of the greatest naval scientific expeditions ever authorized for the United States Navy was undertaken, the Wilkes Expedition of 1838-1842. Lieutenant Charles Wilkes accepted command of a six-ship squadron to explore the world. Many American claims in the Pacific were strengthened by Wilkes' intrepid naval forces.

6. Fremont made two more western expeditions of exploration. In 1846, he returned briefly to Oregon. On May 12, 1846, while camped near the northern end of Klamath Lake, he was attacked by the Klamath Indians in an unusual night battle. The Fremont Party had been divided, sending out noted scout Kit Carson to find the best route for the planned march north. While Fremont's small party remained in camp that night, discussing the news recently brought from California (see below), they were surprised, and three were killed and one mortally wounded. The next day, Carson returned with his scouting party. In retaliation, on May 13, Fremont led an attack on a Klamath village. In an unequal battle of rifles against arrows, Fremont killed fourteen Klamaths.

Prior to these battles, Fremont had received word of impending war with Mexico. On May 8, Lieutenant Archibald Gillespie, U.S. Marines, had overtaken Fremont with orders to proceed to California in anticipation of seizing that province when war broke out. Coincidently, President Polk signed the declaration of war with Mexico on May 13, 1846.

Wilkes departed Norfolk, Virginia on August 18, 1838, with six ships: three sloops, one brig, and two schooners. After one ship sank and another was sent home with progress reports, Wilkes' four-ship squadron explored throughout the Pacific.

On April 28, 1841, the four warships arrived in the waters of British Columbia. From his flagship, the U.S.S. *Vincennes*, which was then the most powerful ship in the waters of the Oregon Country, Wilkes explained his presence as one of exploration. But the British would note that here was an American naval squadron operating unchallenged in Oregon waters.

Wilkes himself visited Fort Vancouver after riding overland from Puget Sound. As he traveled throughout the area claimed by both Great Britain and the United States, there can be little doubt that the British viewed the travels of both the squadron by sea and armed military troops across the land with alarm. While it might truly be a scientific effort, the British were forced to recognize it as a military spying mission as well.

In July 1841, Wilkes dispatched one ship of his squadron, the U.S.S. *Peacock*, to the Columbia River, where soon it added its name to Oregon's Pacific graveyard. Lieutenant William Hudson, commanding, crossed the bar in a light fog. As he saw breakers loom out of the mists, he feared he was too far south of the channel and turned his ship north, inadvertently aiming directly for the north spit. As the ship struck, the fog lifted, and a storm materialized with the sudden power noted by many a mariner on the Oregon coast. Run aground, the captain ordered, "Abandon ship," and the crew lowered the boats. In a remarkable feat of seamanship, Hudson saved his entire crew. In sinking, the *Peacock* gave its name to the northern spit at the great river's mouth.

From the mouth of the Columbia, Wilkes dispatched Lieutenant George F. Emmons (late of the *Peacock*), with a detail of thirty-nine men to explore the Oregon Country. The alarm of the skeptical British increased as they watched the well-armed party of sailors and marines roam across the territory.

Armies and Navies Prepare for War

The British saw the increased American military movement as an alteration in the balance of power. In 1832-35, the Americans had sent Bonneville; Slacum in 1836-37, the Wilkes naval expedition in 1841, including the overland military reconnaissance of Lieutenant Emmons, and the Fremont army expedition of 1843.

Coupled with these official government actions was the large emigration of Americans in the early 1840s—a population that represented a potential militia overwhelming to any force the British had available. The British were rightfully leery of American intentions. In 1843, settlers gathered at Champoeg, Willamette Valley, to determine whether they wished to be part of Great Britain or America. In a close vote, the settlers opted to align themselves with the American government. While not negating the existing treaty between the two countries, the settlers' vote exacerbated British fears.

Oregon Country in the 1840s. 1. Wilkes Expedition, USS *Peacock* sinks; 2. Settlers at Champoeg vote to join the U.S.; 3. HMS *Modeste* and USS *Shark* arrive off Fort Vancouver; 4. San Juan Island (*Author*)

The British reacted to the American efforts. Until the growing threat of American military intervention, the British had relied primarily upon the Hudson's Bay Company to represent the Crown's interest in the Pacific Northwest. However, the Hudson's Bay Company could not be expected to defend British concerns from either American Army and naval forces or militia in the event of an outbreak of formal hostilities.

In the 1840s, sixteen different British ships, representing 350 guns, visited some part of the Oregon Country's waters. At the height of the crisis, the Royal Navy was represented in the Northeastern Pacific by Her Majesty's Ships *America* (50 guns), *Fisgard* (42 guns), *Cormorant* (6 guns), *Herald* (26 guns), *Pandora* (6 guns), and *Modeste* (18 guns). The *America's* draft was too deep to safely cross the Columbia River bar so it took position in Puget Sound. During the critical years of 1844-48, the commander of the Royal Navy's Pacific Station was Rear-Admiral Sir George Seymour. When the *America* arrived in Puget Sound, it dispatched sailors and marines overland to Fort Vancouver, with the determination to "show the British population there 'that our Government is well inclined to afford them Protection (Gough 1969).'" Seymour's report

Ultimatum on the Oregon Question, an American political cartoon published in 1846 satarizing the response from European powers to President Polk's treaty proposal. (*Edwin William Clay, Library of Congress*)

noted that a "considerable force" would be needed to stem the growing threat the emigrant population presented to British affairs.

The Crown sent two officers to conduct a survey to determine what force would be needed. In August 1845, Lieutenant William Peel, Royal Navy, son of Prime Minister Sir Robert Peel, and Captain H. W. Parke, Royal Marines arrived in the Columbia River Valley. They carried a letter from Captain Gordon of the *H.M.S. America* reassuring Chief Factor John McLoughlin that the Royal Navy was in Oregon waters to protect British interests.

Concurrent with the efforts of Peel and Parke, the British government had sent overland two lieutenants of the Royal Marines: Henry Warre and M. Vavasour. While instructed to give the appearance of two private individual travelers, their real purpose was to ascertain Britain's ability to move troops overland, through Canada, to defend the British claim to Oregon. Their detailed report, coupled with Peel's, painted a grim picture for Britain. Warre and Vavasour noted that, in 1845, the population in the Willamette Valley was approximately six thousand, of which no more than one thousand could be considered loyal to British interests.

Further, the Canadian overland route for troops was greatly inferior to the American route through South Pass in the Rocky Mountains. It was during this period of heightened tensions that the Hudson's Bay fort at

Vancouver added a bastion, complete with cannon, as a means of repelling an American attack.

The marine officers pointed out that an 1844 detachment of three hundred U.S. Army dragoons had escorted wagon trains along the Oregon Trail to the Rocky Mountains without difficulty and that there were major forts along the route to support future military expeditions. These American Army efforts illustrated the ability of the Americans to put a sizeable military force in the Oregon Country with relative ease. If the political will of the Americans dictated sending troops, then it could be done with comparative promptness.

The British knew that the 1844 presidential campaign had resulted in James Polk's pledge to "reoccupy" the Oregon Country; all of it. In 1844, Americans rallied to Manifest Destiny with slogans such as, "Fifty-four forty, or fight!" The Americans wanted everything up to the northern boundary of the Oregon Country—54 degrees, 40 minutes north latitude. Both reports from the British officers encouraged a British retreat to the 49th parallel, with retention of Vancouver Island crucial.

In 1844, the *Modeste,* commanded by Captain Thomas Baillie, did cross the mouth of the Columbia and anchored near Fort Vancouver. Responding to the threat to the American community of Oregon City that the *Modeste* represented, the U.S.S. *Shark* was dispatched from the Pacific Squadron in 1846 and proceeded to the lower Columbia River near Fort Vancouver. The *Shark* was a good, if not perfect match for the *Modeste,* should a conflict break out. She carried ten 18-pounder carronades and two 9-pounder long guns, with a complement of approximately seventy men under the command of Lieutenant Neil Howison. The *Shark* would remain on-station until the crisis was resolved.[7]

The Anglo-American "Pig War"

On June 15, 1846, a treaty appeared to diffuse the crisis. The treaty had been suggested by President Polk but originally rejected by the British.

---

7. On September 10, 1846, while attempting to cross the Columbia bar outbound, the *Shark* ran aground on the southern spit, causing her to sink. Her crew was rescued by boats in the waters nearby, including boats sent by the H.M.S. *Modeste.* As the ship ground on the spit, the *Shark* tore apart, with whole sections of the ship floating away. Several portions of the ship, with its cannons still lashed to the planking, floated south onto the Oregon shore. These weapons gave name to the Oregon community of Cannon Beach.

Compromise was ultimately reached, and the treaty was signed and ratified.

The treaty established the continuation of the 49th parallel west as the international boundary with the exception that all of Vancouver Island would remain British. The treaty failed, however, to make a clear distinction where the boundary fell between the mainland and Vancouver Island. In the waters between the mainland and the large island of Vancouver are hundreds of smaller islands, some above, some below, and some on the 49th parallel. But to whom did these islands belong?

In the summer of 1859, on the island of San Juan in the eponymous island group, the last round in the game between the great nations was started by of all things, a pig. When the pig, owned by a Hudson's Bay employee, wandered into an American vegetable patch, it was killed. Seeking restitution, the British citizen turned to British authorities who then attempted to arrest Lyman Cutlar, the American who fired the shot heard, if not around the world, then at least around the island. The British were met by Mr. Cutlar who was armed and willing to kill more than a pig.

As tensions grew, the summer saw each country increase its number of troops on and around the island, with both sides claiming the island a possession of their respective nations. The Royal Marines, also known as the Bootnecks, had established an outpost near the north end of San Juan Island. It was supported by Royal Navy warships, which eventually embarked, at the height of the incident, 2,140 Royal Marines. The Bootnecks were ready to land and reenforce the detachment of fellow Royal Marines who had already built a stockade at the English Camp.

Commanded by West Point graduate George Pickett, the Americans first landed sixty-six infantry men of the 9th U.S. Infantry Regiment. A loyal officer of the United States Army, Captain Pickett warned his men not to fire until they could see the whites of British eyes.

Calling for additional forces to counter the British, Brigadier-General William Harney, in charge of the U.S. Army's Columbia Department, ordered additional 9th Infantry troops as well as elements of the 4th Infantry and 3rd Artillery to reinforce the initial 9th Infantry contingent. Eventually the American strength reached 461 troops of all arms, and fourteen cannons. At one point in the crisis, the Royal Crown Governor, Sir James Douglas, actually ordered the British forces to attack. But, calmer heads in the Great Britain's Senior Service (the Royal Navy) disregarded the order.

Armed conflict remained just one stupid act away. Troops hung poised at each end of the small island, ready to shoot. As the summer passed into fall and then winter, war ardor diminished.

President James Buchanan, greatly displeased with the reports of General Harney's effort to escalate the crisis into war, sent General Winfield Scott to the Northwest to investigate. After consulting with Harney and the San Juan Island commander, George Pickett, General Scott met with the Royal Governor of British Columbia, Sir James Douglas. A

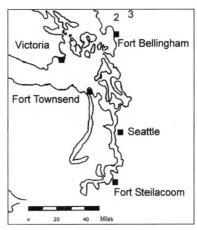

The Anglo-American "Pig War." 1. San Juan Island; 2. Storekeeper shot at border; 3. U.S. Army "invades" Canada at Fort Langley (*Author*)

compromise was suggested of no more than one hundred troops of each side on the island. This peace gesture was quickly accepted. Having kept peace, General Scott returned to Washington, D.C.

Still longing for glory, General Harney tried to escalate the crisis. The following spring, he ordered Pickett back onto the island. This insubordination led to President Buchanan relieving General Harney of command, and Colonel George Wright was assigned to command the district. With war tensions increasing back east, war with England, particularly over a small group of islands in the remote Washington Territory, was unthinkable.

Partly as a result of time to reflect, and partly because civil war loomed as the election of 1860 neared in the United States, the majority of troops were recalled from the island by both sides. While troops from both nations remained on San Juan Island, the Pig War was now a cold war.

That winter of 1859-60, tensions remained taut throughout the region. In 1859, an American soldier stole a gun from a British merchant, who chased him to the American Army camp just south of the mainland border. In turn, the storekeeper was run off and followed into Canada by the trooper's fellow soldiers. While in Canada, the soldiers shot the storekeeper. A protest was made to the American's officer but his reply was jingoistic speech-making rather than his handing over the culprits.

Another "invasion" took place in January 1860, when a U.S. Army officer with an armed force went to the Hudson's Bay's Fort Langley on the Fraser River and arrested two deserters. The detail then retreated back across the international boundary. The officer had threatened to fight any opposition. Despite all the bombast and posturing, the wounded storekeeper and the dead pig were the only casualties throughout that period.

The great game ended with the final treaty of 1872. Kaiser Wilhelm of Germany, having been asked by both nations to act as a neutral judge, determined where the boundary should be drawn, giving the disputed islands to the United States.

While many battles and wars were fought throughout the Oregon Country in the nineteenth century, the Pig War was the only "war" fought between any of the great nations. As Great Britain retired north of the 49th parallel, the United States was left in sole command of the southern half of the Oregon Country that had been created by Anglo-American efforts. The Oregon Country became the Oregon Territory. Now the military would be faced with fighting the nations that were already there before the Americans arrived: The Indian nations.

~

The historical sites mentioned in this chapter have not been well preserved. Some of the forts have been rebuilt; but with one exception, none are original. The Pacific Fur Company forts are gone. The first fort built, Fort Astoria, is marked by a reconstructed block house, part of the palisade, and a historical marker. At present, it can be found in downtown Astoria, Oregon. Other Pacific Fur posts are marked, if at all, by road side historical markers. For example, Willamette Post is memorialized by a roadside marker on Oregon Highway 219, south of the Willamette River, about five miles south of the town of Newberg, Oregon.

Because the North West Company became the Hudson's Bay Company, the two company posts are treated as one. Four Hudson's Bay posts are still visible today, if only as museums or reconstructions. The principle fort that was Fort Vancouver, today, is part of the National Park Service, and has been reconstructed in Vancouver, Washington. The

A reconstruction of Fort Clatsop, Lewis and Clark's temporary structure that established an American military claim to Oregon Country. (*Author*)

reconstruction is on-going, with buildings slated for addition in the future.

The second most important Hudson's Bay fort reconstructed is Fort Langley, east of Vancouver, British Columbia. Located just off Highway 1A, in Langley, B.C., it is a fine example of a fur trading post and has an original building still standing, dating from the 1840s.

Fort Nisqually is another of the Hudson's Bay posts, and is part of the Tacoma's city park system. Any visit to Tacoma must include a visit to this outstanding reconstruction.

A museum at Parma, Idaho, entitled Fort Boise (of the Hudson's Bay Company), details the history of furs as part of its displays. The museum is just off of U.S. Highway 95.

A fort trading fort originally built by Nathanial Wyeth, but sold to the Hudson's Bay, can be found in Pocatello, Idaho. It is an outstanding replica of the post eventually taken over by the U.S. Army.

The other forts are marked, at best, by road side signs. As for the battlefields, most have been lost. None have been located with any great accuracy; general locales can be visited.

The mouth of the Columbia River, scene of the bombardment, has been tamed, but is still worth visiting. The upper reaches of the Snake River can still be imagined as wild. One of the few battle sites of the trapper's era marked is the Jedediah Smith battle, on U.S. Highway 101, north of Reedsport, Oregon.

On San Juan Island in Washington is a National Park Service protected area consisting of two parts. The San Juan Island National Historical

Park has an English Camp and an American Camp site, each preserving the locations of the opposing forces' bivouacs during the Pig War. The English Camp has a blockhouse.

Of the few marked battles fought during this period, a roadside marker indicates the Pierre's Hole battle site, located along Idaho Highway 33 (milepost 143.9), west of the Teton Mountains.

With the approach of 2011, it is long past time to commemorate the first permanent American establishment west of the Rocky Mountains, Fort Astoria. It was here that the Oregon Country started. It deserves to be reconstructed and the history noted. What could be more fitting as the bicentennial arrives than for the National Park Service to create a national monument by reconstructing not only the fort, but a Clatsop village, allowing for the future education of all Americans.

The rest of the sites mentioned within the chapter have been neither preserved nor marked.

Chapter 3

Oregon Divided

The Cayuse Indian War

For the first time, the Oregon Country no longer extended from the 42nd parallel in the south to a northern limit of 54 degrees, 40 minutes of latitude. The great expanse was now divided between the British and the Americans along the 49th parallel. To the north was British Columbia, to the south lay what the Americans would call the Oregon Territory, with its capital located at Oregon City, a settlement where the falls of the Willamette River provided a rich source of water power.

Even as the 1846 treaty created the new territory, huge numbers of American emigrants surged across the Plains, traversed the Continental Divide at South Pass and entered the Oregon Territory. South Pass, a naturally occurring break in the Rocky Mountains located in present-day Wyoming, marked the eastern boundary of the territory where the Oregon Trail first penetrated the new American province.

The Oregon Trail became the path to paradise. Starting in 1841, the Oregon and California Trails funneled pilgrims through the South Pass. Starting with fewer than fifty families in 1841, soon the presence of thousands of newcomers overwhelmed any hopes that the British could counter the swelling American numbers with sympathetic settlers of their own. By 1842, two hundred families had made their way through the South Pass to Oregon; by 1843, the population exceeded eight hundred; by 1844, two thousand; and by 1845, the population was over five thousand.

Starting in 1846, an alternative trail, the Applegate, brought people to southern Oregon. The Oregon Trail ended at the terminus of the northern Willamette Valley, while a fewer number of pioneers opted for the Rogue River Valley just north of the Californian border.

By the 1850s, thousands of wagons brought tens of thousands of pilgrims striving for a new life. Eventually they would spread all over the west, but their first destination was the reported paradise of the Oregon Country. But it was not the entire region that lured the Americans; as the wagon trains entered the Oregon Territory, they passed through many Indian nations, not stopping to settle. Instead, their destination was the fertile, far western locality, the Willamette Valley.

The next great division of the Oregon Territory was the separation of native people from the land. In order to make the new land an extension of America, the American practice and policy from the east was continued. The established method was to deny Indian rights by driving them from their land. Until the establishment of the Oregon Territory, the American policy had been to force the Indians westward. But having now occupied the continent all the way to the Pacific shores, no longer could a policy of westward displacement work.

The creation of an Oregon Territory marked the first major change in American policy, even if it was not recognized as such at the time. It would lead to the eventual adoption of a reservation system—the subjugation of Indian nations and the abandonment of the west as an Indian reserve, not the then-planned-for Indian Territory.

The first Indian nation to experience this unplanned policy ignited the growing white wrath upon themselves. Having withstood the intrusion by western migration, the Cayuse knew their whole way of life was in danger from the new settlers. By inciting the first Indian war of the Northwest, the Cayuse set the pattern of Northwest Indian affairs.

For the next thirty years, there was nearly uninterrupted warfare in part or all of the Oregon Territory. In creating the need for American protection, the Indian wars helped to accelerate and increase pressure for Oregon statehood. It would be a series of Indian wars from 1847 until Oregon became a state in 1859 that created the next division of Oregon. The carnage started with the Cayuse Indian War.

The Opening Rounds

The first permanent American establishments in Oregon were religious. As missionaries entered the Oregon Country, they helped to counter the presence of the British Hudson's Bay Company. Jason Lee's pioneering mission in the Willamette Valley sent word back to the United States of an Eden waiting for the civilizing hand of the white man.

Other missionaries soon followed. One mission was established near present day Walla
Walla, Washington, in the heart
of the Cayuse Indian country.
The missionaries were Marcus
and Narcissus Whitman. While
well intentioned, the Whitmans,
like most missionaries, never
made any attempt to understand
the focus of their efforts, the
Indians. This lack of understanding, coupled with the continued influx of white people,
resulted in the Indian's distrust
of the Whitmans. Ultimately,
the Whitmans were blamed for
many Cayuse misfortunes.

Whitman Mission as sketched by a visitor.
*(Detail from an original at the Oregon
Historical Society)*

When measles struck in the summer of 1847, brought by the wagon
trains passing through, the Indians believed it was intentionally introduced by the whites to destroy them. The half-breed Joe Lewis, who
lived at the mission, told the Cayuse that Doctor Marcus Whitman was
using measles to exterminate the Indians for their land.

On November 29, 1847, the Whitmans and others at the mission
were slain, and word quickly spread. The news of fourteen whites being
killed was inflammatory in itself but the additional details of women,
including Mrs. Whitman, and children being killed only increased the
outrage.

Fears of further atrocities were fueled by the news that fifty-seven
women and children had been taken captive. Within a day, the Hudson's
Bay Fort Walla Walla had heard and sent off a message to the main post
at Fort Vancouver. Word reached that post within a week and the chief
factors at the fort dispatched their most experienced member, Peter
Skene Ogden, to deal with the crisis. On December 7, Ogden left Fort
Vancouver with trade goods to negotiate the release of the fifty-seven
captives still held by the Cayuse.

In Oregon City, the provisional legislature (Oregon was not yet an
official territory of the United States) was in session as word of the mas-

sacre arrived on December 8th. A quick call for militia men was sounded. The next day, forty-six volunteers were sworn in as the first members of the Oregon Rifles. The company was placed under the command of Henry A.G. Lee, of the Virginia Lees. He had traveled to Oregon with a member of another illustrious Virginia family, Charles Pickett, who was instrumental in inflaming passions through his newspaper, the *Flumgudgeon Gazette and Bumble Bee Budget*.

This first company of Rifles, with Lee commanding and with Lieutenants Joseph Magone and John E. Ross as subordinates, immediately departed for The Dalles to stop the threatened uprising of the Wascos and Deschutes in support of the Cayuse.

On December 10, the legislature authorized a force of five hundred members of the Oregon Rifles, a brave move considering the treasury was nearly empty with merely forty-three dollars, and the only recourse to support such a force was through private donations and loans. One such loan would be procured from James Douglas, another of the chief factors at Fort Vancouver. Having authorized the force on the eleventh, the legislature appointed Cornelius Gilliam as colonel and James Waters as lieutenant colonel and second in command. Lee had been given the rank of major.

Gilliam was not a poor choice. He had led a recent wagon train to Oregon, with the peculiar intention of creating a new nation within the Oregon Country with him as its leader. He had previously fought Indians in both the Black Hawk and Seminole Indian Wars. While the leadership already assembled fostered confidence, a lack of volunteers hampered immediate response to the cries to advance against the Indians.

Forces other than war were at work. On December 19, Ogden arrived at the Hudson's Bay's Fort Nez Perce and called for a council with the Cayuse for the twenty-third. Catholic priests had already given hope to the Indians that war might be averted if the Cayuse surrendered their captives and gave up the guilty for punishment. Henry Spalding, a fellow missionary of the Whitmans, but to the Nez Perce tribe, had promised the Nez Perce he would try and prevent the militia from leaving the Willamette Valley. These contrary forces sought to counter the forces for war sweeping through the Columbia Gorge.

The military advanced and Lee's company arrived at The Dalles on December 21. As the troops marched toward the fort, they encountered

A sensationalized drawing of the Whitman massacre. (*Library of Congress*)

a force of Cayuses, Wascos, and Deschutes besieging the stockade. The Rifles immediately strengthened The Dalles as a defensive position, but would need more troops for an offensive. Gilliam was preparing a relief force at Oregon City while Captain William Martin took command of a recently arrived company of volunteers from Yamhill County. Additional forces included the French-Canadians, led by the step-son of Doctor McLoughlin, Captain Tom McKay, with brothers Charles as First Lieutenant and Alex as Second Lieutenant comprising the rest of the officer corps, while Marion County also contributed a company under the command of L.N. English.

Gilliam departed on January 8 from Portland with a force of two hundred and twenty to relieve The Dalles. The succor was needed. Members of Lee's command were deserting now that the initial war fever had subsided and they were confronted by enemy forces.

On the same date as Gilliam's departure, Lee's company skirmished with hostiles at The Dalles. Eight Cayuse and fifteen other Indians of the Deschutes and Wasco tribes made off with a herd of cattle, stolen from immigrant wagon trains. Major Lee led seventeen men in a chase toward the Indians. Catching the herd, a two-hour gun battle ensued, and three Indians were killed. Sergeant William Berry was wounded and Privates Pugh and Jackson were killed, the first combat casualties of the Oregon Rifles.

Passing Gilliam in the Gorge was Ogden. He was en route to Oregon City with the fifty-seven captives whose release he had successfully negotiated on January 2. The news strengthened the resolve of the Oregon Rifles as they struggled through the wintry Columbia River Gorge. Ogden was greeted as a hero when he arrived with the captives on January 10. Meanwhile, the desire to punish the murderers of the Whitmans remained strong. The relief force moved east after creating Fort Gilliam, a supply base in the Columbia Gorge.

On January 23, Colonel Gilliam arrived at The Dalles (now called Fort Lee, or Fort Wascopam) to find Major Lee's company down to a strength of thirteen. The relieving column had approximately two hundred and twenty Oregon Riflemen, and other troops were still marshaling in the Willamette Valley. Colonel Gilliam now commanded four hundred and forty-one men ready to punish the Cayuse.

As the troops arrived, it appeared that some of their stock had wandered away. Actually, some Cayuse had snuck in and hobbled the horses' hooves, making them seem to be grazing. As the soldiers went to move the horses back, the Indians sprang a trap, killing two of Colonel Gilliam's command. The first non-warrior Indian casualty of the war marked the arrival of the rest of the Oregon Rifles. An Indian woman, attempting to enter the perimeter, was shot in the mistaken belief that she was scouting as part of the hostile force, seemingly preparing to attack.

The first major engagement of the war commenced the following day. For the next six days, fighting would take place under Gilliam's direction. Leaving about half of his force at The Dalles to await supplies and reinforcements, Gilliam marched east with a force of about one hundred and thirty men. The terrain had steep gullies and canyons cutting through jagged basalt plateaus with little more than sage brush and the odd juniper tree. It was the same barren country the pioneers had hurriedly crossed as being worthless, but now it was covered with winter snow. The temperatures plummeted with the wind chill of the Columbia River gales as the Oregon Rifles marched through seeking to flush the Indians from their winter villages nestled in sheltered valley floors.

At the Deschutes River, the force proceeded south, upstream, for approximately five miles before establishing their first camp. From that camp, Gilliam's plan was to attack the Deschutes' villages. With that objective in mind, he dispatched a force under Lee to reconnoiter. On

Cayuse War Overview. 1. Deschutes River Campaign; 2. Battle of Sand Hollow; 3. Battle of Tucannon River; 4. Battle of Touchet River. (*Author*)

the afternoon of the 26th of January at around three o'clock, Lee's force was surprised. One Oregon Rifle volunteer, William Stillwell, received an arrow in his hip; the Riflemen then charged the Indians, breaking up the attack. As one private wrote home after the battle:

> The Indians at last, being severely galled by the firing from that place, took advantage of the little party when their guns were all empty and made a charge and run them from their favorite place. In their retreat Perin came very near being cut off. One Indian, mounted on a swift horse, with spear in hand, rushed within 20 feet of him. He was, however, fired on by Captain Lawrence Hall, and was glad to wheel and make his escape.[1]

The Indian village was seized, and destroyed. Overtaking the Indians near the Oregon Trail, one Indian warrior was killed and two women were captured. While retiring, a larger party of Deschutes Indians attacked Lee's detachment. Outnumbered, the force retreated into a canyon and a defensive perimeter. The Deschutes rolled boulders down onto the force. The boulders as well as arrows and bullets flew for several hours of fighting, until dark caused the Indians to withdraw and the Oregon force to escape to the main force.

1. Letter of I.W. Smith, dated February 15, 1848, from a report to the Secretary of War, January 29, 1889, by Captain W. E. Birkhimer, investigating war claims by still living members of the Oregon Rifles.

The next day at Stag Hollow, a canyon off of the main Deschutes River canyon, the Rifles found the Indians had fortified a position on the rim. As the Indians shouted their taunts and insults, Lieutenant T. C. Shaw moved his troops of Company B toward their flank. Shouting to take some scalps, Lieutenant Shaw led his company of the Oregon Rifles in a charge, and the Indians fled.

For the next two days, the Oregon Rifles skirmished further into the Deschutes' territory. Finally, an all but abandoned village was discovered. The only hostiles left were elderly members of the tribe too old to flee, but still possessing cattle stolen from the passing wagon trains. The Indians were left in peace while the cattle was seized and used to feed the hungry troopers.

With his geographic objective reached, a village of the Deschutes, Gilliam ordered the Oregon Rifles back to The Dalles, leaving the enemy force largely intact. The estimated casualties after the fighting was four dead from the Rifles and estimates of twenty to thirty Indians killed.

This first campaign was a draw. But, the Rifles had passed a harsh test. Offsetting that gain was their discovery upon returning to The Dalles that three more of their members had been killed by Indian sharpshooters, one who had been shot while tending livestock.

The War Continues

While the opening battle was taking place, the provisional government had taken steps to avoid further fighting. Based upon the reports of Peter Ogden and Catholic missionaries in the Cayuse Indian homeland, it was hoped that by creating a peace commission, the individuals responsible for the Whitman attack could be forced to surrender and further bloodshed avoided. Provisional Governor George Abernathy informed Colonel Gilliam that a peace commission had been appointed with the government's aim being that "no friendly tribes will be attacked; that all [we] want is the murderers, and restitution of stolen properties." The Governor further ordered Colonel Gilliam to stay in his garrison where he was to remain in The Dalles until the peace commission arrived.

For the peace commission to have credibility with the citizens of the Oregon Territory, the appointees could not be perceived as being sympathetic to the Indians. Consequently, the three men were selected as much for political reasons as for peace-making abilities. Major Henry A.G. Lee, fresh off the fight with the Cayuse and already at The Dalles, was chosen. Lee, age thirty, had respect as a soldier and he had spent his first winter in the territory at the Henry Spalding mission on the Clearwater amongst the Nez Perce, studying their language and customs. This gave him great credit in a society that viewed Indian culture as almost monolithic. Thus, having studied one tribe, Lee was seen as understanding all tribes.

The second peace commissioner was forty-one year old Robert Newell, speaker of the provisional assembly and a man the community greatly respected. He had lived and hunted with several Indian tribes and was considered very knowledgeable of their ways. The third commissioner was the Commissary General of the Oregon Rifles, Joel Palmer. His was an obvious selection, not only because he was admired as an honest man, but he had previously been appointed the Superintendent of Indian Affairs of the provisional Oregon Territory. Peace was impossible without the superintendent's direct and active participation.

On February 3, 1848, Newell and Palmer left Oregon City to join Lee and Gilliam at The Dalles. While en route, the commission was joined by two companies of reinforcements whose supplies included artillery. If peace did not work, additional troops and firepower might. The commission arrived at The Dalles on February 11, where they found Colonel Gilliam eager to advance and engage the Indians.

The commission preceded the main force under a guard of one hundred horsemen. It wanted a smaller armed party to accompany them, but Gilliam insisted on a column sufficient to withstand an attack until he could move up with the main force.

Rumors arrived in camp that all the Indian tribes up river had united with the Cayuse in opposition to the whites. Fortunately, this proved false when emissaries from the Deschutes, having tasted the cost of war, and Yakima tribes arrived and pledged their peace. The rest of the Indian tribes' intentions were not known, but hope had been created that further war could be avoided. Ultimately, only the Palouse and Umatilla would join in the fight as a tribe, although some war-inclined members of the Nez Perce and Walla Walla Indians would fight, too.

Despite these favorable signs, Colonel Gilliam forbade the peace commissioners from riding ahead of the main body of troops. Thus, the Oregon Rifles were lead by a smaller body flying white flags of peace.

As the armed column advanced, they finally entered into Cayuse country proper. The Umatilla tribe, joined by the Cayuse, were led by chiefs Five Crows and Gray Eagle. Chief Gray Eagle bragged of his killing Narcissa Whitman, and Five Crows refused to give up Esther Lorinda Bewley, one of the white woman captives from the massacre, whom he had taken as a wife.

On February 24, the Oregon Rifles entered a small valley known as Sand Hollow. As they did so, the Cayuse finally appeared. Four to five hundred warriors boldly rode into view. The commissioners tried to parley, but the Indians rejected the overture. From their perspective, the Indians had already tried to establish communications. In December, the Cayuse had requested Father Francis Blanchet to send a letter expressing their desire for peace. When the Cayuse met with Peter Skene Ogden, they again pleaded their case for peace and Ogden had promised to relay the message. Finally, soon after the massacre, Henry Spalding had met with the Cayuse and promised that he would try to persuade the Americans to a peaceful resolution and try to see that no armed Americans would enter Cayuse land.

To the Indians, all of these peace efforts had been made even before Major Lee's company had arrived at The Dalles and all had been rejected. Instead, the Cayuse had observed the Oregon Rifles' advance and attacks on other Indians. There would be no peace.

In an attempt to encircle the Indians, the Rifles immediately divided to two wings. Checking the white advance, Grey Eagle led a fierce charge against one of the columns. Repulsing the charge, the Indians retreated as the whites moved forward. After a few minutes, the Indians made another charge, this time against the supply wagons. Protecting their much-needed supplies, the whites formed a defensive circle with the Indians arrayed about them in almost classic Hollywood style.

The Indians cried out that they would kill the whites and march on the Willamette Valley, brave words from Indians that had never encountered whites other than missionaries and emigrants, who often tried to avoid fights because of the women and children accompanying them. But, the Cayuses' chiefs had convinced the warriors that they held magic that would prevent the whites from hurting them.

The battle continued when Five Crows and Gray Eagle advanced against the French-Canadian company of Rifles. Gray Eagle called out that he could swallow the white man's bullets with his magic. Gray Eagle and Five Crows charged toward the opposing line. Seeing someone he recognized, Gray Eagle yelled out, "There's Tom McKay. I'll kill him."

Having heard Gray Eagle's boast to swallow white men's bullets, Tom McKay lifted his gun, aimed, and shouted, "Then let him swallow this one." The bullet missed Gray Eagle's mouth, but hit him in the head.[2] Charles McKay then targeted the other war chief, Five Crows, and severely wounded him. Cayuse morale was severely tested when they saw that the magic protection against the whites was not working.

The Cayuse regrouped and made another serious attempt to cut-off and surround the supplies. To check this attack, Captain H.J.G. Maxon led his company from the right flank, attacking the charging Indians on the left flank. Maxon's company was temporarily cut off and surrounded, but fought their way through, suffering eight wounded.

Capitalizing on the gap between Maxon's troops and the main white defensive position, the Indians made a large V-shaped formation, and swarmed into the hole. The whites counterattacked, driving the Indians back to the hill, thus giving Maxon's command the needed break to fight back into the main lines. To gain further time, more volunteers charged the hilltop that had the Indians' pouring fire onto the command. The whites' war whoops did as much harm as their ineffective fire, but the charge succeeded in driving the Indians away.

From noon until sunset a battle raged on with ineffective artillery fire adding to the din. The Cayuse retired in the night, leaving eight dead, while the Rifles suffered five wounded. Worse for the Indians, the bellicose Cayuse were seen by their potential Indian allies as ineffective.

After the withdrawal of the Cayuse, the Oregon Rifles continued their advance without serious opposition, although the column suffered continual harassment from some Indians, while other Cayuse sought peace.

On February 28, the Oregon Rifles reached the Hudson's Bay Fort Nez Perce. There, peace negotiations were attempted, and other Indians established their own peaceful intentions. Yellow Serpent, also known as Peu-peu-mox-mox,[3] of the Walla Walla tribe, pledged his tribe's support of the Americans. However, as the Americans advanced towards Waiilatpu, the scene of the Whitman massacre, rumors spread that the Cayuse were massing to attack and that the Nez Perce had joined them as allies.

---

2. All sources agree that Tom McKay killed Gray Eagle, but disagree on the weapon (shotgun, musket, rifle). Glassley (1953, 25) is the source of the quotes.

3. Alternately spelled Peo-peo-mox-mox.

On March 2, the Oregon Rifles arrived at the scene of the massacre to find it burned and looted, and the graves of the killed opened by wild animals. The burned buildings black against the snow, with body parts scattered about and wolves howling in the distance was an image that enraged the Rifles. When Indians arrived on March 4, with expressions of peace, it was the image of the devastation that prompted Colonel Gilliam to express that he had come to fight and fight he would.

Nevertheless, Colonel Gilliam was persuaded by Lee and Palmer, both having military rank and credentials, to refrain from war, and the peace commission was given a chance. This chance was largely due to the fact that the majority of the Indians who arrived for the council were Nez Perce. They were given assurances of the American goodwill.

But, the Cayuse amongst the gathered Indians heard a much different message. Joel Palmer's words carried anger and threats. "The land of the Cayuses has been stained with the blood of our brothers... The Cayuses have done it. What shall be done? The Cayuses have forfeited their lands by making war upon the Americans (O'Donnell, 97)." Palmer described the great efforts the Americans had made to secure peace and justice. He went on to say that the Americans did not want the Cayuse land; they wanted the murderers.

The Cayuse war chief, Camastpelo, said that he and his people had nothing to do with the murders and would do nothing to protect the guilty. Underscoring these comments were those of the Nez Perce Joseph, who renounced the murderers, pledging that they would not protect them and that his people were friends of the whites. In return for this pledge, the Nez Perce received an Indian agent and a white promise that no Americans would enter Nez Perce lands without Indian permission.

While the peace commission was successful in reaching one of its principle objectives, the avoidance of a general Indian uprising through an alliance of all the Upper Columbia River Indian tribes, it had failed to achieve the other major objective: the surrender of the Cayuse who had murdered the Whitmans.

Word reached the camp that the guilty were bivouacked on the Touchet River about twenty-five miles from the site of the Whitman mission. On March 9, Colonel Gilliam ordered the Oregon Rifles to move toward that camp for an attack. Met along the way by the Cayuse band under Stickus, who had earlier attacked the fort at The Dalles, Gilliam

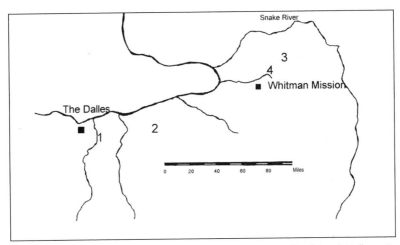

Cayuse War Close-up. 1. Deschutes River Campaign; 2. Battle of Sand Hollow; 3. Battle of Tucannon River; 4. Battle of Touchet River. (*Author*)

wanted to prevent the band's escape into the mountains. The peace commission, still hoping to prevent further bloodshed, prevailed upon Gilliam to allow them to try their efforts with the Stickus band.

Back at the Whitman mission, the peace commission tried to get Stickus to surrender the five suspects hiding within his band, but Stickus refused. Gilliam intervened in an effort to force a concession. Without prior consultation, he said that the five need not be given up if the instigator of the attack, Joe Lewis, who was half-white, half Delaware, was surrendered. The Cayuse refused to surrender Lewis or anyone else. The result of this change in objectives was that it created the final division between the peace commission and Colonel Gilliam.

On March 11, Peace Commissioners Newell and Palmer headed for Oregon City while Colonel Gilliam ordered the Oregon Rifles again into the field to attack the Cayuse.

After a night march, the Oregon Rifles discovered a village near the mouth of the Tucannon River. Indians came out and told the Rifles that they were friendly Walla Wallas. Withholding their fire to determine the truth, the Rifles discovered that the Cayuse had already crossed the Snake River and slipped into the mountains. As the Rifles advanced, they found cattle left behind, unable to be crossed against the swift current. Most of the cattle really belonged to the Palouse Indians, who had helped the Cayuse escape. However, within the herd were cattle with the brand from the Whitman mission. The always hungry volunteers seized the cattle, approximately four hundred head, and started to drive them back to the mission. Wishing to prevent the theft of their wealth, the Palouse attacked. The 158 men of the Oregon Rifles, short of food and ammunition, were faced with over four hundred Palouse and Cayuse warriors.

Surrounded by Indians, the men formed a hollow square. Sergeant Thomas R. Cornelius estimated the command was attacked by about three hundred warriors in the initial charges.[4] As the Rifles fled south, they released the cattle; but that did not deter the Indians. The Rifles suffered ten wounded as they fled south to the Touchet River, near present-day Waitsburg, Washington. There, on March 15, 1848, a fierce covering action took place as the fight for control of the only ford across the Touchet River raged. Captain H.J.G. Maxon of the Rifles reported, "And here I may say that had it not been for the bold and decided stand of a few young men at the most vulnerable point, the army must have sustained a heavy loss in crossing the stream." (Carey, 537)

The fighting was fierce. As one account described some of the fighting, it was literally hand-to-hand:

> An Indian sprang from the bushes, firing. Nathan Olney. . . reportedly rushed up, grappled with the warrior, and pounded him with a club until it broke. They then fought with their fists until Olney finally killed the Indian with a knife. (Ruby and Brown, 140-141)

Finally, the Cayuse and Palouse gave up the chase.

The weary troops still had another day's march facing them in order to return to the safety of the former mission. Across the open prairie, the men wearily trudged. "After the fight was over, we went two or three miles; we were both tired and hungry, and killed a horse and tried to eat it. That night the snow fell about two inches deep on us. We had no tents."[5]

The command of the Rifles arrived back at the site of the Whitman mission and entered into a council. Every item needed to keep the Rifles in the field was now in critical shortage.

4. In a recollection written in 1889, and presented to Captain Birkhimer as part of the captain's investigation.

5. In a recollection written in 1889, by Stephen Allen Holcomb, private in Company D, Captain Lawrence Hall, commanding. Submitted to Captain W.E. Birkhimer as part of his investigation.

On March 18, it was decided that with half the Rifles stationed at the mission, now called Fort Waters, Colonel Gilliam would retire to The Dalles with the rest of the troops to seek additional men and adequate supplies. The plan was to maintain a military presence until Gilliam could return with more troops and supplies to resume the offensive.

James W. Nesmith (*Library of Congress*)

As the main force of the Rifles headed back to The Dalles, a freak accident befell the command. On March 24, 1848, along the banks of the Umatilla River, while pulling on a coil of rope in a wagon, Colonel Gilliam caused a rifle in the wagon to accidentally discharge, killing him.

Command of the retiring force devolved to Captain Maxon. His description of Colonel Gilliam's death, the plight of the troops, and the dire need for supplies was sent in a very moving letter to Oregon City. Subsequently published, the letter caused widespread support for the troops still in the field.

Word reached Oregon City and Governor Abernathy that troubled the government and the population. The news of the death of the respected Colonel Gilliam and the widening of the war as a result of the battle with the Palouse caused great concern within the territory. These events contrasted darkly with the earlier peace commission message of their ability to contain the war.

On April 1, the governor called for three hundred more volunteers. Urged on by the publication of Maxon's letter, patriotic fever ran high. By April 17, Major Lee, having assumed command of the Rifles (later to be taken over by Colonel Waters with Lieutenant Colonel Lee as second in command), reported that two hundred fifty additional troops were ready to head up river. Three companies were raised: one from Polk and Clackamas counties under the command of Captain James W. Nesmith, another under Captain W.P. Pugh from Linn County, and Tualatin County's volunteers under the command of William J. Martin.

At Walla Walla, Lee again held council with the Indians and tried to get the Cayuse to surrender the guilty; unfortunately, they did not. Believing that the Nez Perce were breaking their word given at the March peace council, Lee ordered the Rifles to Nez Perce country to capture the five murderers. This was a violation of the American pledge to the Nez Perce not to enter their country. After a fruitless effort, the Rifles retired to Fort Waters again, critically short of supplies.

Unable to compel the surrender of the guilty through military force, with Captain William Martin, commanding, the Oregon Rifles left one company at Fort Waters and another company at Fort Lee, commanded by Lieutenant Alexander T. Rodgers, located at The Dalles. This effectively ended the Cayuse Indian War.

But, a different war continued by other means. One method used to subdue the Cayuse was the authorization Major Lee gave to white settlers to move onto Cayuse lands. This was enthusiastically met and, in effect, renounced the pledge given earlier that the whites did not seek the Cayuse's land. The constant marching through Cayuse country and the occupation of their land defeated the Cayuse where force of arms had not.[6] The Cayuse feared a general attack against the Indians as a result of their losses against the Oregon Rifles. The chief's magic had failed to prevent the white man's bullets from killing even such a strong chief as Gray Eagle.

The Cayuse War set up much of the basis, as well as pattern, for future Indian-white relations. The Indians heard promises, which were rarely kept by whites, such as they did not desire the Indians' lands, but they still kept coming. While politically and strategically the war was not a success, it was a remarkable military achievement for the fledgling territorial government. The goals had not been the destruction of the enemy, but the prevention of a widespread Indian up-rising and the surrender of guilty Cayuse. Both objectives would eventually be accomplished by a provisional government with neither funds nor having any established bureaucracy ready to raise an army.

The Oregon Rifles were created from scratch in the dead of winter, marched hundreds of miles, supplied in the most adverse conditions, and

6. Fort Waters would remain occupied until early 1849, and Fort Lee had troops continually operating out of it, acting as a constant threat and reminder to the Indians.

never lost a major engagement with hostile forces. They allowed the commissioners to preserve the peace with other Indian tribes and created a situation in which the Cayuse had no home, no friends, no means to trade for supplies, and were in constant fear of attack. The Cayuse had been defeated.

> "War's end found the Cayuse divided. Days of continual chase had forced them to abandon caches of food. They were hungry and they had lost more than five hundred horses. One could write of them: 'The Cayuse as a people were financially ruined. Their prestige as a nation was gone, their leaders went into exile.' Huddled around their scattered campfires in silent fear, they knew that the white man had neither spoken his last word nor fired his last shot." (Ruby and Brown 1972, 143)

The net result of this campaign was that the Cayuse later surrendered five members of their tribe to a detachment of the Oregon Rifles at The Dalles. On June 3, 1850, these five were tried, found guilty, and hanged. Few Indian wars in American history could claim such distinctive achievement; all the objectives for which the war had been commenced had been achieved by the Oregon Rifles, but at a cost that would be paid in blood and war for the next thirty years.

$\sim$

Very few historical places of the Cayuse Indian War have been preserved. The most notable is the Whitman Mission National Historic Site, located seven miles west of Walla Walla, Washington, on U.S. Highway 12. It provides a great deal of background history of the area and the massacre.

No other sites have survived. However, the Deschutes River is designated a Wild and Scenic River, and travel along it will reveal vistas little changed since the 1840s.

Near the mouth of the Walla Walla River, as it flows into the Columbia, stands a historical marker commemorating the Hudson's Bay Company's post, Fort Walla Walla, also known as Fort Nez Perce. Not preserved even so much as by a sign is the battlefield of Sand Hollow. It was fought near where the Umatilla River joins the Columbia and is now covered by the city with the same name. Time has erased all other traces.

The trails west are marked by numerous signs and museums. The the National Park Service has marked the Oregon Trail as a National Historic Trail, but other federal and state agencies contribute to mark the trail well.

Three museums help to explain the experience of the pioneers on the Oregon Trail. The U.S. Forest Service has an Oregon Trail Museum in Montpelier, Idaho, while the Bureau of Land Management has probably the best museum near Baker City, Oregon. A non-profit, private museum commemorates the End of the Oregon Trail at Oregon City, Oregon.

The Applegate Trail, located north of Medford, Oregon in the community of Sunny Valley, is noted with road signs and has a museum dedicated to celebrating its history.

Chapter 4

Transition

The U.S. Army Takes Command

I n the spring of 1849, Oregon changed. No longer was the Oregon Territory solely responsible for protecting itself; it was now part of the United States of America and it came under the protection of the U.S. Army. Another alteration, regardless of who fought, was a shift in the theater of operations.

Manifest Destiny had expanded the country from coast to coast. To meet new demands, the Army added to its command structure by creating a new division, the Pacific, (or Third) Division of the Army. The Pacific Division was commanded by Brevet Major General[1] Persifor Smith, who arrived in San Francisco in February 1849 and quickly took steps to get his command in order. As with the other Army divisions, the Pacific Division was subdivided into geographical departments, and the Eleventh, also known as the Columbia Department, was designated for the protection of the Oregon Country. Brevet Major John S. Hathaway was ordered to take command of the Eleventh Department, and on May 13, 1849, he sailed into the Columbia River aboard the United States Navy ship U.S.S. *Massachusetts*.

---

1. During this period, and until the Civil War, the only references to gallantry on the battlefield were through being mentioned in reports and "brevet" ranks. These were not merely honorary awards. The brevet rank was real, in pay and authority, for certain assignments. However, the system was very confusing. A permanently ranked captain might be forced to serve under a permanently ranked lieutenant if that lieutenant was brevetted twice, and was a Brevet Major. In a service without medals, and glacially slow to promotions, brevets were cherished. The system would last until the end of the nineteenth century.

With just two companies of 1st U.S. Artillery, Major Hathaway was charged with defending a vast territory, part of which was then engaged in the Cayuse Indian War. When Hathaway's troops arrived at the Hudson's Bay post of Fort Vancouver, one company established Columbia Barracks (later renamed Vancouver Barracks) while the other company went north to Puget Sound to establish Fort Steilacoom.

What Major Hathaway found, however, was the end of the Cayuse Indian War. The U.S. Army had arrived too late to contribute to the efforts of the Oregon Rifles. With the issues settled among the Indians in eastern Oregon, Major Hathaway was left to focus his command's concerns on other areas. He had reports of increased problems with the Tillamook Indians on the coast while the Klamaths and Calypooia throughout western Oregon were a growing worry.

During the Cayuse War, a war party of Klamaths and Molalahs had threatened a settler near Champoeg and another company of militia had been raised. March 1848 saw sixty men under the command of militia colonel Daniel Waldo pursued the Indians to a creek called Abiqua (in what is now Marion County). The militia attacked and two Indians were killed. Pursuing the remnant, the whites overtook the rear-guard the following day. The conditions were extremely foggy, adding to the confusion of battle, and shots were exchanged without discrimination. Seven more Indians were killed, including one woman, and an undetermined number were wounded. This was the last major conflict in the Willamette Valley, as the whites displaced the few remaining Indians.

When the U.S. Army took responsibility for defense, Major Hathaway was ill-prepared both logistically and personally for the responsibilities of command. Except for the limited ammunition and supplies carried by his troops, he was not ready to take the field. While still short of troops, supplies reached Hathaway's command in August when the U.S.S. *Henry* arrived with arms and ammunition. This eased his logistical problem.

Personally, Major Hathaway suffered as many frontier soldiers did from the loneliness and the boredom of remote posts. He would be hospitalized within a year with delirium tremens and attempted suicide as a result of his alcoholism.

The Army's arrival had asserted United States sovereignty over the Oregon Territory, marking the first part of its transition. Another contributor to change was an increase in the population and movement of settlers into and through southern Oregon, which had grown with the opening of the Applegate Trail, an alternative route to the traditional Columbia River Oregon Trail. In contrast, the Applegate entered into Oregon's Rogue River Valley from California. Its stimulus to growth was only accentuated when gold was discovered in California, causing large numbers of miners to head south from the Upper Willamette Valley as well as those moving supplies south to support the commercial opportunities of a gold rush. The anxieties of the region's burgeoning white population drew attention away from the subdued Indians of the Columbia Basin to those of the south.[2]

Worrying about the major migration routes, General Persifor Smith ordered two reconnaissances by the Army. In August 1849, Lieutenant G.W. Hawkins led one command from Oregon City, with orders to march to Fort Hall, along the Oregon Trail. He had two missions—first and foremost, to survey alternate routes for the Oregon Trail; second, he would take some of the arms and ammunition recently delivered to the Oregon Territory and meet Colonel William Wing Loring and the U.S. Mounted Rifles Regiment, who were then marching west along the Oregon Trail. (Congress had long recognized the need for additional military support for the Oregon Trail and Oregon. To meet that need, Congress authorized the creation of the Mounted Rifles, whose Oregon deployment had been delayed by their service in the Mexican War.) However, Paiute Indians attacked Hawkins' command, temporarily halting his rendezvous with the Mounted Rifles.

The second command had worse trouble. Captain William H. Warner left Sacramento, California, with his mission to scout new trails from California to Oregon. On September 26, 1849, as he entered southern Oregon, he was also attacked by Paiute Indians. Warner and two others were killed, and one soldier was wounded, in the lake region that came to be named for the slain captain. The Indian "problem" seemed to surround the Oregon Territory.

---

2. The civilian population was largely mid-western and southern, while the Army population was more diverse. The 1850 census showed 251 men at the Columbia (Vancouver) Barracks. All eighteen officers were U.S.-born. Of the 233 troops, only 112 were native-born Americans. The rest showed the place of birth as Germany (55), Ireland (37), England (10), France (7), Scotland (4), Canada (3), Switzerland (3), Wales (1), and Sweden (1).

By October 1849, the Mounted Rifles had reached Columbia Barracks. The command of the Eleventh Department and the defense of the Oregon Territory was transferred to the regiment's leader, Lieutenant Colonel William W. Loring.[3] However, in reality his regiment was stretched the entire length of the Oregon Trail and he had only a few companies in the Oregon Territory; some of those were posted far to the east at locations such as Fort Hall. The citizens of the territory justifiably felt that they could not rely upon the U.S. Army as their sole source of protection.

This lack of confidence was reflected by the Oregon Territory's first territorial governor. Appointed by the president and confirmed by the Senate, General Joseph Lane had served in the Mexican War. After hearing of the Rogue Indians' attack on a party of miners, in 1850, Governor Lane went to negotiate a treaty with the Rogue Indians. He took fifteen of his men and eleven Klickitats. The chief of the Rogue, Apserkahar, arrived accompanied by one hundred unarmed men. This was a positive answer to Lane's request for a peace treaty, but the negotiations broke down when seventy-five more Rogue Indians arrived, armed with not just bows and arrows, but guns. Lane voiced his disapproval through translators; Apserkahar responded by telling his people to show their strength.

Fearing an attack against his greatly out-numbered force, Governor Lane ordered the Klickitats to seize Apserkahar, threatening to kill him unless his demands were met. The Rogues dispersed, brought back property stolen from miners, and agreed to a peaceful coexistence with the settlers.

After signing this treaty, Apserkahar would be known as Joe, either at his own request, out of respect for Joseph Lane, as Lane told of the incident, or out of ease of pronunciation for the whites. This coerced agreement was the first treaty between the U.S. Government and the Indians of southern Oregon. But it would not be the last. Gold was soon discovered on southern Oregon's Illinois River and the area was no longer just a place of transient contact between whites and Indians.

Tensions grew in the spring of 1851. In May, a party of three packers was attacked at Bear Creek, just south of the Rogue River Ford. Escaping to Yreka, a company of volunteers returned to Oregon to punish the

3. In 1851, the regiment was recalled from the Oregon Territory. It was ordered to reassemble at Jefferson Barracks, Missouri.

Rogues. They killed two and took four hostages, including two women. This counter-attack resulted in a series of incidents just south of the Oregon-California line. However, the hostilities quickly returned to the Rogue River Valley in Oregon.

A series of attacks occurred soon thereafter. On the first of June, twenty-six men were ambushed by the Rogues near the Rogue River Ford. The party of miners was able to repulse the Indians, killing one. The next day, at the same location, another party of four packers was attacked.

Throughout the valley, the Rogues continued their attack. One party lost four of their members before fighting off the Indians. A larger party of miners, thirty-two strong, was attacked, but only one member was wounded; in their defense, they killed seven Rogue Indians. But, the Rogues did run off some of their pack animals, which carried supplies, including ammunition, and hard-earned gold, worth over fifteen hundred dollars.

Newspaper accounts reported the attacks by the Rogue Indians against settlers in late June. These and other tales of unprovoked attack and massacre inflamed civilians. Although many of the reports could not be confirmed, by mid-summer there could be no doubt that the tenor of Indian relations had changed.

On June 10, 1851, the first signaling of a shift occurred on the southern Oregon coast. A party of nine armed men under the command of J.M. Kirkpatrick landed at Port Orford to create a settlement. As soon as their ship *Sea Gull* set sail and left, they were attacked by Indians. The assault forced the men to retreat to a tombolo rock, a large stack rock connected to the shore by a narrow natural causeway, which afforded a strong defensive position. It was from this encounter that the geologic feature took its name, Battle Rock.

With the 4-pound cannon they had brought, the settlers succeed in withstanding a fifteen day siege. On the siege's second day, the Indians gathered in front of the rock and did a war dance. After gaining courage from the rite, the Indians started to shoot arrows at the men huddled on the rock. Finally, a party of forty Indians rushed the stronghold. As they charged, the men fired their cannon, loaded with small pieces of lead cut up to act as grapeshot. The blast stopped the Indian charge, resulting in about half the Indians being killed, while two of the nine whites were wounded by flying arrows. On the fifteenth day, another attack was repulsed without casualties, but resulted in the white party deciding to withdraw north.

The need to create a way point between San Francisco and the Columbia forced the *Sea Gull* to return soon to Port Orford and establish a port of sanctuary. The second landing was a true invasion, with a force of seventy men and four cannon. There is some confusion in the historical record between the two Port Orford landings in the summer of 1851.[4]

Less ambiguous was another fight that occurred near present-day Medford, Oregon. Major Philip Kearny commanded two companies of the U.S. Mounted Rifles, who were heading for California, and then to Missouri. The U.S. Army incited the attack. As the party entered Rogue Indian country, the mounted troops were met by citizens asking that a punitive expedition be made against hostile Rogues who had robbed and plundered the area. Without investigating the truth of the allegations, Kearny agreed and swung east with part of his command to get behind the tribe's camp.

On June 17, Kearny's force surprised the Rogues in the vicinity of Table Rock. Dividing his force, Kearny sent Captain James Stuart across the Rogue River to cut off the Indians' escape. Riding with Stuart was his friend, George B. McClelland, later to command the Potomac Army during the Civil War. While pursuing the fleeing Indians, Stuart was mortally injured and two enlisted men were wounded.

Another detachment, under the command of Captain I.G. Walker, attacked and burned the village. Moving to support Walker, Kearny took the balance of his force, seventeen men, and moved forward. There, he was met by a party of nearly three-hundred Rogue warriors. Greatly outnumbered, Kearny ordered his mounted riflemen into a defensive position in the trees. Rather than engage such a formidable enemy, Kearny retreated and rejoined Walker and their baggage train on June 19.

Requesting reinforcements from the miners, Kearny renewed his effort on June 22, with a force increased by about one hundred armed civilians.

---

4. It is the second landing that could account for the revisionist history of the first landing at Battle Rock. Revisionist accounts, written twenty years after the battle, appear to combine both landings. Those accounts had sixty whites from the *Sea Gull* attacking the unsuspecting Indians, thus provoking the encounter. The nine men who escaped north were unintentionally left by their fellow settlers. The second strong force was able to establish Port Orford while maintaining Battle Rock as a defensive position.

Battle Rock on the Oregon coast near the present-day city of Port Orford. (*Author*)

For the next few days, Kearny's force attacked the Indians wherever they found them and destroyed as much of their belongings as possible.

On June 23, General Joseph Lane, arriving with reinforcements, located Kearny's camp and the attacks were continued. Lane claimed that fifty Rogues were killed, an undetermined number wounded, and thirty women and children were captured. No male prisoners were taken as the Rogues fought to the last. Lane reported that the Rogues were "completely whipped in every fight." (Schwartz, 38)

The succession and rumors of attacks as well as counter moves made the summer of 1851 a season of war for southern Oregon. However, there were peace overtures, too. Joseph Lane's successor as territorial governor, John P. Gaines, was in the Rogue River Valley attempting a peace treaty in June 1851 when Kearny's attacks thwarted his efforts. Wanting revenge for the unprovoked attacks, the Indians would not initially have peace. Eventually, Governor Gaines helped set the stage for Indian Agent Alonzo Skinner's efforts, which resulted in a successful treaty[5] with Apserkahar's tribe of the Rogue Indians.

In exchange for protection and the return of women and children taken prisoner by Major Kearny, the Rogues agreed to yield all that they

5. One recurring problem was what defined a treaty. The only treaty which had the power of law was a treaty ratified by the United States Senate. If the treaty was not ratified, it was not law. Worse, local officials or Army officers often would sign a "treaty" with Indians, which was little more that a promise. These treaties often confused the Indians and caused them to have continuing doubts about the white man's word.

had taken in raids and to be peaceful. While it is doubtful that this treaty could have been enforced, it was never given an opportunity to be tested as other Rogues continued hostilities.

On August 24, a party of civilians set out up the Rogue River to establish an overland route from Port Orford to the valley. When supplies ran low about half the party returned to Port Orford, while the other half pressed on. Both parties would be attacked in separate incidents, the last occurring on September 14, 1851. Of the original twenty-three explorers, only five would escape.

Coincidentally, Lieutenant August Kautz[6] and a twenty man company of dragoons arrived at Port Orford and created the U.S. Army post of Fort Orford. Arriving with Kautz was Oregon Territorial Indian Agent Anson Dart.

On September 20, prior to receiving word of the attacks on the explorers, Dart negotiated two treaties. The first had the local bands of Rogue Indians cede all the land between the Rogue and Coquille Rivers and between the crest of the Coast Range and the Pacific Ocean. The second treaty covered the area twenty miles south of the Rogue River. Neither of these bands of Indians were responsible for the earlier attacks. To create a policy of carrot (a treaty) and stick (the Army), it was decided to punish those who attacked the explorers. The new commanding general of the Pacific Division, Ethan Allen Hitchcock, ordered more dragoons to Fort Orford to do just that.

Thus in October, Colonel Silas Casey landed with 130 troops—all arms: infantry, dragoons, and artillery—and eighty-seven horses for a punitive campaign. The first plan for attack, on October 31, was against the Coquille Indians at the mouth of the river of the same name. One company marched north while parts of two other companies tried to surprise the Indians by making an amphibious landing. The surf was so rough, the sea-borne force commander, Lieutenant George Stoneman,[7] ordered the men to return to Fort Orford to make the same march over the beach. The three companies were reunited on November 3.

6. Kautz had a long history with the Pacific Northwest. He became the officer-in-command of the Department of the Columbia when he returned as a Brigadier General in September 1891. He retired the next year and moved to Seattle, where he died in 1895.

7. George Stoneman would one day be elected the governor of California.

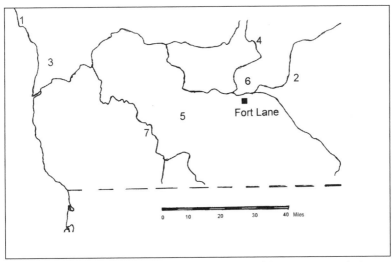

Period of Transition. 1. Battle Rock; 2. Kearney's Battle of the Rogue; 3. Col. Casey's attacks on coastal Indian villages; 4. Evans Creek Indian village attacked; 5. Williams Creek Indian village attacked; 6. Battle of Table Rock; 7. Illinois Valley Indian skirmishes. (*Author*)

On November 5, from opposite banks of the Coquille River, about 150 Indians exchanged fire with the troops on the south shore. Building rafts, parts of two companies crossed in hope of catching the Indians, while the remaining troops, under Lieutenant Henry W. Stanton, continued on the south bank. The effort was fruitless. However, it convinced the force's commander, Colonel Casey, for the need for boats to cross the rain swollen river. Useless in the dense rain forest of the Coast Range, Casey ordered Lieutenant Stanton[8] and the dragoons to return to Fort Orford. Stanton then had three boats sent to Colonel Casey.

After several weeks spent marching in search of the foe, the troops found evidence of the Indians' camp. Lieutenant Thomas Wright led a party of soldiers up the north fork, but found no enemy. Lieutenant Stoneman took his party up the main river in a boat, with some of his men following on shore. As his command moved up river, it was ambushed. He prudently ordered a retreat to report to Colonel Casey.

8. Lieutenant Stanton took Company C, First Dragoons, as escort for Lieutenant Robert S. Williamson. His mission was to forge a trail to the interior. His failure at that mission at least resulted in creating an accurate map of the area.

Colonel Casey moved his entire command rowing the three boats up river, with some troops marching along each bank. Achieving surprise, the command assaulted the Indian camp on November 22. Lieutenant Wright charged out of concealment, and opening fire, chased the Indians out of their camp. Seeing where the Indians had fled, Lieutenant Stoneman's troops opened fire. Colonel Casey, giving encouragement to his troops, yelled, "Boys, take good sight, throw no shots away, give them hell [Beckham, 67]!" Fifteen Indians and two privates were killed. No one ever determined that it was the same camp of Indians who killed the overland explorers. More probable is that it belonged to a band that had signed the recent treaties.

Tensions remained high throughout the winter of 1851-52 and on into summer. Lone travelers of both races were in constant danger of being killed. Legitimate grievances were voiced by both sides and ignored. One such complaint led to confrontation near Jacksonville. A settler named Ambrose, misunderstanding the Indians' trade system, feared the Rogues wanted his child. The Indians, believing the white settler was homesteading on land already theirs, complained. Adding to this combustible situation came word of whites killing Indians in northern California. When white travelers who had camped near the Ambrose farm heard the Indians demand to be treated fairly, they drew the worst interpretation. On July 15, 1852, eighty volunteers from Jacksonville mustered under the command of John K. Lamerick to fight the Indians "threatening" the peace.

Indian Agent Alonzo Skinner rode out the same day to meet with the local chief, Toquahear, who promised that the Rogues were not seeking war. The next day, a party of about a dozen Californians rode into the camp with a Rogue Indian who they believed had, in the company of another Indian, killed a white man in California. The Californians had tracked the fugitive to the Indians in the valley and demanded that the Rogues turn him over for justice to be hung. Into this volatile situation rode the Jacksonville volunteers.

Agent Skinner crossed the river, near the present day town of Gold Hill, to meet with Toquahear, who had been joined by Apserkahar, both of whom had long experience with white justice. The Indians felt safer in the deep valleys dense with scrub brush, and wished to avoid the open north slopes of the hill sides, where the whites could more easily follow them. Skinner persuaded them to parley and they rode to the river to cross back over. As they crossed they viewed the entire white contingent, nearly one hundred strong, lined up as if to charge. Still seeking a peaceful resolution, Skinner convinced the whites to stack their arms and the two chiefs rode into the white camp with a party of about two dozen. A request was made to have the rest of the Rogues join the meeting but they were reluctant to cross from the relative safety of the far side of the river. Toquahear and Skinner rode across to bring the rest of the Rogues to the council.

Friends of Skinner tried to warn him that the whites were readying an attack. Riding back to keep the peace, he was confronted by the whites' eagerness to start a fight by killing the Indians who had already crossed the river. Skinner persuaded the Americans to make them prisoners instead, but one Indian fled and was shot down. The volunteers then opened fire upon all Indians who had remained, killing four. A gunfight raged across the river as both sides discharged weapons. The Indians fell back, but were chased for nearly thirty miles, suffering additional casualties of two or three killed and several wounded. The whites, using the element of surprise and treachery, suffered no casualties. The battle ended when the Indians reached a natural defensive position that prevented the whites from attacking without suffering unacceptable casualties.

On July 18, at the mouth of Evans Creek, Lamerick's company attacked an Indian village. He succeeded in killing some of the women in the camp, but caused the rest to flee into the mountains.

Seeking peace, Toquahear went to speak with Skinner. The Rogues did not want war and were willing to enter into a peace treaty. The Rogues would establish themselves at the camp near Table Rock, and asked only to be left in peace. Agent Skinner took a census of the Rogue Indians and found that only 1154 remained alive.

The battle satisfied white blood lust that summer of 1852, and peace returned to southern Oregon's Rogue River Valley. It was a peace based upon the Indians' hope that the Army and Agent Skinner would protect them and upon the assumption of the whites that if anything went wrong, it was caused by the Indians.

As wagon trains came to Oregon along the Applegate Trail, some were attacked by Indians. One infamous attack was a train that was ambushed by Modocs. Without warning, the Indians attacked the wagon train, and sixty-two men, women, and children were massacred. Two young girls were taken captive (and lived for several years until they were killed by Modoc women), and one man escaped to bring word of the massacre. The attack site, located east of Tule Lake just south of the Oregon-California border, was named Bloody Point.

In response to calls for help, a company of volunteers were mustered at Yreka, California. The volunteers selected as their leader a known Indian killer, Ben Wright.[9] While attempting to reach the attacked pioneers, the volunteers were ambushed. Despite the losses, the Yreka volunteers continued to fight. Scouring the country, Wright's men came upon another wagon trail being attacked, once again at the infamous Bloody Point.[10] Riding to the rescue, the Yreka men drove the Modoc off. When the saved train reached Jacksonville, Oregon, Wright was praised as a hero; but reports of his out-numbered command spurred calls for more troops. A company of twenty-two was formed under the command of John E. Ross, a veteran of the Oregon Rifles.

On September 13, the Oregon volunteers marched east, and joining with Wright's command, spent two months subduing the Modoc. In one barbarous attack by Wright, he surprised a village killing forty-one Indians, then mutilated their bodies.[11] By November, the two commands had declared success and returned to their homes.

Assuming the source of any white death to be by an Indian, the summer of 1853 was bloodier than that of 1852. The heavy spring rains of 1853 flooded rivers, delaying contact with remote miners, some of whom

9. Wright first fought Indians as part of the Oregon Rifles during the Cayuse War. He frequently expressed his hatred of all Indians, stemming from the death of a young girl on the wagon train he had accompanied to the Oregon Territory. Punctuating his hatred, one report had Wright purchasing strychnine so as to poison the Modoc. His plan was to open negotiations with the Indians for the release of the captive girls by offering them a feast under a flag of truce. When the Modoc refused to eat, the plan failed.

10. Three of Wright's men had been riding along the trail to warn trains and miners of the danger of the Modoc. They came upon a wagon train besieged by the Modoc at Bloody Point. The three joined in the defense, but it soon appeared that the train would be overwhelmed. Fears grew more intense as first the Modoc torched the grass, and then a dust cloud could be seen coming from the west, the area from which the Modoc had come in their first attack. Fearing the end as more Indians reinforced the attackers, the homesteaders instead felt elation as the pioneers recognized the mounted riders as whites, led by Ben Wright.

were reported missing. Evidence suggested that they had been drowned by flooding, but the Rogues received the blame; it was claimed that the Indians had killed them. A mob rode throughout the valley looking for Indians. Four were found and hung. Two others were forced to run with their hands tied behind their backs and used for target practice, being shot to death.

A man named Edwards was found dead in his cabin in the first week of August. He had been shot, his throat cut, and his head sliced with an axe. Based upon the injuries, the verdict of the coroner's inquest was that he had been killed by Indians. Again, local volunteers swept the valley for the guilty and hung four more Indians.

The settlers were ready to believe the Indians were abusing the whites, and any act of misfortune was labeled an act of Indian violation. Whites injured, whether by arrow or gunshot, were said to be victims of the Rogues. Burglaries and livestock killing were also blamed on the Indians. Another white man was killed and this, too, was blamed on the Indians. *The Oregon Statesman* reported that this was proof of the Indian's "avowed determination to exterminate the whites and regain possession of the country." (Schwartz, 54) Fearing Rogue Indian attacks, the residents of Jacksonville petitioned the Army for protection.

On August 7, Captain Bradford R. Alden of Fort Jones,[12] just across the Californian border, marched north with ten of his men. With his regulars as a corps of dependable and steady soldiers, he then enlisted 110 less reliable volunteers from Jacksonville. Alden now had a large enough force to seek out the threatening Indians. Prior to assaulting an Indian

11. That attack occurred on the Sprague River, north of present-day Klamath Falls, along U.S. Highway 97. Captain Jack, a Modoc leader during the 1860s and 1870s, was in his mid-teens at the time of the attack and was one of the few who escaped. His father, then the chief of the Modoc, was one of those killed in the onslaught. In their later dealings with the whites, the Modoc often referred to the treachery and bloodthirstiness of Wright as a reason for their distrust and discontent with whites.

12. Captain Alden was part of the 4th U.S. Infantry, sent west in 1852. Regimental Headquarters was established at Columbia Barracks (Fort Vancouver) with Colonel Bonneville in command. Major George Wright was at Fort Reading, California; Major Gabriel Rains was at Fort (The) Dalles, Oregon; Major Larned was at Fort Steilacoom, Washington; and Lieutenant Colonel Buchanan was at Fort Humboldt. Brevet Captain U.S. Grant was part of the 4th Infantry assigned to the Columbia Barracks.

camp near Table Rock, reports reached Alden's encampment that the Rogues had struck first, killing two whites and burning a farm. While unconfirmed, it was sufficient to prompt some volunteers to flee in order to protect their homes.

Alden tried to rally his volunteers as he received more reports of Indian attacks. This made raising them easier, but also made it open season on any Indian found by any American.

More reports were heard of Indians being killed. One company of volunteers not under Alden's command had attacked an Indian village on Sterling Creek, on August 10. Two days later, Rogues attacked the same company at Williams Creek. This increased white fears and demands for Army protection. After reconstituting his volunteer force, on August 16, Captain Alden marched onward. He had three companies of volunteers under the command of John Lamerick, James P. Goodall (with a company of Yreka Volunteers), and John Miller. Discovering the Rogue's camp on Evans Creek, the troops marched to the area and made camp on the 17th, in the dense brush common throughout the stream valley of southern Oregon. Using the cover, the Indians surprised the camp, killing two whites, and forcing the volunteers to retreat to a ridge. The Rogues kept the troops pinned down for three hours, killing four more, and wounding four, until relief arrived, though they made off with their supply horses, complete with guns and ammunition.

General Joseph Lane, recently elected territorial delegate to the U.S. Congress, marched south with additional volunteers and took command on August 21. Lane noted that the rumors in the north were that not only had the Rogue Indians started a war, but they had been joined by the Klamaths and Shastas.

Searching the area around Table Rock, Lane divided his four companies into two wings. While he commanded one with Captain Alden's regulars, the other, with Lamerick and Miller's companies, was under the command of Colonel John Ross (late of the Oregon Rifles and the Modoc campaign). Signs of Indians were frequently found. Troops followed trails, but were often hampered by Indian delaying actions, such as chopping down trees to block the mounted troops advance.

On August 24, Lane found an Indian village north of Table Rock on the upper reaches of Evans Creek. While Captain Alden led a frontal assault with Goodall's and Jacob Rhodes' companies of Yreka volunteers, the rest of the men, commanded by Lane, flanked the peaceful village.

As the whites charged, the Indians
swiftly mounted a stiff defense. Leading
the charge, Captain Pleasant Armstrong
was shot dead at thirty paces from the
Indian camp. Alden was wounded and
Lane was shot as he led a charge into
the Indian's defensive position.[13] Lane
lay on the field for three hours, directing
the fire fight. During a lull, the Rogues
asked for a parley, as all they wanted was
peace.

The Indian chiefs of Apserkahar,
Toquahear, and Anachaharah met with
the general and agreed to sit with the
whites at Table Rock in a week for formal peace talks. Lane observed that

Joseph Lane (*Library of Congress*)

there were two hundred well armed Indians in a strong defensive position. While they talked, Colonel Ross' force arrived on the battle front.
Despite reinforcements, Lane decided to accept the arrangements for a
peace conference.

The whites suffered four dead and four wounded, including Lane and
Alden. This probably contributed to the reluctance to continue the fighting. Lane reported twenty-eight Indians killed or wounded. Of significance to establishing the moral foundation of the combatants, once the
fighting stopped, the Indians aided the whites by supplying water and litters for the wounded, as well as men to carry the litters.

Prior to the peace council, more troops were arriving. Captain Andrew
Jackson Smith and his 1st Dragoons arrived from Fort Orford. Help also
arrived from Fort Vancouver. Lieutenant Augustus Kautz brought a
twelve-pound howitzer and Oregon Territorial volunteer James Nesmith.

The peace conference met on September 3. Even as they palavered,
the Americans continued to sweep the valley searching for Indians to
attack. Volunteer Captain Owen and a party found five Indian houses on
Grave Creek. Using the guise of wanting a parley, Owen seized the
Indians, tied them to trees, and shot them.

---

13. Captain Alden would suffer for two years with his wound, and would die from
complications resulting from his injuries.

Genuinely seeking an end to the hostilities, accompanied by a party of ten unarmed men, General Lane agreed to meet with the Indians in their camp. One of the ten, James Nesmith, protested this decision vehemently:

> Against those terms I protested, and told the General that I had traversed that country five years before, and fought those same Indians; that they were notoriously treacherous, and in early times had earned the designation of "Rogues," by never permitting a white man to escape with his scalp when once within their power; that I knew them better than he did, and that it was criminal folly for eleven unarmed men to place themselves voluntarily within the power of seven hundred well armed, hostile Indians in their own secure encampment. (Nesmith, 216)

Despite such strong advice against a parley, General Lane was determined to end the bloodshed. He had Captain A.J. Smith draw his dragoons across the valley in a show of strength, and then General Lane rode forward with ten of his principle leaders. Placing trust in the Indians, Lane was accompanied by Joel Palmer, Superintendent of Indian Affairs, Captain Smith, Colonel John Ross, James Nesmith, Lieutenant Augustus Kautz, and others.

General Lane asked the Rogue chiefs why they had taken the path of war and their response rang with credibility. They had done so upon the general reports of the whites killing Indians. Despite their just cause for defense, the Rogues were viewed as the aggressors. The talks progressed and two treaties were reached, in effect causing the Rogues to give up most of the Rogue River Valley for sixty thousand dollars, of which fifteen thousand had to be paid back to the whites as war debts. Further, the Rogues believed they were retaining a reservation north of Table Rock, but the whites' interpretation was that the reservation was a temporary one until a more suitable reservation could be found. It was this misunderstanding that would add to the injustices already laid upon the Rogue Indians.

The treaty successfully brought a temporary peace to the interior valleys of southern Oregon. However, distrust remained high. Even higher were the levels of white greed and hatred. On patrol along the Applegate Trail, Captain Miller's Yreka volunteers were sent east after the Table Rock Treaty, and discovered a village of Modoc on Tule Lake. Choosing to believe the Indians guilty of an attack on a white train, the Yreka volunteers attacked, murdering all of the inhabitants, including women and children; it was an attack of pure hatred.

The search for mineral wealth also continued to transform the region. Gold had been discovered near the southern Oregon coast in 1852, and by the summer of 1853, miners created a town called Randolph, numbering nearly a thousand inhabitants.

The search for ore took miners deeper into Indian country. On September 12, miners panning for gold on the Illinois River, a tributary of the Rogue River, were attacked. In the Applegate Valley, another volunteer company, under the command of Robert Williams, battled until dark, wounding many Indians, but not forcing them to surrender.

Responding to these outbreaks, Captain Smith and his dragoons moved into the Illinois Valley. He killed fifteen Indians and captured some of their horses and much of their supplies, at the loss of two Americans killed and four wounded. Smith's attack drove the Indians into the hills.

To help respond more quickly to the troubled interior valleys, a new fort was created on the south bank of the Rogue River, near Table Rock. Captain Smith named the new post Fort Lane, and the new commander was Captain George W. Patten.[14]

The killing continued into winter. On January 18, 1854, a party of nineteen miners jumped an Indian village on the Illinois River. The Indian men were gone when the whites swept in, thus enabling the miners to kill one woman, two children, and wound three women and another child.

Other miners in the area protested that the Indians were hostile. When four miners were killed, a volunteer company was formed, commanded by Captain Greiger. It trailed after the Indians, believed to be Shastas, but Greiger found his men out-numbered. The volunteers sent word to Fort Jones and Captain Judah joined the punitive raid. Chasing the Indians to an unassailable cave, a howitzer was sent for, and the Americans waited until it arrived with Captain Smith and reinforcements.

14. Fort Lane and Fort Jones both were administered by Major George Wright, from Fort Reading, California. Communications were difficult and slow.

On January 27, the troops attacked behind howitzer fire. Captain Greiger, the only white casualty, was shot from his horse. Finally, the Indians wanted a parley. The Shastas said they had killed the miners in retaliation for the attack on the village on January 18. Captain Smith accepted this statement, thus ending the battle. The volunteers, disgusted with the lack of bloodthirstiness of the regulars, vowed not to seek the Army's help in future problems, and the volunteers went looking for revenge.

When more "attacks" occurred, rather than call upon the Indian agent or the 1st U.S. Dragoons, under Captain Andrew Jackson Smith, the miners created a volunteer company under the command of George Abbott. On January 28, the miners ambushed a peaceful village of Coquille Indians. They killed fifteen, for such crimes as having "ridden a horse without permission," (Beckahm, 135) burned the village, and took as prisoners women, children, and old men, without suffering any injury themselves.

Indian Agent F.M. Smith noted that there had been fewer than fifty Coquille Indians and over 300 miners. The remaining thirty Coquilles went with Agent Smith to seek protection at his Port Orford agency.

At the mouth the Chetco River, the Indians had long had a village and a ferry. Americans settled nearby, but after gold was discovered the commercial value of the village site and ferry became vividly clear to the whites. They simply moved in and took over. When the Indians protested, the settlers threatened arson and brought in armed men. To deal with the Indian competitors, early on the morning of February 15, 1854, a war party of ten men, made a surprise attack on the Indian village. As the Indians emerged from their homes they were shot dead. Some Indians remained inside their houses and returned fire. The houses were burned, and in all, the settlers killed two dozen men and women.

Throughout the rest of 1854, there were peaceful Indian relations because the Indians were afflicted with epidemics and hunger, and they needed all of their efforts just to survive. But the injustices still festered and contributed to the next Indian wars. In just one year, the entire Northwest would erupt in total war. The Rogue Indians would rise again, their wrath fueling the widespread war flames. While the simultaneous unleashing of Indian war made it seem as if the Rogues were cooperating with other tribes from throughout the Northwest, it was really a continuation of their previous struggle. They fought not merely for justice but for survival.

~

M any of the natural features of the area, although changed by man-made development, can be visited. It allows the visitor to step back into time and imagine the country as it was when fought over. The single most impressive natural feature in the central Rogue River valley is Table Rock. Easily seen from the south and east, it is located north of Central Point, Oregon. In the same part of the valley, two other natural features often cited are the Rogue River Ford and Evans Creek. The easiest crossing in the central valley is simply referred to as the Rogue River Ford, and the river slows to manageable speed near Gold Hill, Oregon. The mouth of Evans Creek, near the community of Rogue River, flows from the north and then swings east around the north side of Table Rock.

Two man-made historical sites are also located with the central valley. The town of Jacksonville, site of murder and intolerance, is a historical community that has preserved its past. A walk through town is a trip through time to the gold rush days of Jackson County.

The other significant establishment of the valley, Fort Lane, has not been preserved. Once located on the south side of the Rogue River, a plaque commemorates its significance. The plaque is on the north side of the river, north of Interstate 5 (exit 35, Blackwell Road north and west to Gold Ray Road).

Most sites mentioned on the Oregon Coast are not commemorated in any way. The rivers mentioned, such as the Chetco and Coquille, are easily reached, and still have much of the appearance each had during the days covered by this chapter. One site mentioned and preserved is Battle Rock, a city park and traveler's rest area in the town of Port Orford.

Further north, away from the coast, are two sites linked to the history covered in this chapter. Vancouver Barracks is part of the Fort Vancouver National Historic Preserve and easily visited in Vancouver, Washington, when visiting the Hudson's Bay post, Fort Vancouver.

The other site is near Fort Lewis, Washington, between Olympia and Tacoma, Washington. The Fort Lewis Military History Museum is immediately off of Interstate 5 and can be reached by following the well-marked direct signs. While it covers the entire history of the Army's involvement at Fort Lewis up to the war on terrorism, the sections on the Army's earliest efforts in the Northwest will be of great interest to the reader.

Lastly, in reference to the fights with the Modoc, Bloody Point is a designated landmark along the Applegate Trail. It is located south of the California-Oregon border along what is the old east shore of Tule Lake, due east of the town of Tulelake, on county road 104, near its intersection with country road 114.

Chapter 5

The Great Outbreak

Puget Sound, Rogue, Yakima, and Spokane Indian Wars, 1853–1858

F or the United States, the year 1853 marked a major change in Oregon Territory. Migration to the area had grown steadily and Washington, D.C., recognizing the need to divide the territory into small-er regions that would soon be ready for statehood, separated Washington Territory on February 8, 1853, from what would eventually become the State of Oregon, the first stage toward transforming the contested wilder-ness into a permanent part of the Union.[1]

For the Indians, it was an ominous year. White immigration contin-ued unabated while Indian populations continued to decline. At the time of the Lewis and Clark expedition, the Indian population in the Oregon Territory had been estimated at approximately 45,000 people. By 1853, the U.S. Army estimated the combined population of all Indians within Department 11 of the Pacific Division (the Oregon Territory), as being only 25,000. In contrast, when the Washington Territory was carved out of the greater Oregon Territory, the white population in Department 11 was estimated in the mid-thirty thousands. By 1859, with statehood for Oregon, Oregon's non-Indian population alone would be estimated at 53,000.

The Indians saw immigrants stream west along the Oregon Trail, north along the Applegate Trail, and by sea through the Columbia River

---

1. The estimate for pioneers arriving over the Oregon Trail in 1850 was 15,000; 1851, 6,000; 1852, 25,000; and 1853, 10,000. Population centers were found throughout the Oregon Territory, not just the western valleys.

and Puget Sound. They understood that their whole way of living was threatened by the inundation of settlers.

In the eventful year of 1853, with an appropriation, the Territorial Governor for Washington, Isaac I. Stevens, ordered the newly promoted Captain George B. McClellan to start construction of a military road across the Cascades from Puget Sound to the Columbia River. The road was the first to cut across the Washington Cascades instead of the typical route up the Columbia River.

In meeting with the Indians, McClellan found hostility and distrust. He reassured the Indians the road would be used only to pass through their country, and that the whites were not coming to take their land from them.

This year also witnessed the emergence of one of the greatest Northwest Indian chiefs. Kamiakin, war chief of the Yakimas, was a voice of Indian unity in a manner not heard since the days of Pontiac or Tecumseh, thousands of miles away and generations earlier. His words brought confidence or fear, depending on the audience.

Kamiakin was reported to have told his allies, "Heretofore, we have allowed them [whites] to travel throughout our land unmolested, and we refused to help the Cayuses make war against them, for we wanted to live in peace and be left alone, but we have been both mistaken and deceived." (Neils, 76) In the coming years, as events unfolded, to many whites it seemed clear—if mistaken—that the Indians heeding Kamiakin's call for unity were acting in coordination to fight the whites.

Among those affiliated with the Yakimas was the feared warrior tribe, the Klickitats. They had invaded the Willamette Valley in the previous two decades, easily overwhelming disease-decimated tribes such as the Calypooia and Molalah. Recognizing their prowess as warriors, whites often used them as mercenary auxiliaries. Respected and feared as warriors, when word started reaching whites of Kamiakin's call for Indian unity, it was noted with trepidation. If the Indians heeded Kamiakin's call for a union against the whites, the two sides would be able to field armies of similar size. If lead by Indians such as the Klickitats, a Kamiakin inspired coalition would bring a war of terror.

In the summer of 1854, the Yakimas called for an Indian council and many tribes gathered in the Grand Ronde Valley of northeastern Oregon. In that spring, the still-divided tribes were anticipating Governor Stevens' call for a peace council.

Isaac I. Stevens, left, Territorial Governor of Washington. Yakima Chief, Kamiakin, right, from a sketch made in 1852. (*Library of Congress*)

Three tribes favored a treaty with the whites: the Nez Perce, Cayuse, and Spokanes. The rest were opposed to any accommodation. Kamiakin told the gathered Indians, "We wish to be left alone in the land of our forefathers, whose bones lie in the sand hills and along the trails, but a palefaced stranger has come from a distant land and sends words to us that we must give up our country, because he wants it for the white man. Where can we go?" (Neils, 77) Many thought that when McClellan had told them of the road through their country, he had lied to them. Instead of passing through, the whites now came asking for their land by writing treaties.

The Indians heard Kamiakin's vision of the Indians acting united against the white invasion, and some were even prepared to act. However, the Indians at council decided upon a peaceful alternative. They would meet with Governor Stevens and tell him there were no lands not occupied, thus none were available for the whites to buy and, therefore, no whites could enter the Indian country and no treaty would be needed. It was a shrewd if impractical plan.

Governor Stevens was determined not to have any Indian problems during his governorship. In December 1854, at the Medicine Creek Council, and January 1855, at the Point Elliott and Point No Point Councils, he signed treaties with the Indians of Puget Sound, leaving a population of 8,500 Indians on little more than 4,000 acres. It was not long before Chief Leschi of the Nisqually Indians began traveling from Indian village to village, where he spoke of the whites' desire to destroy the Indians, warning that the reservations were a trap.

Having seemingly secured his western front, the Governor prepared to settle the eastern Indian problem. Acting as the Superintendent of Indians for the Washington Territory, along with Joel Palmer, Superintendent of Indians for the Oregon Territory, Governor Stevens would sign treaties in order to end the Indian problem forever. They would create reservations and corral the Indians within them.

While the Cayuse War had seemingly subdued those Indians, others menaced. The great Indian council of 1854 had prepared many Indians to act on Kamiakin's vision. On August 29, 1854, a band of Snakes attacked a five-wagon immigrant train on the Oregon Trail, about ninety-five miles east of the Hudson's Bay post, Fort Boise. They killed three whites and made off with the caravan's horses.

The next day, before word of this attack could spread, another band of Snakes jumped a wagon train seventy miles further west. A fierce fire fight erupted when an Indian attempted to steal a horse; all the white men were killed. The women were raped, tortured, and then killed, along with their children. Only two children survived, one severely wounded. As the carnage continued, another wagon train happened upon the scene. As they attempted to rescue the women being raped, they were repelled with one dead, leaving the women to die by the Indians' hands, embodying the fear of every white pilgrim.

Moving fast, Captain Nathan Olney led a company of Oregon Militia to track down the Snakes. Four were ultimately captured, but were killed "while escaping" prior to trial.

In contrast to the Oregon Militia's success, Major Granville Haller and his smaller company of 4th U.S. Infantry regulars marched about in a fruitless search. Even though Haller would redeem the Army's pride in 1855 when he captured three more of the Snakes identified as attacking the wagon train and had them hung at gallows especially erected at the site of the graves of the massacred women, the difference in results of the two commands' efforts underscored the settlers' belief in the ineptness and incompetence of the U.S. Army, and the need for them to provide their own defense.

Peace had to be established with the Indians or, the whites feared, war would constantly threaten the settlers and their hopes for statehood. Thus, Governor Stevens and Indian Superintendent Joel Palmer arranged to meet with the Indians in the valley of the Walla Walla, near Mill Creek. While many tribes refused to come, most notably the Palouses and Couer

Nez Perce arriving at Fort Walla Walla for a peace confernece in May 1855. (*Bureau of American Ethnology collection, Smithsonian Institution*)

d'Alenes, others came. When the white party arrived in late May 1855, they found approximately five thousand Indians waiting to create a treaty. The Indians had planned that the land was already theirs. This was to be met by the whites' plan to get the Indians to agree to reservations.

After arriving on May 21, the first talks were informal and preliminary. The council opened officially on May 29. Words, expressing both sides' feeling, were exchanged. Peu-peu-mox-mox of the Walla Walla, growled to the whites, "You have spoken in a manner partly tending to evil." (Carey, 576)

The whites promised trade goods for the Indians' assent to the reservation, but the great chief of the Walla Walla was not impressed. "I know it is not right; you have spoken in a round-about way. Speak straight. I have ears to hear you and here is my heart. Suppose you show me goods; shall I run up and take them? Goods and the earth are not equal." (Carey, 576)

The negotiation deadlock broke on June 4, 1855. While Peu-peu-mox-mox demanded to know where the "lines" of the reservation were to be drawn, many young Indian men became restive and agitated with all the talk. Many wondered if the young men were not trying to build up to an attack.

The aptly named Nez Perce chief, Lawyer, gaining a larger reservation in return for his cooperation, informed the whites that the Cayuse were preparing to lead an attack. Lawyer promised Nez Perce protection. His report of treachery finally allowed the treaty to be concluded. The Indian superintendents discredited the war-inclined Indians, and forced their acceptance of white terms.

The Cayuse believed they had been mistreated and lied to, a result of the Cayuse War. As they talked of a plan to kill the whites at the council and then move west to The Dalles to kill more whites, they found receptive audiences with the Yakimas and Walla Wallas. The surprise attack might have been successful had not spies reported back to Lawyer.

As the negotiations continued, Looking Glass, a Nez Perce, rode in. His words were, "My people, what have you done? While I was gone you sold my country." (Richards, 221) Looking Glass was the spokesman for the Nez Perce not wishing to be limited to the reservation agreed to by Lawyer. Both Indian factions had strong emotions, and each Indian tribe wished to gain as much prestige and influence for themselves as possible.

With the prominent Nez Perce agreeing to a treaty, the other tribes signed one of the three treaties on June 12, 1855. Some tribes, such as the Yakimas, signed, but only when threatened. Kamiakin refused to sign until Governor Stevens threatened his tribe with bloodshed. As William Cameron McKay,[2] witness and translator, noted, "When the Indians hesitated, the Governor said to tell the chief, 'if they don't sign this treaty, they will walk in blood knee deep.'" (Ruby and Brown, 1972, 203) Only then did Kamiakin sign, saying, "Well let it be so. It is well. I will make the treaty as you wish." (Richards, 221) But unlike other chief-signatories, Kamiakin refused the gifts offered by Stevens, believing that if he did not accept the gifts (payment), then the treaty was not valid.

The Klickitats, who had refused to attend the treaty council, were mandated by the whites, without the Klickitats' knowledge or consent, to be one of the tribes under the authority of Kamiakin, and thus "signed." Of the three treaties completed during the negotiations, the Nez Perce treaty guaranteed the largest reservation. The 5,000 square miles allowed the Nez Perce contrasted starkly with the smaller allotments for the other, less cooperative tribes. While the Cayuse treachery was never proven, the report did allow the Nez Perce to be seen favorably by the whites.

Governor Stevens then rode north towards the Canadian border to negotiate, or force, treaties with Indians such as the Kootenais and

---

2. Son of Thomas McKay, trapper and Cayuse Indian fighter, and grandson of Alexander McKay, of the Astorian party fame.

Flatheads, while Palmer headed south to make treaties with the more favorably inclined Deschutes, Tyghs, and Wascos. By mid-summer white officials believed that, notwithstanding growing Indian threats, peace had been assured with treaties in southern Oregon, Puget Sound, eastern Washington, and central Oregon. Stevens said that the treaties' "effect on the peace of the country hardly admits of exaggeration." (Richards, 223)

Despite Governor Stevens' pride in his accomplishments, events soon proved a forlorn boast. Without waiting for ratification by the U.S. Senate, whites opened Indian territory for settlement. Gold, recently discovered in northeastern Washington, sped white inflow. Their avarice prompted the miners and settlers to ignore treaty promises. In spite of Stevens' and Palmer's efforts for peace, the war fuse had been lit and, in August 1855, the opening explosion was heard.

Modern War

From 1855 to 1858, the Oregon Country was at war. The war was fought from the border of British Columbia in the north, to California in the south; and on the salt waters of Puget Sound in the west, to the sage brush plain of the Snake River in the east.

War Department records show that nearly 6,000 troops—over 850 regular U.S. Army troops and over 5,100 militia troops of the Oregon and Washington Territories—took the field. The number of troops represented approximately twenty percent of the entire white population in the Pacific Northwest. It did not count the civilians who took up arms in defense without formal induction into the regular Army or informal territorial militias. Thousands of civilians were directly threatened, attacked, or killed, while the entire white population felt the war's effects. The entire populations of the warring sides were involved.

The scope of the combat was unprecedented in Northwest history. While there were skirmishes with small forces, major battles were fought with one side fielding nearly a thousand combatants and even more on the other. Casualties were heavy, often exceeding twenty percent killed and wounded. In modern combat, losses of five to eight percent are thought grievous.

Noncombatants on both sides were killed, including the aged, women, and children. Prisoners were killed rather than taken, and both sides engaged in atrocities of torture, mutilation, and desecration. Both combatants intentionally attacked homes and sources of sustenance as a tactic of war. Remarkably, armament for the armies was closely matched, with the Indians frequently better armed than the whites. The Indians often displayed better leadership, while the white advantage lay in better organization, supply, and artillery. It was a total war.

Summer, 1855

Although peace had been declared as a result of the June 1855 treaties, tensions immediately started to grow. Whites expressed fear that the treaties were a sham and that the Indians were planning a general uprising. Almost immediately there seemed to be evidence of a conspiracy.

In the Rogue River valley, miners and settlers were waging a private vendetta against the Indians, who responded in kind, fueling the fires of further vengeance. Throughout August and September, the disputes cost both sides property and lives, with twenty-five Indians killed by gunshot or hanging in the Rogue River Valley alone.

Peaceful Indians, as well as Indians using the peaceful Indians as a refuge, sought protection from the U.S. Army at Fort Lane, which was quickly surrounded by angry whites who demanded the Army turn over the Indians.[3] Civilians, calling themselves The Independent Rangers, that the Army was charged to protect, besieged Fort Lane, until a fleeting return to sanity prevailed.

Fearing problems from the Modoc Indians again, a company of volunteers patrolled the Applegate Trail from the Rogue River Valley to beyond Tule Lake and back. Their efforts killed an additional thirty to forty Indians.

With some volunteers marching against the Modoc, tensions remained high in the interior valleys. One of the most notorious bands of Indians was a group led by Tipsey. Throughout August and September 1855, Tipsey's warriors pillaged the Siskiyou and Cascade Mountains' valleys. On September 25, a wagon train of supplies for miners was

---

3. Many whites had peaceful interactions with Indians, including some taking Indian women as wives. But, racial prejudice was very strong, and self-righteous whites often used peaceful white-Indian interactions to accuse whites of being overly sympathetic to Indians. A case in point: In 1854, Captain Andrew J. Smith had a child born to a Rogue River Indian woman named "Betsy Smith" while both were at Fort Lane. There were some accusations that Captain Smith was too protective of Indians when some whites were calling for their extermination.

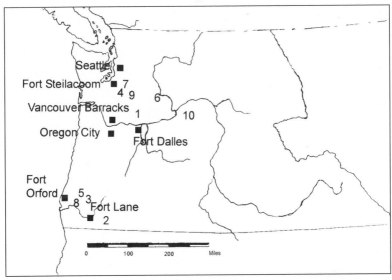

The Great Outbreak: 1855 Overview. 1. Haller attacked. 2. Lupton's Massacre. 3. Battle of Galice Creek. 4. White Valley attacked. 5. Battle of Grave Creek, or Hungry Hill. 6. Yakima River Battle. 7. Battle of Bittings Prairie. 8. Battle of Black Bar. 9. Battle of Puyallup Valley. 10. Battle of Frenchtown. (*Author*)

attacked; two whites were killed. Another miner was killed on September 26, and word spread of Indians raiding the valleys. The Yreka volunteers rode north to revenge the attacks, commanded by Major James Lupton, formerly of the Oregon Rifles. Tensions increased on both sides.

Meanwhile, on the Oregon coast, an Indian was arrested on suspicion of assaulting a white. The Indian agent, believing that the local sheriff was untrustworthy, asked the Army to provide an escort to the court trial. As the troopers did so, the aggrieved white man and his associates attacked the party. In the ensuing gunfight, two Indians were killed, as were three whites. Such incidents contributed to a sense that the Indians were planning something, and that the U.S. Army was an untrustworthy protector.

On the eastern front, gold had been discovered in north-central Washington, and miners were moving north from the Columbia River toward the mining town of Colville. In August, word spread of one party of miners missing while crossing the Simcoe Mountains and Yakima Valley area. When a second party was attacked, word came from a wounded surviving member who staggered into an outpost to report the massacre. The local Indian agent, Andrew Jackson Bolon, who had worked with George McClellan on his survey, believed that the murderers could be brought to justice through his personal intervention with Chief Kamiakin.

Soon after riding north from The Dalles, Bolon was overdue. Word was carried by a Deschutes Indian to Fort (The) Dalles that on September 23, 1855, members of the Klickitats had killed Bolon. "Kamiakin. . . was said to have expressed regret only that the killing of Bolon had anticipated his plans for a later well organized and widespread uprising." (Carey, 581) But, Kamiakin sought justice, not war. The great chief dictated a letter to a priest, Father Charles Pandosy, to give to the Americans.

> If the soldiers and the Americans after having read the letter and taken knowledge of the motives which bring us to fight, want to retire or treat [us in a] friendly [manner], we will consent to put [our] arms down and grant you a piece of land in every tribe [as long as you] do not force us to be exiled from our native country, otherwise we are decided to be cut to pieces and if we lose, the men who keep the camp in which are the wives and children will kill them rather than see them fall into the hands of the Americans to make them toys. For we have heart and respect ourselves. Write this to the soldiers and the Americans and they [may] give you an answer to know what they think. If they do not answer it is because they want war. (Kip, 152)

There was no answer. Suspicion and fears of summer turned into the guns of fall.

Autumn, 1855

Events progressed rapidly with the igniting news of Indian Agent Bolon's murder. The acting commander of the Eleventh Department, Major Gabriel Rains, ordered a two-pronged response. Brevet Major Granville Haller, in command of Companies I and K of the 4th U.S. Infantry at Fort Dalles, was to take a detachment north to investigate Bolon's murder and apprehend, if possible, those responsible. Lieutenant William Slaughter, along with other 4th U.S. Infantry troops stationed at Fort Steilacoom, near present-day Tacoma, Washington, would march across the Cascade Mountains on the McClellan Military Road and enter the Yakima Valley from the Northwest.

The rugged Siskiyou Mountain range in southwestern Oregon where Indians and settlers skirmished in 1855. (*Author*)

As Major Haller's force of eighty-six men entered the Yakima Valley, on October 6, 1855, they were attacked near Toppenish Creek by nearly five hundred Yakima and Klickitat Indians.[4] As the four day battle raged, Major Haller ordered his howitzer spiked and buried, and his troops to retreat. He was met by a relief column of forty-five men of the 3rd U.S. Artillery, under the command of Lieutenant Day, who had marched north when friendly Indians brought word of Haller's battle. Haller reported five infantry men killed and seventeen wounded—a twenty-six percent casualty rate. Lieutenant Slaughter's unit of fifty men had marched to the Natches Pass when word reached him of Haller's defeat. He prudently retired to Fort Steilacoom to await further orders.

Fearing a widespread uprising, Major Rains asked the two territorial governors to summon militia for federal service. Rains requested four companies from Oregon and two from Washington. Washington's Acting-Governor Charles H. Mason placed the two militia companies under federal authority and asked for additional volunteers to protect the Puget Sound settlements. Mason also called on the United States Revenue Cutter, *Jefferson Davis*, a forerunner of the modern Coast Guard vessel, for munitions, and for protection against water-borne Indian raids.

Governor George Law Curry of Oregon exceeded the Army's request, calling up eight companies of militia. Within the month, he would call

4. Other estimates ranged as high as 1,500 warriors, including other tribes such as Cayuse and Walla Walla Indians, led by Peo-peo-mox-mox. (Ruby and Brown, 1972, 207)

out an additional nine companies, as events unfolded elsewhere. He placed the Oregon Mounted Volunteers Regiment under the command of Colonel James Nesmith, who had served with the Oregon Rifles during the Cayuse Indian War, as well with General Lane in southern Oregon in 1853. It is worth noting that Governor Curry refused to place the Oregon militia under federal command. Not only were the federal troops seen as inept, they were perceived by the settlers as lacking the élan to close with the enemy. Nesmith assembled his men and marched to Fort Dalles.

On the southern front of what was now a regional war, the first battle was fought only two days after the start of Major Haller's defeat. Settlers heard rumors that Indians camped on the banks of Butte Creek were planning to raid the valley. A company of Oregon Volunteers, under the command of Major James. A. Lupton, proceeded to the camp.

On the morning of October 8, the volunteers surrounded two camps and opened fire in a surprise attack. At least twenty-three Indians were killed; more possibly, as many wounded were carried off with the escaping Indians. But upon entry into the camp, it was discovered that most of the killed were old men, women, and children. Major Lupton was struck by a poisoned arrow, killing him and his promising political career as the representative of Jackson County in the Oregon Territorial Legislature. The second company's attack was less bloody, killing one woman and two male children. One of the participants expressed the regret of many that so few Indians had been killed.

Lupton's attack prompted Indians throughout the valleys of southern Oregon to take up arms. Raiding parties of Indians quickly revenged the Lupton Massacre, and by October 9, they had killed sixteen white men, women, and children in isolated settlements.

With only three units of regular Army in southern Oregon for protection,[5] Governor Curry called for nine more companies of militia to be formed into two additional regiments. By October 20, fifteen companies commanded by Colonel John Ross had been recruited for the unit now called the 9th Regiment of Oregon Militia.

Arms and ammunition were very scarce. Oregon's governor requested supplies from the Army, but the Army's high command refused to supply

5. Fort Lane had two under-strength troops of dragoons—a small detachment at Fort Orford, and one of infantryman escorting a railroad survey party in the Umpqua River Valley.

or support the state unless its militia was first placed under federal command. This hampered the Oregon companies from taking the field quickly, and created some hostility toward the federal government and the U.S. Army. Nevertheless, cooperation between militia and federal troops was common once in the field.

Action came faster in the south, as the white population was greater and the threat more immediate. On October 16, militia (Company E) under the command of Captain William B. Lewis arrived at the mining camp of Galice Creek and awoke the next day to find themselves surrounded by Indians. As the troops took cover in the miners' cabins, the Indians launched burning arrows into the camp, lighting a house on fire. After a twenty-four-hour battle the larger Indian force retired, leaving four militiamen killed and eleven wounded.

Meanwhile, U.S. Army Lieutenant August Kautz had a party of soldiers who were finally establishing a route through the Coast Mountains to connect Fort Orford with the main valley trail. As the command neared a junction with the Oregon-California Trail on October 24, they were attacked by the Rogue Indians. The surprise attack had an immediate impact, as Lieutenant Kautz was seemingly struck down by an Indian bullet. Seeing their commander fall, the troops panicked. However, the bullet had lodged itself in a small book inside his coat; Kautz got to his feet and ordered a counterattack. Repelling the Indians, the party reached Fort Lane with two dead. With his retreat, Kautz brought news to the fort of his inadvertent discovery of the Indian gathering place. He had stumbled on the main concentration of Rogue Indians.

Fights broke out as the volunteers searched for any Indians to kill. On October 25, a company of volunteers attacked a peaceful village of Indians along the Umpqua River in an area known as Looking Glass Prairie. Four men and a woman were killed before the Indians could escape into the surrounding trees.

Fort Lane quickly became the center of military activity in southern Oregon. By the end of October, three hundred militia had arrived to augment the ninety troopers of the 1st U.S. Dragoons, under the command of Captain Andrew Jackson Smith. Among his command was Lieutenant George Crook, who was to gain his greatest fame as an Indian fighter after the Civil War.

After more volunteers arrived, it was decided to attack the camp of Indians known, by Lieutenant Kautz's discovery, to be concentrating at

Grave Creek. The plan was to split the force into three divisions and attack the camp from the front and rear simultaneously. One of the repeated criticisms made by pioneer militia of army troops was that they did not know how to fight Indians. This battle reinforced the civilian conviction that the regulars were weak Indian fighters.[6]

October 31 was a cold fall day, as Captain Smith's force arrived early at the rear of the Indians camp. To take the chill off, Smith had fires lit, forfeiting any chance for surprise, spurring the Indians to evacuate their camp and prepare for combat.

Andrew Jackson Smith, commander of 1st U.S. Dragoons during the Great Outbreak. (*Library of Congress*)

The first salvo of the battle came from four miles north. The Indians, seeing Captain Smith's fires, had retreated to what later became known as Hungry Hill. Captain T.S. Harris ordered his men to attack, and cover the movement of Colonel Ross's force and the supposed movement of Captain Smith's dragoons. With Ross' arrival, the Indians retreated to a ridge and Captain Smith finally ordered his dragoons forward. Ross and Smith's forces united in a frontal assault on the ridge top stronghold. After taking heavy casualties, they cleared the ridge. Pursuing the Indians into the valley on the far side, the troops entered the thick woods, only to be pinned down by

6. There was some justification to the belief that the Army did not know how to fight Indians. All of the volunteers were hardy pioneers, recently arrived after gaining experience crossing on the Oregon Trail or other pioneer routes. The Army's fighters were often green. For example, when the 9th U.S. Infantry was created in 1855, the field grade officers, major and above, were experienced. Colonel George Wright came from the 4th U. S. Infantry; Lieutenant Colonel Silas Casey from the 2nd U.S. Infantry; the 3rd U.S. Artillery contributed Major Edward Steptoe; and the 1st U.S. Dragoons contributed Major Robert Garnett. In contrast, the company grade officers, captain and below, were about half political appointees directly from civilian life, without prior military experience, and the raw troops were raised primarily from Maine, Connecticut, New York, New Jersey, Pennsylvania, Virginia, Ohio, and Tennessee.

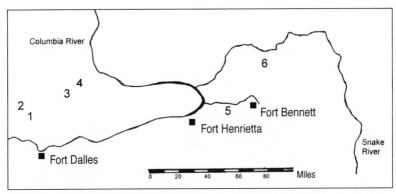

The Great Outbreak: 1855–56 Eastern Front. 1. Agent Bolon killed; 2. Major Haller attacked; 3. Yakima River battle; 4. Twin Buttes skirmish; 5. Battle of Frenchtown; 6. Battle of Tucannon River Mouth. (*Author*)

heavy fire. Every advance was repulsed with the wounded left to their own salvation. The wounded crawled to the valley floor seeking water, thus giving the canyon the name of Bloody Springs. All that night the troops were trapped.

The next morning, All Saints Day, the Indians attacked and more losses were taken. Dragoon Lieutenant Horatio Gibson was shot in the leg, one of the twenty-six wounded in the fight. When the Indians retired, twelve troops were dead or left dying. The troops left the field to the Indians. This was the third battle of the war since Lupton's surprise attack, and all three had been Indian victories.

November 26, 1855, saw a battle in the south with yet another Indian victory. Three hundred and eighty volunteers commanded by Major James Bruce, and fifty regular U.S. Army troops under the command of Captain Henry Judah attempted to capture 200 Indians at Black Bar, on the Rogue River. The troops failed in their objective when they were unable to cross the river under intense Indian fire. The plan had the two forces divide to catch the Indian village in between. Finding the Indians on the other side of the river, the volunteers started to chop down trees to build rafts. However, the sound alerted the unsuspecting Indians. Catching the troops exposed on the opposite shore, about to launch their rafts, the Indians opened fire. After six hours, the expedition retreated with one dead and four wounded. Once again, the Indians had repulsed a white force, this time twice their size.

Smaller actions continued. On Christmas day, two different volunteer companies discovered and attacked Indian camps. On Little Butte Creek, Captain Miles Alcorn charged, killing eight Indians and capturing some Indian livestock. On the Rogue River, Captain E.A. Rice made a surprise attack on another village, killing all the men, and capturing the women and children.

As the Battle of Hungry Hill raged in the south, the next major action was shaping up on the eastern front. On October 30, Major Rains, now a brigadier general in the Washington Volunteers, as appointed by Acting-Governor Mason, marched north from Fort Dalles with a force scraped together from every nearby post. This force included parts of Companies G, H, I, and K of the 4th Infantry; Companies B, L, and M of the 3rd Artillery; and a detachment of 1st Dragoons under the command of Lieutenant Phillip Sheridan, who would later gain fame during the Civil War. In addition to the two hundred regulars, two companies of Washington Territorial Volunteers accompanied Rains in federal service, bringing Rains' total strength to 350 men.

Acting as an independent command, Colonel Nesmith marched north on November 1, with Companies C, D, E, F, and G of Oregon militia, representing another 450 troops invading the Yakima Valley. While not in coordination, both forces remained in close contact, which developed as a two-pronged advance.

On November 8, while attempting to ford the Yakima River near Toppenish Creek, Major Rains' command was attacked by a force of fifty warriors, led by Kamiakin. Unable to repulse the attack with his force divided by the river, Rains summoned reinforcements from Colonel Nesmith. Two companies of Oregon Mounted joined with Sheridan's dragoons to make a mounted attack into and across the river, clearing the ford for Rains' advance. The next day, near Twin Buttes, the command was again met with small-arms fire. Seeing the Indians on the ridge, General Rains ordered his howitzers to open fire, then had his men charge the ridge. Several companies, both regular and volunteer, charged, led by Major Haller and Captain Ferdinand Augur. The ridge was successfully cleared without loss of life, as none were reported by either side.

Sweeping the plains of the valley, the two forces made no more contact with enemy forces, but did burn supplies much needed by the Indians to survive the winter. Kamiakin, recognizing the overwhelming firepower facing him, led his people across the Columbia to safety. A

A reconstruction of the Fort Henrietta bastion. (*Author*)

move up the valley toward Naches Pass, led by Colonel Nesmith and Lieutenant Sheridan, failed to find any hostile forces. Finally, the two frustrated white forces pulled back to Fort Dalles.

Earlier in November, Major Mark Chinn had taken two companies of the Oregon Mounted into the Deschutes Indian country to compel peace. Chinn heard from other Indians that the Cayuse, traditional allies of the Deschutes, had been attempting to bring them into the war, notwithstanding the treaty recently negotiated by Joel Palmer, Indian Superintendent of the Oregon Territory. Having passed through the Deschutes country unmolested, Chinn's two companies marched east.

Friendly Indians brought rumors that the Cayuse planned to attack Washington Territorial Governor Stevens as his party rode west from the Spokane Indian country. Hearing the reports, Governor Curry, having the only independent forces available, ordered Colonel Nesmith to move into the Walla Walla Valley to stop the Cayuse threat.

As a preliminary move to that effort, Major Chinn built a fort at the crossing of the Umatilla River near Wells Springs. Naming the strong point Fort Henrietta, in honor of Major Haller's wife, who had given the command her wagon to help them carry their supplies, Chinn awaited reinforcements before taking any actions in the field. Three companies of Oregon Mounted arrived by late November, under the command of Lieutenant Colonel James Kelley. This raised Fort Henrietta's combined strength to 350. But, garrison duty would greatly reduce the force when the Oregon Mounted moved toward the valley of the Walla Walla.

On December 2, Lieutenant Colonel Kelley led a night march from Fort Henrietta to the now abandoned Hudson's Bay Company's Fort

Walla Walla, hoping to surprise any Indians in the area. Having determined that the fort was not being used by Indians, the Oregon volunteers
divided their force. Colonel Kelley marched with about two hundred
troops directly to the mouth of the Touchet River, while Major Chinn
brought up the baggage train.[7]

As Colonel Kelley marched, his command encountered the Walla
Walla chief, Peu-peu-mox-mox. He and five other Indians rode forward
from his band of forty warriors under a white flag. Peu-peu-mox-mox
desired to parley, asking why the soldiers had entered their country. To
punish the Indians for their wrong doings, replied Kelley. Peu-peu-mox-
mox asked for a truce until the next day when he would sign yet another
peace treaty.

Ahead, in the narrow canyon of the Touchet, was a Cayuse and Walla
Walla village, near where French-Canadians of the Hudson's Bay
Company had settled. The area was known as Frenchtown. The Indians
encouraged the whites to camp within the village. Fearing a trap, Colonel
Kelley refused to advance and refused a truce unless Peu-peu-mox-mox
remained as hostage. The Walla Walla chief agreed, with the condition
he could send a messenger to tell his people of his decision to have the
Cayuse and Walla Walla sign a peace treaty. Kelley agreed.

The next morning, December 7, the Oregon troops found the Indian
village near Frenchtown deserted. The troops looted the hastily abandoned camp of the food supplies. Having had time to catch up, Major
Chinn and the baggage trained arrived. The reunited command marched
toward Waiilatpu, the site of the Whitman Mission massacre eight years
earlier. As the command advanced, Indians, both Cayuse and Walla
Walla, sniped at the column, seemingly confirming the suspicion that
Peu-peu-mox-mox had told the messenger to have his people ready for
war. After twelve miles of sniping, the advance guard came upon the
Walla Walla and Cayuse arrayed between the river on their left and brush
covered hills on their right. The forthcoming battle would roil back and
forth across the river valley.

7. A small garrison was left at Fort Henrietta to protect the outpost. On
December 4, having watched the main body leave, Indians raided the fort. Private
William Andrews, who was guarding the horse corral, was killed; after which,
they scalped him and skinned his face, leaving a bloody head on the mutilated
corpse. Word of this reached the troops fighting in the Walla Walla Valley, which
undoubtedly contributed to an atrocity committed later by the whites in the fight.

The first charge was made by the fifty-man advance guard. In an attempt to force the Indians to yield way, Captain Charles Bennett of F Company, and Lieutenant J.M. Buroughs[8] of H Company, died, along with three of their men. The Indians repulsed this attack and made a slight advance.

Gathering more troops, another attack was made against some Indians who were occupying a settler's cabin as a fortified position. The Oregon troops charged, which successfully drove the Cayuse back two miles, but at the cost of Captain Alfred Wilson, A Company, and two enlisted killed. Many more were wounded and treated by the regimental surgeon, Dr. Shaw, at another settler's cabin. It was decided that Peu-peu-mox-mox and the other hostages would be tied up and held at the cabin rather than have soldiers stand guard over them. As they were being tied, the Cayuse and Walla Walla hostages resisted, and in the fight, were killed. Their captors mutilated their bodies, with particular evil attention given to Peu-peu-mox-mox.[9]

The battle resumed the next day with the Volunteers charging and retreating. The Indians gained some momentary advantage when nearly one hundred Palouse joined the fray. Consequently, both sides were forced to send mounted troops to the north to protect their flanks from sweeping attacks. Lieutenant Charles Pillows led Company A, while Lieutenant A.B Hannah had Company H; both charged the flank to protect the main body of troops. Finding more Indians than they had thought, with the timely arrival of the Palouse, reinforcements were called upon for support by Companies F, B, I, and K, commanded by Lieutenants A.M. Fellow, Jeffreys, Charles B. Hand, and Captain N.A. Connoyer, respectively.

The four companies made a hard rush into the wooded hills in their front, pushing the Cayuse and Palouse back, but the charge finally ended in another stalemate. Both sides dug rifle pits, with the Indians performing in an unusually well coordinated and persistent defense. The Cayuse had obviously learned how to fight the whites since the time of their last

8. Alternatively spelled Burrows.

9. For his reported actions against Haller's command, and to revenge Private Andrews, killed at Fort Henrietta. Peo-peo-mox-mox's ears were cut-off and he was reported to have been skinned.

war against the Oregon Rifles. One side would attempt to outflank the other and either force a retreat or retreat themselves. The battle literally moved forward and back as each side gained momentary advantage. This continued through December 9, with both sides retiring each night to regroup and replenish.

On December 10, two companies of reinforcements arrived from Fort Henrietta, allowing for a general advance. Lieutenant James McAuliff led Company B in a charge against the Indians rifle pits and breastworks. The Cayuse-led coalition retired from the field, but most certainly were not driven from it. Thirty-nine dead Indians were found, but it was supposed a large number of dead had been carried off.

On December 11, the Oregon Mounted advanced and built a fortification named Fort Bennett, near the former Whitman mission site, in honor of the fallen captain. Leaving the fort guarded, the balance of the command pursued the Indians. Advancing through an abandoned village the scouts counted 196 extinguished fires, an extremely large village, more than was thought to be the population of the Cayuse tribe of the valley. Later, it was learned that the Cayuse had been joined in the fight by Palouses, Umatillas, Yakimas, and Deschutes, alongside the known Walla Walla.

While U.S. Army General John Wool was critical of the Oregon Volunteers for widening the war (and mutilating Peo-peo-mox-mox), Washington Territorial Governor Isaac Stevens was rich with praise. After attempting to negotiate treaties with other Indians, Stevens arrived in the Walla Walla Valley from the east on December 20, 1855. Governor Stevens was convinced that the Oregon Volunteers had saved his party, as he had heard that the Indians of the area were prepared to ambush him. It was General Wool's unwillingness to provide an escort for the Governor which led, in part, to the Washington Territorial troops no longer being placed under federal control throughout the rest of the war.

Others contended that the Oregon Mounted Volunteers merely expanded the war needlessly. Many Indians had been unwilling to join the Yakimas, until the attack on the seemingly peaceful Cayuse and Walla Walla, which was seen as unprovoked. Further, the treatment of Peu-peu-mox-mox, taken under a flag of truce, and then mutilated, was the provocation that sent many tribes, or at least their young men, into the war parties attacking the whites.

As the war in the east continued, so did the conflict in the south. After a series of Indian raids, a company of volunteers tracked the Indians to their village near Olalla. On December 4th, the company attacked the village, killing two warriors and wounding an undetermined number, without any casualties of their own.

Other companies scoured the valley, searching for any Indians to kill. Finding two bands on Butte Creek, site of the previous battle, the whites entered professing their friendship. The peace overture was a ruse merely to allow the leaders to scout the Indian camps. On Christmas Eve, the volunteers attacked and the surprise was complete. Nineteen warriors were killed, and the winter supplies for the survivors were destroyed.

Patrols throughout the lower valleys encountered small ambushes and snipers. Both sides lost a comrade or two in each incident, keeping tensions high.

Winter, 1855-1856

It was the Oregon Mounted Volunteers who maintained the only force in the field that very cold winter. The season was so bitterly cold, the Columbia River froze solid, denying river boat transportation of needed supplies. Grass was either covered with snow or wind-burned brown, making poor forage for the troops' horses. The weather made any military movements that much harder to endure for the weary soldiers.

On December 21, after Colonel Nesmith had resigned to take up elected office in the Oregon Territorial legislature, Colonel Thomas R. Cornelius, the company commander of D Company, and a sergeant in the Oregon Rifles during the Cayuse War, assumed command of the Oregon regiment. However cold it was that miserable winter, the Oregon Mounted remained active.

In February, they made a foray across the Snake River into Idaho. The mission accomplished nothing directly, but forced the Indians to recognize that there would be no peace, even in winter, from so determined an enemy.

In March 1856, five more companies of reinforcements arrived from the Willamette Valley; the force quickly took the field. One company conducted a sweep shortly after arriving, moving to track down hostile Palouse Indians. Near the mouth of the Tucannon River, the Oregon troops seized the Indians' livestock, killing nine Palouse who resisted the seizure. But, without the support of ammunition from the U.S. Army, it was impossible to maintain the Oregon Mounted in the field indefinitely. It was decided to retire to the Willamette Valley via a two-column march, leaving troops to man Forts Bennett and Henreitta.[10]

On March 16, 1856, the columns started west, one on the south bank of the Columbia River, and the other on the north bank. Lieutenant Colonel Kelley took the south bank and returned home without incident. Colonel Cornelius took five companies and marched west along the north bank.

On April 9, 1856, again near Toppenish Creek, a two-day minor battle resulted in the death of Captain Absalom J. Hembree. It was believed that the Indians encountered were retiring from the Battle of The Cascades (see below), and must have viewed Colonel Cornelius' command as interminable pursuit. After this battle, the Oregon Mounted Volunteers, as a regiment, was disbanded, leaving independent companies operating in the field.

But, these were not the only actions that winter.

Puget Sound

The northern front was equally tense, with rumors of the Puget Sound Indians planning to join in the threatened uprising in the autumn of 1855. The earlier treaty seemed to be holding. When Major Rains ordered troops from Fort Steilacoom, they were assembled and marched to assist Major Haller's expedition in October of 1855. This was not seen as stripping needed protection from the Puget Sound area to support Major Haller's troops in the field. Shortly after Lieutenant Slaughter had left Fort Steilacoom, Captain Maloney, 4th U.S. Infantry, left with an additional seventy-five men and was joined by a company of Washington Territorial Volunteers under the command of Captain Gilmore Hayes. While the troops were nearing the summit of the Cascades, the Indians attacked. But, the seemingly well planned attack was not against the troops.

---

10. The continued occupation of the forts kept tensions high. On April 20, 1856, sixty Indians raided Fort Henrietta. They killed and scalped one soldier, Private Lot Hollinger, and successfully drove off the fort's horses. Two companies of volunteers had reached the fort on April 16, and gave chase to the raiding party; but their mounts, tired from their recent march to the fort, were too weak to overtake the Indians.

On October 28, 1855, Indians attacked settlers in the White River valley. Eight were killed; one child was missing and presumed killed. Express riders quickly spread word of the attack and sought the protection of the U.S. Army. Adding to the panic, the temporary commander of Fort Steilacoom, Lieutenant John Nugen, believing a force of 250 Indians was about to attack, sent word for his perceived need for reinforcements.

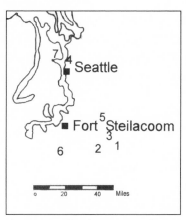

The Great Outbreak: Puget Sound Area. 1. Indians Attack White River Valley; 2. Battle of Puyallup Valley; 3. Slaughter's camp attacked; 4. Battle of Seattle; 5. Battle of White River Valley; 6. Battle of Connell's Prairie; 7. Battle of Port Gamble. (*Author*)

Once the troops had retired from the Cascades, when word reached them of Haller's defeat, reinforcements arrived with Company M of the 3rd Artillery with Captain Erasmus D. Keyes, commanding. This allowed Captain Maloney, once again in command at Fort Steilacoom, to muster a field force.

The arrangements were made so that the entire area would be covered to intercept any marauding Indians. On November 3, as the forces moved to deploy to strategic locations, Lieutenant Slaughter and Captain Hayes, each with about fifty soldiers, fought a small action on the White River plain. The action forced the Indians to scatter, allowing for the planned manning of strategic points to continue.

A company of Washington volunteers, under Captain C.C. Hewett, left the tiny sawmill town of Seattle, and marched to the area of the Green and White Rivers. Captain Hayes' Washington Volunteers were near Muck Prairie on the Nisqually River, while Captain Wallace's volunteers were in the Puyallup Valley.

On November 24, as Lieutenant Slaughter, joined in the field by U.S. Revenue Service Lieutenant Harrison of the U.S.R.S. Cutter *Jefferson Davis* (named for the then Secretary of War), marched up the White River, his command was attacked at Bittings Prairie by Klickitats, Nisquallies, Green River, and Biscope Indians. In the fog, Slaughter's command lost no men, but the Indians made off with forty horses.

In the Puyallup Valley, Captain Wallace's command was attacked on November 26 with one man killed and another wounded. Wallace shifted to closer proximity to Slaughter's command so that the two commands could work in close coordination. On that same date, Lieutenant McKeever's twenty-five-man command of the 3rd U.S. Artillery joined Slaughter's force. Wallace made repeated sorties and patrols in an attempt to drive the Indians into open combat.

Slaughter then took sixty-five men, including five Washington Territorial Volunteers, to meet Captain Hewitt's force. On December 4, 1855, Slaughter's 4th U.S. Infantry were engaged at night in a surprise attack by a combined force of Indians near the present-day city of Auburn, Washington. Killed in combat was the unit's commander, Lieutenant William Slaughter and three soldiers, with four additional wounded. Among the dead Indians were members of the Green River and Nisqually tribes, and most significant to the whites, members of the Klickitat tribe. The presence of the Klickitats seemed to confirm the conspiracy of a coordinated Indian uprising both east and west of the Cascades. The Indians dispersed after the December engagement and it appeared that combat had ended for the winter.

On January 25, 1856, the apparent cease fire of winter ended. Chief Leschi of the Nisquallies and Chief Owhi of the Upper Yakimas, another tribe from east of the Cascades, attacked the town of Seattle, then a village of fewer than one hundred permanent citizens. Their plan was to destroy Seattle and then march on Fort Steilacoom. All day the Indians poured fire into the town, originally defended only by volunteers; two settlers were killed. In late morning, the U.S.S. *Decatur* arrived and opened fire with the ship's guns. Commander Guert Gansvoort sent ashore the ship's U.S. Marines, accompanied by sailors, to man a howitzer and assume the defense of the town. At nightfall, the Indians burned several houses and retired.

The Battle of Seattle was over. While it caused very few casualties (two whites were killed and an unknown number of Indians) and little damage, the shock value was immense. No city or town was safe.

The lack of safety was emphasized again in early March, 1856. On March 1, two hundred Indians attacked Captain Kautz's 9th Infantry company as he advanced up the White River Valley. Captain Keyes, with a company of the 3rd Artillery, was sent to relieve the embattled infantry. Together, the regulars stormed a ridge, suffering two killed and nine

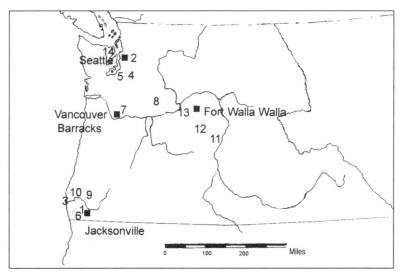

The Great Outbreak: 1856 Overview. 1. Applegate Valley Indian villages besieged. 2. City of Seattle attacked. 3. Gold Beach besieged. 4. Battle of White River Valley. 5. Battle of Connell's Prairie. 6. Battle of Eight Dollar Mountain. 7. Battle of the Cascades. 8. Battle of Toppenish Creek. 9. Battle of Battle Bar. 10. Battle at Big Bend. 11. Oregon Ranger's Battle of Burnt River. 12. Battle of the Grande Ronde Valley, or Shaw's Massacre. 13. Battle of Pepper's Crossing. 14. Battle of Port Gamble. (*Author*)

wounded, including Captain Kautz, shot while leading the charge. The Indians fled the field.

Next, a short distance from Fort Steilacoom, Indians again attacked settlers, killing several. A company of Washington Volunteers hastened to the area of the raids, and on March 8, engaged a superior force of Indians at Connell's Prairie. The volunteers successfully repelled the Indians, killing thirty, and suffering four wounded in return.

Throughout the spring and summer of 1856, six companies of infantry, two U.S. 9th Infantry, and four Washington Territorial Volunteers patrolled the Puget Sound area, engaging in small skirmishes. In addition, thirty-three blockhouses were built and manned at strategic locations, denying the Indians freedom of movement. To further deny them movement via canoe on Puget Sound, the U.S. Navy maintained a squadron, with the flagship U.S.S. *Massachusetts* patrolling the sound and eliminating the salt waters as a route of travel.

By July 11, 1856, Lieutenant Colonel Casey, 9th Infantry, commanding the regular forces in the Puget Sound area, was able to report that the area was once again at peace.

War Resumes East and South

Throughout this period, General Wool, in command of the Pacific Division, was critical of civilian authority and actions. He believed that the war was a result of poor civilian policy of intentional hostility toward the Indians. Notwithstanding cooperation at local and small unit levels, Wool was adamant that he would not support the two territorial governors' efforts to combat the Indians. However, as attacks spread, civilian demands for protection increased. With spreading war throughout the Northwest, General Wool could not ignore the threat to settlers, even if he thought they had brought the menace upon themselves. By late 1855, Wool ordered reinforcements for the Eleventh Department.

In January 1856, Colonel George Wright arrived with eight companies of the U.S. 9th Infantry[11] with orders to march east, up the Columbia River, and headquarter at Fort Dalles. He would use his troops to occupy not only the Columbia River Valley, but the valleys of the Yakima and the Walla Walla. Wright aimed to reestablish peace with the Indians without additional combat. As his troops took to the field to establish their new posts, other theaters of the war heated up.

While the U.S. Army sent reinforcements to sparsely populated eastern Oregon and Washington territories, the more populated west needed protection. Puget Sound was still threatened, and needed troops throughout 1856 to maintain calm.

In southern Oregon, the Indians remained a real threat with reports, real and exaggerated, of killing and plunder. In response, Major Bruce led the volunteers into the Applegate River valley in pursuit of some Indians reported as having raided white settlements. Accompanying the volunteers was a detachment of regulars, under Lieutenant Underwood, with a howitzer.

On January 2, 1856, the troops discovered the Indians had occupied abandoned miners' cabins, and had made them into a fort. It would later be found to have been stoutly built, with rifle pits in each corner of the cabins, allowing the Indians to fire out of rifle slits near ground level. The heavy snow prevented the howitzer to be brought up, and the first two

---

11. The 9th's arrival brought the strength of the Pacific Division to approximately 2,400 troops, all branches, though the vast majority were in the Pacific Northwest. Of General Wool's thirty-three companies within his division, twenty-seven were engaged in fighting the Great Outbreak in the Northwest.

days were a siege. The volunteers suffered one killed and three wounded. Finally, on January 4, the howitzer arrived and opened fire. A cabin
was shelled, killing one Indian warrior, and wounding two children. The
camp was surrounded, and sporadic artillery fire continued without
noticeable effect. Near midnight, an Indian attack through the lines
allowed most of the Indians to escape, and the rest managed to evade the
surrounding troops when they gathered near camp fires the next morning
to ward off the severe cold of fresh snow. Captain Alcorn gave chase.

The pursuing company discovered the fleeing Indians four days later,
and summoned reinforcements. Captain O'Neal and Lieutenant
Armstrong arrived, joining Alcorn on Williams Creek, and attacked the
Indian village. The volunteers suffered one killed and three wounded,
but managed to destroy much of the Indian winter supplies while inflicting an unknown number of casualties. These battles added to the pressure to provide greater protection to southern Oregon.

To answer those demands for protection, Governor Curry authorized
two new battalions of Oregon Volunteer Infantry[12] to be raised, which
was accomplished by February 1856. Brigadier General John K.
Lamerick led them to southern Oregon to subdue the Indians of the
Rogue River Valley.

The urgent need for the troops was quickly demonstrated. On
February 22, 1856, Indian Agent Ben Wright,[13] along with Captain John

12. These battalions were created, in part, to offset the demobilization of Colonel
Ross' 9th Regiment of Oregon Militia. It had been ordered disbanded partly as a
result of party politics. The Know-Nothing Party was viewed as anti-slavery/pro-
Indian while the Democrats were seen as the pro-Indian war party. Party politics
also hampered the recruitment of troops, and the two battalions were joined as
the Southern and Northern Battalions of the 2nd Regiment of Oregon Mounted
Volunteers with Colonel Robert Williams commanding, and Lieutenant Colonel
William J. Martin, formerly a captain in the Cayuse Indian War, as second in
command.

13. Wright had been a strange selection for an Indian agent. Joel Palmer had
selected him to replace Josiah Parrish as agent at Port Orford. Wright had been
the head of the Yreka Volunteers who fought the Modoc tribe, and had a reputation as a fierce Indian killer. He had traveled the Oregon Trail with Palmer, who
knew he would carry out his assigned duties, even to support the Indian case for
justice. Palmer's faith was well placed when he assumed office, as he was diligent
in his efforts to protect his charges.

Poland of the Oregon volunteer unit, Gold Beach Guards,[14] were killed near Gold Beach, Oregon. Worse, the Indian who killed and viciously mutilated Wright's body, was widely thought to be a member of a tribe from east of the Cascades, fueling the fear of a coordinated uprising.

No sooner had Wright been killed than the Indians swarmed throughout the area. First attacked was a twelve man unit of the Gold Beach Guards, under the command of Sergeant Barney Castle; seven were killed. Before gaining shelter, twenty-three more settlers were killed. The survivors quickly retreated to a stockade where they were besieged for thirty-five days. On February 25, the Indians made a direct attack on the fort, but were repulsed. Sixty homes were burned before the Indians' rampage ended.

The closest U.S. Army unit was just a few dozen miles away. The artillery unit, under the command of Major John Reynolds (who was to die a major general at the Battle of Gettysburg) was too small to relieve Gold Beach and keep Port Orford protected. Eight volunteers from Port Orford attempted to aid the besieged fort by rowing to the area. As they rowed ashore, their boat overturned in the surf. Six men drowned, and the would-be rescuers needed to be rescued by the citizens trapped in the fort. A group of armed men rushed out to cover others as they dragged the two survivors out of the ocean.

Food became an issue and the citizens looked for any sign the Indians had left the area. Believing that the siege was over, another party left the protection of the fort, and moved toward a potato patch a short walk away. As the seven men made their way to get food, the Indians opened fire. Besides those killed in the opening ambush, others fell as they returned fire and retreated. Only two made it back to the safety of the fort's walls, and without the needed food.

Relief would soon come. Word had reached Crescent City and Fort Humboldt when Captain William Tichenor, of Battle Rock renown, sailed down the coast and had seen for himself the devastation the Indians had left of the settlers' farms. A call for more troops was spread throughout the region.

Captain E.O.C. Ord brought troops to reinforce Captain Delancey Floyd-Jones' command at Crescent City, uniting under Lieutenant

14. Later designated Company K, 2nd Regiment, Oregon Mounted Volunteers.

The site of the Gold Beach Massacre. (*Author*)

Colonel Robert C. Buchanan's command, who ordered an overland march from Fort Humboldt near Crescent City, California. Other reinforcements came from Fort Vancouver, when Captain Christopher C. Augur brought seventy-four needed troops to support Fort Orford. A two-prong relief force set out on March 15—one north from California, and one south from Fort Orford. Also moving to the relief was a column of Crescent City Volunteers under the command of George Abbott.

Having chosen not to wait for the troops, Abbott led his men quickly north. The haste allowed the volunteers to fall into another ambush. On March 18, at Pistol River, Oregon, the Indians struck down one man in the opening volley, and pinned the rest down until the regular army arrived.

The relief force moving south from Fort Orford also found a battle to fight. On March 19, at Euchre Creek, Captain Augur's troops attacked a village. The attack scattered the Indians into the forest, though five were killed. The two forces finally arrived at Gold Beach on March 21, 1856, and the siege was lifted.

With the regulars combating the coastal Indians, the Oregon Volunteers were left to defend the interior without meaningful support from the regulars. General Lamerick wrote to Governor Curry, "I have reason to believe that General Wool has issued orders to the United States Troops not to cooperate with the volunteers." (Carey, 598) This left the Oregon Volunteers acting independently, and on March 25, they engaged a mixed force of Rogues, Shastas, and Umpquas near Eight Dollar Mountain, in the Illinois River Valley of Josephine County.

To follow up this battle, General Lamerick divided his force so that half would proceed up river, each on one side of the Rogue River. The command carried two canvas boats to ease crossing the river. The terrain forced the command to rejoin, and on the night of April 26, they found themselves on the wrong bank, as the Indians were camped at Battle Bar on the south side of the river, downstream of Horseshoe Bend on the lower Rogue River.

The fighting started on the morning of April 27, when Colonel John Kelsay's men gained a ridge on the south side, overlooking the Indian encampment at an area called Little Meadows. Concealed by heavy fog, Kelsay opened fire to force the Indians north and into the main body of troops under General Lamerick. Instead of retreating, the Indians took defensive positions and returned fire to cover the escape of their women and children. Major James Bruce's 150 troops joined in the fight and were reinforced by Captain Abel George's company. Throughout the day, the Indians were heard to call for a cease-fire; they had grown weary of war. But the volunteers refused to stop the attack. At nightfall the Indians escaped, leaving nearly thirty dead, while the Oregon Volunteers suffered one casualty.

The next morning, Colonel Kelsay attempted to cross the Rogue River near Quail Creek, approximately three miles downstream from Battle Bar. His crossing was contested by the Indians, and a three-hour firefight resulted. Although Kelsay was successful in driving off the Indians, they forestalled his crossing, and Kelsay's command retreated with one wounded.

On the third day, April 29, General Lamerick successfully crossed his entire command, only to find the Indians had departed, leaving behind a village with seventy-five cold campfires. Recrossing the river, he built Fort Lamerick and left one company to deter Indians from using the area, called Big Meadows, one of many similarly named locations along the river.

Companies of Oregon Volunteers from Coos Bay, Gold Beach, and Port Orford roamed throughout the mountains during the spring. They rarely saw any Indians, but kept the Indians moving to avoid combat, denying them the opportunity to gather food. One of their few engagements was an ambush set up by the Gold Beach Guards. Hidden among the boulders of the Rogue River, near Lobster Creek, the volunteers set their trap. The next morning, on April 22, two canoes paddled down

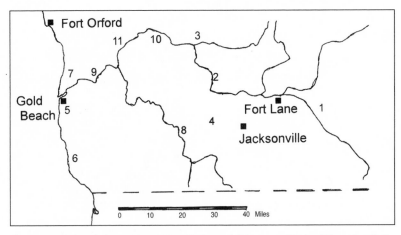

The Great Outbreak: Rogue River Front. 1. Lupton's Massacre, Battle of Butte Creek. 2. Battle of Galice Creek. 3. Battle of Grave Creek, also known as Battle of Hungry Hill. 4. Applegate River Valley Indian villages beseiged. 5. Gold Beach siege. 6. Battle of Pistol River. 7. Battle of Euchre Creek. 8. Battle of Eight Dollar Mountain. 9. Skookum House Prairie villages attacked. 10. Battle of Battle Bar. 11. Battle at Big Bend. (*Author*)

stream. The Guards opened fire, killing twelve of the fifteen men and women in the canoes.

While unplanned, the regular U.S. Army joined the strategy of the volunteers of keeping the Indians on the move. After relieving the Gold Beach civilians, Colonel Buchanan began a campaign of Indian harassment. On March 26, 1856, Captain Edward O.C. Ord took 113 men and destroyed an Indian village eleven miles up the Rogue River on the north bank, at an area called Skookum House Prairie. On the south bank, supporting Ord, was Captain Christopher Augur with seventy-two troopers. As the order came to burn the abandoned village, sixty warriors charged out of the woods. Lieutenant John Drysdale, defending the pack animals, fended off the first attack. Captain DeLancy Floyd-Jones then attacked the Indians on a ridge. A final combined attack drove the Indians off, leaving eight dead. The Army suffered two wounded.

During late March 1856, Captain Andrew Jackson Smith led his 1st U.S. Dragoons on a march across the mountains from Fort Lane to the Pacific Ocean. He never had more than a skirmish with any Indians, suffering two wounded, and joined with Lieutenant Colonel Buchanan's command near the mouth of the Illinois River. Colonel Buchanan's combined force of 343 men marched up the Illinois River Valley, in effect trapping the Indians between his force and the volunteers of General Lamerick to the east. The Indians feared the volunteers more because of their unwillingness to take prisoners. If the Indians were to surrender, they would much prefer the more honorable regular U.S. Army. Word spread among the Indians of how volunteers had attacked some friendly Indians near Port Orford, killing twenty, and taking the surviving women and children as prisoners.

Tecumtum, Elk Killer, also known as Chief John, around 1863 following his release from prison. (*Detail from an orginal at the Oregon Historical Society*)

Neatly coinciding with the arrival of the U.S. Army were the messengers sent by the Indian Superintendent Joel Palmer seeking peace. Having been hounded all winter and spring, many Indians were tired of war. It seemed that here was a chance to find peace.

On May 15, 1856, at Oak Flat, about four miles up the Illinois River from its confluence with the Rogue River, many of the chiefs met with Colonel Buchanan. After negotiation, most chiefs agreed to surrender, lay down their arms, and receive protection by the Army with an escort to a reservation. A date and place was fixed for the surrender. But not all the Indians agreed to this plan, among them, Chief John. His speech to Colonel Buchanan was remarkable:

> You are a great chief. So am I. This is my country. I was in it when those large trees were very small, not higher than my head. My heart is sick with fighting, but I want to live in my own country. If the white people are willing, I will go back to Deer Creek and live among them as I used to do. They can visit my camp, and I will visit theirs; but I will not lay down my arms and go with you on the reserve. I will fight. Goodby. (Carey, 599)

Despite the Chief John's promise to fight, the rest of the chiefs agreed to surrender on May 26 at Big Bend on the Rogue River.

On that same date, Captain Smith's dragoons, reinforced with infantry, under the command of Lieutenant Nelson B. Sweitzer, 4th U.S.

The Rogue River battlefield. The area has changed very little from the time of the Great Outbreak. (*Author*)

Infantry, for a total strength of ninety-six men, arrived at Big Bend, near where Foster Creek flows into the Rogue River. No Indians were found. Instead, an Indian brought word that Chief John was planning to attack because as the Indians were moving to meet Smith at Big Bend two days earlier, on May 24, the volunteers attacked them, inflicting many dead and wounded. Not wishing to give up hope on peace, Captain Smith did not retreat but instead ordered defensive works built.

The morning of May 27 found Smith's command completely surrounded. The Indians said they had come to surrender, but they were all well armed, and Captain Smith declined permission for them to enter his defensive works. At around eleven that morning, the Indians attacked. Although the command had a howitzer, their small arms were inferior to those of the Indians. Dragoons of the 1850s were equipped with musketoons, a short range carbine weapon easily fired and reloaded from horseback, but ineffective as an infantry weapon. The Indians continued to pour in accurate long-range fire, which the Army was unable to return. At the end of the day, Captain Smith's force had already suffered nearly thirty-percent casualties.

The next day, May 28, Chief John ordered repeated charges. As the battle raged, Smith's ammunition supply dwindled. Word of the battle had reached Colonel Buchanan's camp when one of Smith's guides, who had escaped in the opening charge, reached the main force. Buchanan ordered Captain C.C. Augur, with fifty-four men, to the relief of the besieged Captain Smith's command.[15] At four o'clock in the afternoon, Augur arrived and drove the attackers off. As the Indians retreated toward their canoes, Lieutenant Sweitzer ordered his infantry to charge and block the way to the Indian canoes, forcing them to head into the woods. That effectively ended the Battle of Big Bend.

Other troops continued the war. The plan was to force the Indians to the peace council. Major John Reynolds attacked a village on the Rogue on June 5, killing four Indians. Captain Augur, in a rare instance of a coordinated attack with volunteers on the coast, found two camps near Painted Rocks on the Rogue River. While the Gold Beach Guards made one attack, the regulars made an attack on the other village. Fourteen Indians were killed, while others drowned attempting to escape in canoes, which were capsized in their haste. The continued attacks encouraged the remaining Indians to come to Colonel Buchanan's peace camp. While the volunteers continued to kill Indians when they found them, the U.S. Army ceased active campaigning in June.[16]

With the cease fire, the organized resistance of the Indians of southern Oregon ended. With Chief John's defeat, the tired and hungry Indians slowly came in to surrender to the Army. They were moved to a distant Indian reservation on the Siletz River, augmenting the Umpqua Indians already moved to the Grand Ronde River in northern Oregon's

15. Captain Smith would serve in the Civil War, obtaining the rank of colonel in the Regular army and being appointed Brevet Major General. After the Civil War, he reverted to his Regular army rank, as did all of the Civil War command, and was appointed to be the colonel of a cavalry regiment. He helped to develop a crack regiment but was relieved of direct command to assume responsibility of the District of Upper Arkansas as a Brevet Major General. His regimental leadership was assumed by the regiment's lieutenant colonel. Of note were the regiment and its lieutenant colonel, the 7th Cavalry and Lieutenant Colonel George Armstrong Custer. One can speculate as to the change in history if Andrew Jackson Smith, experienced Indian fighter who had already dealt with being surrounded by a large body of hostile Indians, had been in command on June 25, 1876, at the Battle of the Little Big Horn.

16. The southern front continued throughout the summer of 1856. Much of the fighting was sporadic, against unorganized resistance or Indians not part of the warring tribes. Patrolling the Applegate Trail, Modocs were attacked as late as September 1856.

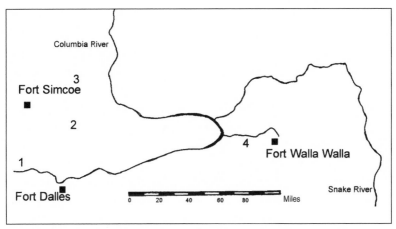

The Great Outbreak: 1856 Eastern Front. 1. Battle of the Cascades; 2. Battle of Toppenish Creek; 3. Wright skirmishes on Naches River; 4. Battle of Peppers' Crossing. (*Author*)

Yamhill County.[17] While the southern front was successfully concluded, the war still continued.

The Eastern Front, Spring and Summer of 1856

The Klickitats had been the masters of combat in the Willamette Valley before the advent of the whites. However, by the 1850s, they had been forced to the north side of the Columbia River, east of the Cascades. The Klickitats, along with the Yakimas and their war chief, Kamiakin, who dreamed of pushing the whites out of the Indian homeland, knew that the war had to be taken to the west and populous Willamette Valley. In the spring of 1856, Kamiakin planned for an invasion of the Willamette Valley.

Contrasting Kamiakin's plans were the plans of the U.S. Army. In southern Oregon, Colonel Buchanan had been forced to react to the strategy put in place by General Lamerick of the Oregon Territorial Infantry. The war had been taken to the Indians, if not always in combat then in steady harassment. Colonel Wright of the 9th Infantry had a dif-

17. The reservation was guarded by three U.S. Army forts: Yamhill, Hoskins, and Umpqua. While stationed at Fort Hoskins, Second Lieutenant Philip Sheridan lived with one Rogue River Indian named Frances, and may have fathered a child with another Indian woman.

ferent plan, which was based upon limited involvement of territorial forces, either from Oregon or Washington. The plan was to avoid combat if possible, in order to foster peace by placing troops at strategic locations, interfering with the Indians' movement and their gathering of traditional food sources. Denied their way of life, Wright reasoned, the Indians would seek peace without further bloodshed.

About a third of the 9th Infantry was put under the command of Lieutenant Colonel Silas Casey and placed in the Puget Sound region. As noted above, a series of blockhouses were erected denying the Indians freedom of movement. In the eastern parts of the two territories, a number of forts were manned or built to maximize the disruption of Indian life. Fort Dalles would be the springboard for operations of the 9th Infantry directly under the command of Colonel Wright. He would have Major (Brevet Lieutenant Colonel) Edward Steptoe march to the valley of the Yakima River to establish Fort Na-Chess (later spelled Natches), eventually built on June 20, 1856. Later, Major Steptoe would build Fort Walla Walla, in the valley of the same name, while Major Robert S. Garnett would construct Fort Simcoe, on the Yakima Plains. These forts, along with blockhouses manned at key points, would be the basis for Wright's planned interference with Indian life. However, before any of these forts could be built, Kamiakin almost changed the whole war.

In early March 1856, Colonel Wright marched east from Fort Dalles with Companies A, E, F, and I of 9th Infantry, L Company of the 3rd Artillery and one detachment of the 1st U.S. Dragoons. They were planning to march to the vicinity of Fort Bennett in the valley of the Walla Walla, then occupied by Lieutenant Colonel James Kelley's command of the Oregon Mounted Volunteers. Wright's command marched east and had crossed the John Day River when word came of a major Indian attack, and they quickly turned back in relief.

At the narrowest portion of the Columbia River Gorge was a natural crossing point near the rapids known as the Cascades of the Columbia. On the Washington side of the river was a saw mill and a storehouse named for its owner, Bradford. A few miles away was a blockhouse named Fort Rains. Sergeant Matthew Kelley commanded a nine-man squad drawn from 4th Infantry's H Company. On March 26, in an unusual display of discipline and coordination, the Indians launched a simultaneous surprise attack at both the Upper Cascades, that is, Bradford's Storehouse, and at the Lower Cascades, Fort Rains. At the Lower

Cascades, one soldier was killed in the initial rush and another was cut off from the blockhouse and was later killed. The rest of the squad made it to the blockhouse and, with civilians who had sought shelter, held off the Indians' attack.

At the Upper Cascades, the situation was more precarious. Three settlers were killed in the first onslaught, including one woman. As the Indians dashed towards the Columbia River, settlers quickly retreated to the stoutly built Bradford Storehouse. Forty men, women, and children found protection inside, but only eighteen men and all four women were capable of

Lt. Philip Sheridan commanded a company of dragoons during the Great Outbreak. (*Library of Congress*)

fighting. Inside the storehouse were wounded men and children. At the river itself, the steamboat *Mary's* crew held off the Indians until steam was raised and it could head up river to The Dalles. Upon reaching The Dalles, a rider was dispatched to overtake Colonel Wright's column. Other escapees had taken a canoe and quickly paddled west to Vancouver Barracks.

Meanwhile, the Indians pressed both prongs of their attack. For two days and nights, they kept the two buildings under siege, even attempting to burn the whites out, but the two isolated groups of guardians maintained their defensive redoubts.

From the east, Colonel Wright quickly counter-marched. From the west, two relief forces were ordered assembled. From the barracks at Vancouver, Lieutenant Philip Sheridan's company of Dragoons quickly boarded a steamer named *Belle* and headed up river. In Portland, a company of Oregon Territorial Volunteers, under the command of Captain L.G. Powell, was assembled and followed the dragoons a day later. In a rare bit of good fortune, both relief forces, east and west, arrived on March 28. In the east, Wright's 250 men swiftly lifted the siege at Bradford's Storehouse. In doing so, they found fourteen killed, including the woman killed at the beginning, and twelve wounded.

To the west, a few hours later, Sheridan's force arrived. The first order of business for Sheridan was to find out what the enemy strength was arrayed against him.

> After getting well in hand everything connected with my little command, I advanced with five or six men to the edge of a growth of underbrush to make a reconnoissance. We stole along under cover of this underbrush until we reached the open ground leading over the causeway or narrow neck before mentioned, when the enemy opened fired and killed a soldier near my side by a shot, which, just grazing the bridge of my nose, struck him in the neck, opening an artery and breaking the spinal cord. He died instantly. (Sheridan, 55)

As the Indians attacked, Sheridan's command stormed up the hill, but was forced to retreat against the heavy resistance. At the river's edge, Sheridan's force dug rifle pits and fought off Indian attacks. As Sheridan's force held the river, the steamboat *Fashion* arrived and the Oregon Volunteers roared ashore. With the combined forces, Sheridan attacked uphill towards Fort Rains. At approximately the same time, Major Steptoe arrived from the east with part of Wright's 9th Infantry. The Indians, trapped between two superior forces, quickly retreated into the forest. The siege was lifted.

Wright built and manned two more blockhouses, calling the new post Fort Cascades, and then proceeded north to march through the country of the three tribes responsible for the attack: Klickitats, Yakimas, and Cascades. Chief Chenoweth of the Cascades was captured with eight others and hung, though unsuccessfully. As the rope did not kill him, he was shot in the head to stop him from suffering. The rest of the Cascades were removed to an island in the Columbia as a reservation. As had been become typical in the aftermath of such a conflict, friendly Indians were also indiscriminately killed in the haste of some to seek vengeance.

As Colonel Wright marched north, Major Garnett, with four additional companies of 9th Infantry, came across the Natches Pass of the Cascades. Suddenly the Indians' home country was swarming with regular U.S. Army troops. Wright's force, reinforced with Garnett's, marched through the Wenatchee, Yakima, and Kittitas River valleys. Kamiakin and three hundred Yakimas and Klickitats avoided confrontation with such a large and well armed force, seeking refuge to the northeast with the

Spokane Indians. But, in their desire to avoid the U.S. Army, the Indians accidentally ran into the returning Oregon Mounted Volunteers, under Colonel Cornelius.

In this engagement, the Indians, fleeing Wright, must have believed that they were surrounded by hostile troops. Kamiakin quickly led his Indians away from the fight while the Oregon troops, too depleted of strength and supplies from wintering in the Walla Walla Valley, were unable to pursue. Nevertheless, the impact of the Oregon Mounted Volunteers' battle magnified Colonel Wright's march through the Indian country.

Continuing the pressure, Colonel Wright led his troops north. On May 11, near the Naches River, Wright was confronted by nearly 1,500 warriors, led by Kamiakin. Wright was able to recognize numerous tribes, from both west and east of the Cascades. Seeing this large confederation facing him, Wright sent for reinforcements. However, after a brief firefight, even without additional troops, Wright was able to scatter the Indians.

To capitalize on his succession of largely victorious encounters, Wright built forts. Major Steptoe established Fort Na-Chess in June and Major Garnett, with G and F Companies of the 9th, established Fort Simcoe in August 1856, not far from Major Haller's first fight a year previously. These forts, plus the efforts of Wright's and Cornelius' marches through the heart of the Indian country, subdued the central Washington Indians for the rest of 1856.

The two territorial governors were not content to leave the fighting to the regulars, whom they often saw as timid and overly sympathetic to the Indians. The Washington Territorial Legislature answered Governor Stevens' call for the removal of General Wool for his failure to protect civilians and his refusal to support the territorial troops by writing a joint declaration, enacted by both houses of the Washington Territorial legislature, sent to Washington. In Oregon, the Territorial Legislature voted favorably for a memorial, a piece of non-bind legislation, to Washington, D.C., which requested the removal of General Wool, too, stating, "He has remained inactive and refused to send troops to the relief of the volunteers." (Carey, 607) Territorial governments were prepared to protect their citizens if the U.S. Army was not.

Oregon's Governor Curry raised a regiment named the Oregon Rangers, commanded by Major Davis Layton, and directed it to patrol the Oregon Trail from the area of Fort Dalles to Fort Hall in Idaho. The Rangers were joined by a company of Washington Territorial Volunteers under the command of Captain Goff, and this combined force maintained vigilance over the trail throughout 1856 without significant loss of life.

The Rangers' one major engagement occurred on July 15 and 16, 1856. Finding a band of hostile Indians by the Oregon Trail near the John Day River, they gave chase over the Blue Mountains, finally coming to combat at the mouth of the Burnt River. After a punishing attack, the Rangers returned to the trail, the protection of which was their primary purpose.

Governor Stevens of Washington received word in the late winter of 1856 that warlike Cayuse, Walla Walla, and Umatilla Indians, who recently fought with Oregon volunteer forces under Lieutenant Colonel Kelley, were on the move. Fearing they would overwhelm the forces guarding the Oregon Trail, he was authorized by the territorial assembly in February 1856 to raise more troops. Stevens ordered the Second Washington Territorial Volunteers, commanded by Lieutenant Colonel B.F. Shaw, to southeastern Washington and northeastern Oregon. Reaching the valley of the Walla Walla by early July, Shaw discovered no hostile Indians within the boundaries of the Washington Territory. Guided by the information obtained from friendly Indians, Colonel Shaw marched south into the Oregon Territory.

On July 17, 1856, Stevens found what he believed to be hostile Indians in the valley of the Grand Ronde River. In a running battle that covered over a dozen miles, the Washington soldiers charged, fighting with revolvers rather than rifles in close combat. At the first charge, Shaw ordered his troops into two wings. As some Indians ran for the protection of trees along the river, the troops believed an ambush was being prepared, and opened fire indiscriminately into the bushes. Hiding there were mostly women and children.

Capturing the Indians' supplies and horses, the troops kept the food, and shot two hundred horses. The mounted troops kept pursuing and killing Indians until early afternoon. Approximately sixty Indians were killed, many of them women and children, and the old men trying to defend them. While Governor Stevens lauded it as a great victory, having destroyed their food, ammunition, and more than two hundred horses, to others it was simply a massacre. To the Indians, it was a bloody continuation of white betrayal.

At around the same time, Colonel Wright had finally succeeded in getting the Indian leaders to meet with him. Chiefs including Kamiakin of the Yakimas, Skloom and Owhi of the Upper Yakimas, Leschi of the Nisquallies, and others told Colonel Wright of their long desire for peace. Each chief told Wright that it was other chiefs who were for war and he needed time to bring them to a peace council. Little came of Colonel Wright's efforts,[18] other than his not attacking the Indians, but the territorial forces continued to harass the Indians. By late summer, as a result of the persistence of territorial troops, nearly a thousand Wascos, John Days, Tyghs, Deschutes, and other Indians had surrendered and been placed on reservations.

In August, Colonel Wright ordered Major Steptoe to take four companies of the 9th to the valley of the Walla Walla. There, he established another fort. Major Steptoe, sympathetic to the Indians, ordered all white settlers out of the valley as the treaty of 1855, granting whites settlement rights, had not been ratified.

On September 19, Fort Walla Walla was dedicated as an established post. Nearby, the old Oregon Mounted Volunteer's fort had been supplanted by the Washington Territorial Volunteer's Fort Mason, named for the Lieutenant Governor of the Washington Territory, occupied by Colonel Shaw's command.

Governor Stevens, in his capacity as the Superintendent of Indian Affairs for the Washington Territory, arrived in the valley of the Walla Walla in an attempt to negotiate another treaty with the warring Indians. Many of the Washington Volunteers were due to be released from their six-month enlistment so Governor Stevens asked Major Steptoe for two

---

18. One result of the meeting was Wright's successful persuasion of several Nisqually chiefs to return to their homes on the Puget Sound. They went west with letters from Wright protecting them from Army prosecution. The letters were not binding on civil authority, and Governor Stevens ordered they be arrested for trial for war crimes. Chief Leschi was betrayed by a relative and was hung, despite a personal plea from Colonel Wright that he be pardoned. Chief Quiemuth was murdered in the governor's own office, after voluntarily surrendering himself.

companies of the 9th Infantry to escort him to his meeting with the Indians. Steptoe refused, claiming it would inflame the Indians, and be directly contradicting General Wool's orders not to help the territorial forces; this despite the fact that Stevens was acting as a federal officer in his capacity as Superintendent of Indians. Governor Stevens turned to Colonel Shaw's depleted command and was assigned Captain Goff's company as escort.

On September 11, Stevens opened another council not far from where he had negotiated the treaties just a year before. The Indians were not in a mood to compromise, and were openly hostile. Many tribes held war dances at their camps each night. Again appealing to Major Steptoe for protection, Stevens was told he would not receive any troops from the Army, and if he needed protection, to move his camp to Steptoe's. Fearing attack, Stevens' camp moved. But as they neared Steptoe's protection, they met Kamiakin with a band of warriors en route to attack Stevens and his few volunteers. The attack was averted by seeking Steptoe's protection.

By September 18, it was apparent that the council would accomplish nothing, and Governor Stevens and the Washington Volunteers started the march for The Dalles. Major Steptoe was preparing to winter in the valley, and asked for another council with the Indians. The request for council was ignored.

The grasslands around Steptoe's camp were set on fire and the Indians moved west in pursuit of Stevens. At Pepper's Crossing of the Walla Walla River, on the afternoon of September 19, the Indians attacked the Stevens' party. The Washington Territorials repelled the attack, but could neither advance nor retreat. Fearing they were being out-flanked, Colonel Shaw charged with twenty-four men. It was a trap. The Indians had planned to lure the whites into pursuing them down a ravine, and past a side gully, which hid more Indians. However, the trap was sprung too soon. One elderly Indian, seeing the warriors apparently fleeing before the charging whites, screamed at them, "You band of squaws, what are you running from a few white men for? Turn on them and kill them all." (Ruby and Brown, 1972, 250) Although the whites were quickly surrounded by approximately 150 Indians, they avoided even more Indians hidden in the gully and fought their way back to their own lines. As dusk settled, both sides rested on the field of battle. The whites started camp fires, but soon extinguished them as the Indians used them to sight in on the whites standing before them, pouring musket fire into the camp. Fearing annihilation in the morning, a courier slipped out of the camp and made his way to Steptoe's troops to appeal for help.

On September 20, Major Steptoe sent a relief column of dragoons and artillery. Arriving around two in the morning, the Army troops pushed forward, which succeeded in driving off the Indians. It was reported that Kamiakin believed the Army would not support the volunteers, and felt betrayed by Steptoe's intervention. The Stevens' party lost one killed and two wounded. The Indians were reported to have suffered thirteen killed and wounded. Finally, Governor Stevens and the Washington Volunteers were able to retire to The Dalles.

Governor Stevens' terms to the Indians at his September 11 council had been unconditional surrender. The governor stressed the need for the Indians to trust the Great White Father's justice—merely place their families and lives in the hands of the troops, and justice would be done. It was little wonder that the Indians rejected Stevens' peace offer. Of note, one result of the fight was a change in Major Steptoe's attitude. He no longer was in accord with the Army's official belief that the cause of the Indian troubles was white misconduct. He wrote to Colonel Wright, "In general terms, I may say that in my judgment we are reduced to the necessity of waging a vigorous war, striking the Cuyuses at the Grande Ronde, and Kam-i-ah-kan wherever he may be found." (Ruby and Brown, 1972, 252)

Meanwhile, Colonel Wright still wished to bring peace to the area, in accordance with General Wool's plan, so he called for another peace council. While not as large as the council of 1855, forty chiefs did attend. Their position was that they were dissatisfied with the treaty signed with Stevens and Palmer just a year ago, that they had been duped, and wanted peace, but with a new treaty. The legal authority to enter into treaties, however, rested with the Superintendent of Indian Affairs, a unit of the Interior Department, and not with the War Department nor its U.S. Army.

Therefore, without the presence of the Washington Territory's Indian Superintendent, Governor Isaac Stevens, and Oregon's Indian Superintendent, Joel Palmer, to make a treaty legal, Colonel Wright entered into a new quasi-treaty of promises. He promised the Indians immunity for their conduct of the last year, and that no white men would be allowed into their territory until a new treaty had been negotiated. The Indians misunderstood his words of "the bloody shirt shall now be washed and not a spot left on it." (Ruby and Brown, 1972, 253) They believed it meant that the old treaties were no longer in effect. It would be another case of white men's words seeming to contradict each other, or, more simply put, white men lie.

Governors Stevens and Curry were outraged. Colonel Wright's new treaties further damaged relations between the Army and the civilian governments of the two territories. Colonel Wright told the Indians that he did not believe the U.S. Senate would ratify the 1855 treaties, that is, Governor Stevens' treaties. Worse, he made new promises that all but contradicted the law and the stated policy of both territories. By closing the Indian lands to white settlement, General Wool unilaterally negated the Oregon Donation Land Law passed by Congress in 1850. Not only was the U.S. Army soft on punishing the hostile Indians in the minds of many settlers, it was anti-American—that is, anti-white—in denying settlers the free land Congress had granted them.

Reassured by Wright's promises, the Indians pledged their peace. The Army was so willing to believe this that, on December 18, 1856, General Wool announced that peace had officially been restored.

The closing act of 1856 did not take place in the east, nor was it fought either by the U.S. Army or even by territorial troops. The final battle of 1856 was fought by the U.S. Navy.

In November of 1856, a large number of coastal Indians from southern British Columbia raided throughout the area of Puget Sound. When the Indians attacked a lumber camp near Fort Steilacoom, Lieutenant Colonel Casey ordered troops to the area, only to find the Indians would stand off with their canoes, out of reach of Army muskets. Casey asked for the Navy to assist. Commander Samuel Swarthout, captain of the U.S.S. *Massachusetts*, responded. Upon arriving at the lumber camp, Commander Swarthout found that the Indians had fled north and pursued them to the area of Port Madison.

On November 20, he found them close to Port Gamble, and sent a party under Lieutenant I. Young ashore to persuade them to return to British Columbia. The Navy lieutenant faced a war party of 117 men, plus a few women and children. As his landing party neared shore in small boats to talk with them, the Indians rushed forward threatening to shoot anyone who landed.

Commander Swarthout enlisted a resident doctor known to local Indians to attempt another peaceful settlement. Under a flag of truce, Lieutenant Young took the doctor to speak with the Indians. Their response was that they would leave when they were ready. Faced with Indians bent on war, the Navy responded and throughout that night, preparations were made. A gun was transferred from the *Massachusetts* to a merchant ship named the *Traveller*, and both ships covered a different part of the shore. In addition, a party of sailors and Marines were put ashore under the command of Lieutenant Semmes and given a howitzer.

On the morning of November 21, the Indians were given one more opportunity to leave, under naval escort, peacefully for British Columbia. They refused. Both ships opened fire, with the *Massachusetts* firing a full broadside of both grape and round shot. The shore party of Marines charged while the sailors fired the howitzer. After destroying the canoes, huts, and supplies, the shore party returned to the *Massachusetts*. For the rest of the day, the *Massachusetts* bombarded the woods where the Indians had taken refuge. At nightfall, the Navy ceased firing and sought the Indians' surrender. They refused.

On November 22, Commander Swarthout prepared to open fire again, but the cold November rain had changed the Indians' desire to fight to the last warrior. The Indians had twenty-seven killed and twenty-one wounded, while the Navy and Marines had suffered one killed and four wounded. The Navy man killed was Coxswain Gustave Englebrecht, the first U.S. Navy sailor killed in action on the Pacific Coast. The Indians were taken aboard the *Massachusetts* and dropped off on Vancouver Island.

1857

General Wool may have declared peace, but a high tension still encircled the entire Pacific Northwest. On the southern front, the U.S. Army gathered the Indians at Fort Orford and transported them to the new Siletz reservation, guarded by three forts, and declared victory. The northern front remained peaceful with one exception. Another raiding party from British Columbia briefly sortied south, beheading a Whidbey Island settler in August. The blockhouses erected the previous year had stopped roving bands of Indians, and allowed the northern front to remain largely calm.

The eastern front was slightly different. Although there were no direct conflicts between Indians and troops either regular or territorial, tension remained high. That summer, the Palouse raided Fort Walla Walla and stole the command's horses. More dramatically, they killed miners around Colville, and the citizens petitioned for troops. The Army wanted time for General Wool's plan of intervention in the Indian lifestyle to work. Some respite was achieved when vastly smaller numbers of emigrants traveled the Oregon and Applegate Trails in 1857, as a result of the newspaper reports of the fighting in 1856.[19]

Even after Wool left the command of the Pacific Division in early 1857, his successor, Brigadier General Newman S. Clarke, endorsed his plan. When Clarke visited the Northwest in June 1857, he amplified the program by permitting no white settlements east of the Salmon River in Washington, and the Deschutes River in Oregon. In fact, the U.S. Army forcibly removed settlers who attempted to settle in the area.

General Clarke made other attempts to end the war. He met with the new Superintendent of Indian Affairs for the Oregon and Washington Territories, James. W. Nesmith, former colonel of the Oregon Mounted Volunteers. At the meeting at The Dalles, Nesmith named two primary causes of Indian unrest in the eastern territories. First, Bolon's murderers were still at large after two years of intense fighting. Second, the Indians feared enforcement of the 1855 treaties. Clarke shared Major Steptoe's opinion that if any attempt were made to enforce the treaties, open warfare would resume in the Walla Walla Valley. Still, many Indians misinterpreted any appeasement as weakness, which added to their contempt of the whites.

Religious bigotry added hardship to the troubled land. Troubles between the Army and the Mormons in Utah kept rumors flying that the Mormons were trying to distract the U.S. government by inciting the Indians of the Northwest to resume their war. Rumors of Mormon instigators were reported from Fort Walla Walla, and from Fort Simcoe's Major Garnett. Anti-Catholic rhetoric accused priests ministering to the tribes as being instigators of Indian hostility, supplying them with ammunition and weapons, and even directing their activities.

19. The trails had seen steady travel. In 1854, 6,000 reached the Pacific Northwest, and 1855 and 1856 each saw about 5,000 more emigrants travel the trails to the Pacific paradise.

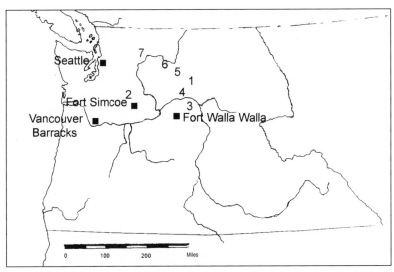

The Great Outbreak: 1858 Overview. 1. Steptoe's Battle. 2. Lieutenants Allen and Crook capture seventy Indians. 3. Colonel Wright's pack train attacked for the first time. 4. Wright's pack train attacked for the second time. 5. Battle of Four Lakes. 6. Battle of Spokane Plains. 7. Battle of Okanogan River. (*Author*)

Finally, the Indians of northeastern Washington remained intent on keeping the whites out of their country. The Couer d'Alenes and Spokanes swore that they would not sign any treaty, and gave refuge to disgruntled Indians such as the Yakima's Kamiakin. Father Charles Pandosy fled his mission, writing of his concern that war would soon breakout. Another Jesuit missionary, Father Joseph Joset, sent word that Kamiakin and the Palouse chief Tilcoax, were trying to bring the Coeur d'Alenes to the warpath.

While 1857 passed largely without incident, the war could not truly be called over. The hated 1855 treaties still stood. Moreover, no formal reservations had been created to contain and protect the Indians from white settlers who would come. By January 1858, General Clarke instructed his command, in particular Major Steptoe's Fort Walla Walla, to ready the troops for extended operations in the campaign season of 1858.

1857 had been merely a respite for the final effort from both sides. That effort that would result in the two largest single engagements ever fought in the Pacific Northwest and the crushing of the remnant Indian coalition.

The winter of 1857-58 passed and spring brought renewed war.

1858

Major (Brevet Colonel) Edward Steptoe led the opening movements. Ordered to move north toward Colville, his job was to meet the Indians and determine their proclivities. Steptoe's expedition was not punitive, as he prepared his 158 men to march, carrying only routine patrol issued amounts of ammunition.

On May 6, 1858, Major Steptoe set out with three undermanned companies of 1st U.S. Dragoons, Companies C, E, and H, and one part of E Company, a company of the 9th Infantry. E Company, 9th Infantry, with Captain C.S. Widner commanding, was the best armed, carrying the standard infantry weapon, the 1841 rifle. While having the utmost accuracy, the long infantry weapon was incapable of being reloaded from horseback. The foot soldiers also freighted two mountain howitzers. Most of the dragoons slung the ineffective standard-issued musketoons across their saddles. This was true of Captain Taylor's C Company and E Company, led by Lieutenant William Gaston. H Company, however, led by Lieutenant David Gregg, had been issued ten carbines to field test as a replacement for the short-barreled, limited-range musketoon. The 1841 rifles and carbines would be crucial in the unfolding events.

Clearly Major Steptoe was not preparing a major combat campaign. He had left behind at Fort Walla Walla B Company, under the command of Captain Frederick. J. Dent (brother-in-law of U.S. Grant), the rest of E Company, both of the 9th Infantry, and Captain William Grier's I Company, 1st Dragoons, acting as the post's commanding officer in Steptoe's absence. A typical combat force would have fielded two of the remaining three companies.

Complicating the situation, three of the leading officers were ill. The column's commander, Major Steptoe, had suffered a stroke in 1855, leaving him unable to ride a horse, at least temporarily that year, and his health was precarious.

No less fragile was the health of two other officers. Captain Winder had just finished a two-year medical leave of absence and Lieutenant William Gaston had cancer steadily growing within his neck. Believing it to be fatal, Gaston had often expressed to his fellow officers a desire to die a warrior's death rather than be slowly consumed by the agonizing cancer.

As the column marched north, signs of Indian activity increased. Although this was Palouse country, Steptoe's command noted other

Indians as well. Near the Snake River the column met with friendly Nez Perce, who told of a large gathering of Palouse ahead. Making sure that he was not going to be cut off, Steptoe sent a rider to Fort Walla Walla to have Major Grier send troops to protect his Snake River Crossing. Having secured his rear, Steptoe ordered the column on. Rather than take the most direct route toward Colville, the column swung further north, nearly entering the Coeur d'Alene country.

Many Indians, professing peace and friendship, made contact with the column as it pushed north. A few Indians warned the troopers that the tribes ahead were listening to agitators, such as Kamiakin, who called for the whites to be stopped. However, inflaming matters, Steptoe's Nez Perce scouts often would taunt the Indians the column made contact with, saying, "Coeur d'Alenes, your wives, your horses, your goods shall very soon be ours." (Burns, 205)

Taking a long Sunday rest on May 15, 1858, the column was still at Pine Creek camp when a large party of warriors appeared across the rolling hills. Nearly 1,500 Indians of the Coeur d'Alenes, Spokanes, Palouse, and even the Yakimas rode up. Their leaders said they had heard that Steptoe had come to destroy their nations. If that was his mission, the Indians were prepared to defend themselves. Steptoe proclaimed his peaceful intent and desire to talk, but the Indians had no trust in the white man. Some chiefs, seeking peace, had sent word for a Jesuit missionary, Father Joset. Arriving on the Sunday, Father Joset argued for peace, but inadvertently merely persuaded the Indians not to fight on the Christian Sabbath.

Attempting to fulfill his mission, Steptoe spoke to the Indians, but found no listeners. Fearing the Indians' intent, Steptoe had an Indian rider, Wie-cat, take word back to Fort Walla Walla requesting reinforcements. The message was never delivered. Believing that the command would be wiped out, Wie-cat returned to the Walla Walla valley, but not to seek help for Steptoe. Instead, Wie-cat tried to rally the Cayuse and Walla Walla Indians to attack the weakly defended fort. Even with the belief that help might be coming, the troopers remained for several days surrounded by Indian camps full of warriors dancing around flames and singing their harrowing war songs.

Finally, on the morning of May 18, Steptoe started his march back to Fort Walla Walla. After the troops broke from their defensive camp position, they took to a marching column, stretching out across the rolling grasslands. Father Joset tried for one more peace conference, but the chiefs now wanted war.

The column had covered three miles and was exposed, when the Indians opened fire at eight o'clock in the morning. A column of dragoons guarded each flank. In one of the first charges, the troopers dropped three of the Coeur d'Alenes' chiefs, which further enraged the Indians. If there had been any hope for a mere rearguard skirmish, the death of the three chiefs brought it to an end. As one Indian leader explained after the conflict, "I [Chief Vincent] had no intention to fight, but at seeing the corpse of my brother-in-law I lost my head." (Burns, 221) As more Indians joined around noon, a serious foray was made against the column's pack train where a few of the mules were captured.

The dragoons tried to cover the infantry and then surge ahead to a high point, holding it until the column moved up, and then repeated the maneuver. After six hours of continuous fighting, Steptoe ordered the troops to circle in defense, where the command sought high ground near the present day town of Rosalia, Washington. Under covering fire, the column scrambled to the top of a low hill. In the firefight, Captain Taylor of the dragoons, on the right flank, was shot through the neck. Lieutenant Gaston of E Company of the 9th, protecting the left flank, and two privates of H company were killed. Gaston's desire to die a warrior's death had been fulfilled.

The struggle became extremely fierce as troopers dismounted to recover Captain Taylor's mortally wounded body, and the Indians swarmed upon them.[20] The fighting was hand-to-hand, with the Colt revolver of particular use in close combat. Covering the retreat, Sergeant William C. Williams was mortally wounded leading his dragoons in a rear-guard action. Another of his troopers, Victor De Moy, swung his empty rifle as if a sword. The former French army captain was heard shouting, "My God, for a saber!" De Moy was shot from his horse, then shot two of his attackers with his revolver as they came at him, and as the troops climbed to the top of the hill, leaving him behind, he saved the last bullet for himself.

From the hilltop, in a strong position, Steptoe's command held off the Indians until nightfall using the long range 1841 rifles and the recently

20. Captain Taylor lived long enough to convey his undying love to his wife and two children who had recently joined him at Fort Walla Walla.

The Steptoe battlefield has changed little since the time of the Great Outbreak. (*Author*)

issued carbines. The Spokanes and Coeur d'Alenes attacked Steptoe's back from the north. In his front were the Palouse, with the other tribes, in much smaller numbers, filling in where they might. Arrows soared in, causing more casualties, and the musket fire was steady, cutting men down. The desperate troopers fired back, holding the Indians at bay. The heavy fighting had reduced each man to just three rounds of ammunition a piece. Twice the Indians made frontal attacks, but were staved off. Another attack by the Indians would finish the command off. Fortunately, as dusk fell, the Indians slackened their efforts.

Later Indian reports spoke of Kamiakin being present with the Yakimas, and how he urged an immediate night charge. His failure saved the command. Now surrounded by burning camp fires and shouting Indians, the troopers were faced with the terror of the night. Calling for a final stand, Steptoe's officers persuaded him that they must try to escape. If the command was wiped out, the only recourse left for Fort Walla Walla would be to retreat to Fort Dalles, since they were too weak to hold out. The column had to try for Walla Walla. Hastily burying his dead as well as his howitzers, Steptoe, with the lightened force, made a stealthy retreat in the darkness. The departure was well timed. Shortly after midnight, the Indians made an unusual night attack, only to find the whites gone.

A night march of eighty miles to the Snake River brought the command to Captain Dent, who met them with a column of sixty-six men as

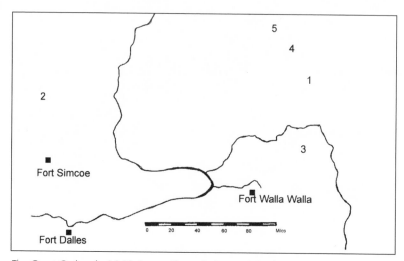

The Great Outbreak: 1858 Eastern Front. 1. Steptoe's Battle. 2. Lieutenants Allen and Crook capture seventy Indians. 3. Colonel Wright's pack train attacked for the first time. 4. Battle of Four Lakes. 5. Battle of Spokane Plains. (*Author*)

part of the previous plan to protect the river crossing, to help them cross to relative safety. Steptoe lost eight killed, eleven wounded, and reported one missing.[21] Indian sources put their casualties at nine killed and forty wounded. According to one historian, "Steptoe had managed one of the cleverest retreats in Indian-fighting history." (Burns, 228)

General Clarke was now persuaded that the plan to avoid hostilities and bring peace had failed. Restraint was seen as weakness. Those misinterpretations would be quickly corrected. From Vancouver Barracks in June, Clarke gave his command, "You will attack all hostile Indians with vigor; make their punishment severe, and persevere until the submission of all is complete [Utley, 203]." Just as the earlier Haller defeat had

21. Missing was First Sergeant Edward Ball, Company H, 1st U.S. Dragoons. As the column made their escape from the hilltop at night, a small group was left behind to keep the fires lit in order to trick the Indians into believing the command was still there. Not wanting to allow the Indians to gain the medicinal alcohol in the pack train, it was ordered destroyed. Ball accomplished his mission in a manner that does credit to the capacity of the frontier soldier to drink. When the rear-guard troops snuck out, Ball was passed out in the bushes. The Indians missed him as he hid, or believed him to be dead, and Ball walked back to Fort Walla Walla, arriving six days late. For his gallantry, his misconduct was overlooked.

spurred a gathering of forces, now Steptoe's defeat required a similar concentration of power.

Lieutenant George Crook commanded Company D of the 4th Infantry during the Great Outbreak. (Library of Congress)

From California came reinforcements. Three companies of the 3rd Artillery (A, D, G) joined the three already in the Northwest (B, L, M), acting as infantry, under Captain Erasmus Keyes. Part of the 3rd created a fort at the mouth of the Tucannon River, covering its confluence with the Snake River. They named the base Fort Taylor in honor of Steptoe's dead captain of dragoons. An additional company of the 4th Infantry, Company D, commanded by Lieutenant George Crook, was drawn from Fort Jones in California and one from Fort Umpqua in southern Oregon. These were added to the concentration of troops from the rest of the Pacific Northwest. One further company was raised, Nez Perce scouts commanded by Lieutenant John Mullan, 2nd U.S. Artillery.

Clarke sought the peaceful surrender of the Indians. He sent word to Father Joset of his three demands: First, acknowledgment of U.S. authority by letting troops move throughout the region unmolested; second, the acquiescence to the construction of a military road through their territory; and third, admission of their crimes, surrendering of the guilty, and the return of their plunder. If peace failed—which it did when the Indians rejected the terms, especially the surrendering of the "guilty" and the return of their plundered booty—then Clarke planned a two-pronged attack.

From Fort Simcoe, Major Garnett led 9th Infantry Companies C, G, and I, commanded by Captains Archer, Frazer, and Black, respectively, as well as Company D of the 4th Infantry, commanded by Lieutenant George Crook—a total of 315 officers and men. Garnett's job was to hunt down the known hostiles of the Yakima Indians.

Major Garnett's column left Fort Simcoe on August 10. Having no dragoons, ten men were drawn from each company and placed on horseback, under the command of Lieutenant Jesse K. Allen. The first encounter was on August 13, when Garnett surrounded a Yakima village. In the attack, one officer, Lieutenant Allen, was mistakenly killed by his own men in the dawn light. Seventy Indians were captured; five were identified as instigators of the uprising and were executed. Dogging the Indians wherever they could be found, Lieutenant Crook led one company up the Wenatchee Valley, where he captured and executed five more Indians. Meanwhile, the rest of the command headed toward the Okanogan region.

Reunited with Crook's troops, Garnett's column had a brief melee with the Indians on September 10 along the Okanogan River, forcing the Indians to flee. Again dividing the force into two wings—Garnett and Crook with a wing each—the body of troops headed back to Fort Simcoe. Neither wing became caught up in any more fights, but Garnett's actions kept many Indians occupied who would otherwise have joined the main resistance, directed at Colonel Wright's command.

On August 7, Wright's first troops departed Fort Walla Walla as a vanguard. Their mission was to prepare a defensible crossing of the Snake River. Wright ultimately followed with a command of 570 troops. His column consisted of four companies of 1st Dragoons, Brevet Major William Grier, commanding; five of 3rd Artillery, Captain Keyes, commanding;[22] and two of the 9th Infantry, Captain Frederick J. Dent, commanding; plus thirty Nez Perce scouts and one hundred civilian teamsters using pack animals instead of the typical wagons.

Indian raids continued. Thirty-six oxen were taken by the Indians in a raid on August 8, against Fort Walla Walla. Lieutenant Henry Davidson, of the 1st Dragoons, rode in pursuit. On August 13, an Indian raid to cut off the pack train from the column was beaten off. Camp was erected and peace feelers were extended through the Jesuit missionaries; but the Indians felt confident that they would kill any white who entered their country, and were ready to fight.

22. The artillerymen, acting as infantry, were very well equipped. They had the new 1855 Springfield .58 caliber rifle, capable of firing a Minnie ball accurately farther than anything the Indians had. Of note, when serving as infantry, artillerymen were called "red-leg infantry." Each part of the army had a color to designate their branch: yellow for cavalry, light blue for infantry, and red for artillery. Hence, the red stripe down the pants of the artillery resulted in the "red-leg infantry."

"After the Steptoe disaster the Indians had reportedly said that 'the white soldiers were women and could not fight and the more that should be sent into that country the better they would like it, for they would kill them all.' They were confident that U.S. troops could not stand up to them. Being well supplied with arms, ammunition, and provisions, they expected another easy victory." (Schlicke, 162)

The Spokanes, Coeur d'Alenes, Yakimas, Palouse, and Pend d'Oreilles gathered together. After the construction of Fort Taylor where the Tucannon flows into the Snake, Wright's column crossed on August 27, riding and marching directly toward the gathering Indians confederacy.

As the column advanced, the Indians readied to attack. "They [the Indians] meant to harry Wright's force, allowing it no time to reach any objective, dictating the terms of battle by striking first and decisively." (Burns, 284) Bands of them could be seen on the hills, out of rifle range, and on August 30, the Indians attempted to burn the grasses surrounding the troops. A backfire by the troopers quickly stopped that threat, increasing the vigilance of the sentries. Shots were exchanged by the pickets that night, as the Indians probed the camp. The next day, the Indians attempted a raid against the pack train. First, they raided against the Nez Perce scouts at the front, drawing a company of dragoons away from the column to ride to the rescue. This exposed the baggage train and the Indians swooped in. Infantry made a square around the animals and held off the attackers.

On September 1, the Indians attacked at Four Lakes, southwest of present-day Spokane, Washington. "The Indians had planned their strategy carefully and chosen the field for battle." (Schlicke, 165) They were arrayed directly in front of Wright, atop a treeless hill. Covered by a squadron of dragoons under the command of Lieutenant Henry Davidson, the infantry under Captain Ord, and artillerymen under Lieutenant Morgan, acting as infantry, charged in-line up the hill, taking the crest. Grier brought more dragoons, around what is now called Battle Butte to try to cut off the escape of the Indians. Directly below were about 500 Indians with clear signs that more were in the trees to the flanks.

On the plain below us we saw the enemy. Every spot seemed alive with the wild warriors we had come so far to meet. They were in the pines on the edge of the lakes, in the ravines and gullies, on the opposite hillsides, and swarming over the plains. They seemed to cover the country for some two miles. (Kip, 55)

One account has the Indians lined up by tribes, as if in military formation.

> According to Chief Stellam of the Coeur d'Alenes, reminiscing perhaps inaccurately thirty years later, the braves had begun their battle in roughly tribal grouping. The prominent figure at their right wing was Kamiakin with his Yakimas and Palouse. The Spokanes and other tribes had gathered particularly on the left. Among those in the center were the Coeur d'Alenes. (Burns, 291)

Dent's 9th Infantry advanced into the trees to flush the Indians out while Keyes' 3rd Artillerymen advanced, supported by Grier's First Dragoons. The Indians would spring out of the tree line, attack the advancing infantry, and then retire. Keyes' troops were armed with the new 1855 rifle, and so provided effective fire, even at 600 yards. No Indian firearms could match the greater distance, and they suffered unavenged casualties.

Meanwhile, Dent's infantry advanced into the trees, covered by artillery fire, driving the Indians out onto the plains. As the Indians fell back into the open ground, Grier ordered his four companies of dragoons to attack. Walking their horses through the long line of infantry skirmishers, Grier ordered them mounted and led them with his cry of, "Charge the rascals!" The dragoons laid into the Indians with pistol and sabre. "We saw the flash of sabres as they cut them down. Lieutenant Davidson shot one warrior from his saddle as they charged up, and Lieutenant Gregg clove the skull of another." (Kip, 57) Approximately sixty Indians were killed and an unknown number were wounded. Among the dead were two chiefs of the Spokanes. Further, many of the Indians' horses and supplies were captured as the dragoons swept in. Wright suffered no casualties at all. If the Indians thought the white men fought like women, the Battle of Four Lakes was a rude awakening.

Retreating about fifteen miles, the Indians gathered once again to resist the invasion of Colonel Wright. The next battle was fought on the Spokane Plains, just north of what is now Fairchild Air Force Base. As Wright advanced on September 5, he was met by approximately 700 warriors. "The Indians had chosen their terrain well. The ground was so broken that dragoons could not operate effectively." (Burns, 294) Bringing his pack train forward, Wright surrounded it with two companies of infantry—one from the 9th Infantry, under Dent, and one from the 3rd Artillery, acting as infantry, under Lieutenants Howard and Ihrie—with dragoons led by Lieutenant Davidson, ready as a mobile reserve. The Indians were unable to penetrate to the valuable supplies. But neither could Wright effectively deal with the attacking Indians. The Indians torched the tinder-dry grasses, letting the wind blow the flames toward Wright's troops.

> We had nearly reached the woods when they advanced in great force, and set fire to the dry grass of the prairie, so that the wind blowing high and against us, we were nearly enveloped by the flames. Under cover of the smoke, they formed round us in one-third of a circle, and poured in their fire upon us. (Kip, 63)

Closing up his scattered command, Wright ordered Keyes to advance his artillerymen as skirmishers on one flank and his center. Using one company armed with the long range rifles and his howitzers, Wright ordered his command forward, and they marched into the billowing black smoke of the burning grass.

Having the Indians again in the trees, Wright ordered his howitzers once more into action. Shelling the forest, the barrage killed or wounded many of the Indians who had sought shelter. Among the wounded was the great Yakima chief, Kamiakin.

As the infantry advanced, they drove the Indians ahead of them. Through four miles of timbered country the infantry shouldered forward. The Indians, finally driven back onto the plains, were charged once again by Grier's dragoons. As the dragoons charged, the fighting became fierce.

> Among the incidents of the fight was one which happened to Lieutenant Pender. Firing his pistol as he charged, just as he dashed up to the side of an Indian he discovered that his revolver had caught on the lock and was useless. He had no time to draw his sabre, and was obliged, therefore, to close with his enemy. He grappled the Indian and hurled him from his horse, when a soldier behind him dispatched him. (Kip, 65)

The chase continued. Whenever the Indians rallied to a defensive position, the howitzers opened fire and the infantry cleared the position.

After a twenty-five mile battle, the Indians fled across the Spokane River. Wright suffered one wounded. Besides the unknown killed and wounded, Wright destroyed 900 Indian horses, leaving the Spokane and Palouse effectively horseless in a country where survival demanded horses, and severely damaging their morale.

In the Indians' eyes it was incredible that a warrior could be indifferent to the basis of wealth in an Indian society: horses. First the Indians believed the whites could not fight, and now two battles had chased the Indians from the field. Further, with a vast amount of Indian wealth, 900 horses, here was an enemy so callous that they would kill all of the horses. The Indians were in shock and peace overtures were extended within days of their defeat.

Wright met with several tribes over the weeks as he continued his advance. He promised each tribe that if they would talk peace with him, no one would be hurt. But, many of the chiefs were seized by Wright, even under a white flag, and used to force the tribes to agree to his terms by moving on to reservations.

Fifteen principal instigators of the troubles were captured during the truce and hanged, while others were placed in irons and taken prisoner. Among the captured were Chief Owhi and his son, Qualchin, whom the Indians identified as having killed Indian Agent Bolon in 1855.

Wright's expedition returned to Fort Walla Walla victorious on October 5, 1858, almost three years to the day of Major Haller's defeat in 1855. Many of Wright's command would go on to become generals in the Civil War, either for the Union or the Confederacy.[23] Officers serving the Union to reach general rank included Keyes, Ord, Gregg, and Tyler. For the Confederacy, Wright's future generals included Winder, Davidson, and Pender.

General Clarke's two-pronged battle plan had effectively ended total war in the Pacific Northwest. Never again would Indians rise up in war west of the Cascade Mountains. Never again would the Walla Walla, Palouse, Yakima, Klickitat, Spokane, or other tribes of the Indian confederacy east of the Cascades rise up against the whites.

In 1859, the iniquitous 1855 treaties were ratified by the U.S. Senate, adding the final defeat to the Indians' resistance. Not since the earliest

23. Seventeen officers would wear general's stars in the Civil War—twelve for the Union, and five for the South.

colonial days had any area of America been so totally engulfed in Indian war. Nearly one third of the white population was directly involved or threatened by Indian attacks, and the rest felt the specter of destruction. Nearly every Indian tribe in the Pacific Northwest felt the sting of war, either as hostiles, allies of the whites, or innocents killed just because they were Indians.

Kamiakin is not as well known as Sitting Bull or even Pontiac, but his dream of uniting the Indians in total resistance came closer to reality than most chiefs. He escaped capture by Wright and was later discovered in 1870. When he was found living not with his Yakimas, but south of the town of Spokane, he was described as being "a large, powerful man, about fifty years old and six feet high . . . but he does not go much among the whites, and seems broken-hearted, having lost his former energy." (Utley, 209) Kamiakin had lost more than his energy; he had lost his country.

~

As the history of the Great Outbreak was divided geographically, so are the historic sites to visit. The place to start is in the south.

The dominant feature of the war with the Rogue River Indians is the very river named for the tribe. The Lupton Massacre ignited the war, and it is a fitting place to start as the drama moved west from this tragedy. The village attacked by Lupton was located on the South Fork of the Rogue River, easily traveled on Oregon Highway 140. The closest significant settlement to the site is Brownsboro. The area is still very scenic, and recalls how the American Indians saw the land before the advent of whites.

After the two major forks of the Rogue River join in the central valley, several geographic and historic sites are easily seen. As mentioned in an earlier chapter, Jacksonville is worth a visit to step back to the gold-rush days. Table Rock still stands as the dominant topographical feature of the valley. Fort Lane was located near Table Rock on the south side of the river. Near Jacksonville is the scenic Applegate Valley and one battle site on Williams Creek.

Just north of Sexton Mountain Pass, Interstate 5 crosses Grave Creek. Several engagements occurred on or near this stream, the most significant being the Battle of Hungry Hill. Take exit number 76 off of Interstate 5, and start from the Historic Wolf Creek Tavern. Hungry Hill is to the west, about six and a half miles from the Wolf Creek Tavern, accessible by foot. The area is still rugged and heavily wooded.

The back roads from Wolf Creek also head south along Grave Creek to the old mining town of Galice, on Galice Creek, and the site of one early engagement in the Rogue River Indian War. Nothing marks the spot, but it is easy to see in the mind's eye the cabins along the river where Galice Creek tumbles into the fast flowing Rogue.

It is from Galice that drivers may take a paved, but very windy U.S. Forest Service road across the Siskiyou Mountains to the coast. Vistas open up allowing the traveler to see how extremely rugged these mountains, and how steep the valley walls are dropping to the Rogue River. For more adventurous souls, a hiking route follows along the Rogue River itself, and many of the actual sites are commemorated by markers. The battles sites of Big Meadows and Big Bend can be walked upon by using this trail. Other sites, such as the Black Bar of the Rogue, Battle Bar, Horseshoe Bend, Quail Creek, Fort Lamerick (nothing remains), Lobster Creek, and Skookum House Prairie are all available to the hardy traveler who is willing to take the river trail.

Near the confluence of the Rogue and Illinois Rivers is the community of Agness, which can be reached by boat, foot, and car. From this town it is a short hike from a nearby trail head to the grounds of the Battle of Big Bend. Or, if the traveler heads south to the Illinois River, it is four miles up river to Oak Flat, a site of one engagement. A few miles further is the very steep mountain that marked another engagement in the Illinois River valley, Eight Dollar Mountain. It is located near the town of Selma, immediately west of U.S. Highway 199.

Proceeding west from Agness, the road leads to Gold Beach, Oregon and the Pacific Ocean. To the south, the Pistol River historical marker is located at the site of the skirmish fought by George Abbott and the Crescent City volunteers as they marched north to relieve the besieged settlers at Gold Beach. To the north is Euchre Creek, where troops from Fort Orford attacked an Indian village while en route to help lift the siege of Gold Beach.

This tour from east at Brownsboro to the Pacific Ocean covers the majority of the Rogue River Indian War terrain. Despite the encroachment of civilization, much of the country is as it was during the war, absent the Indians who were removed to a reservation further north.

Two of the forts created to protect the reservation have sites commemorating the establishment of the posts. Fort Hoskins has a Benton

A replica blockhouse of Fort Yamhill at Dayton, Oregon. (*Author*)

County park marking the site, and is reached by traveling Oregon Highway 223, then taking the Luckiamute and Fort Hoskins roads, following well marked signs. Fort Yamhill has a replica of the blockhouse located in Dayton, Oregon, on Oregon Highway 221, just south of the Junction with Oregon Highway 18. The actual site of Fort Yamhill has been developed by the Oregon Department of Parks and Recreation, and recently opened in the summer of 2006.

In the far north, the central feature is Puget Sound and the rivers that feed into it. Port Madison is on Bainbridge Island, west of Seattle, and just to the north of it is the Port Madison Indian Reservation. A bit further north is Port Gamble, site of the naval attack and the Port Gamble Indian Reservation.

Between Seattle and Tacoma are three significant rivers: the Green, the White, and the Puyallup. To the south of Tacoma is the Nisqually River. On the White River, near the city of Auburn, is the location of the engagement at Bittings Prairie; nothing marks the fight now. Further south, on the Nisqually, marks the skirmish of Muck Prairie. Again, time has erased any hint of the fighting. Finally, east of the town of Bonney Lake marks the engagement of Connell's Prairie. This site is marked just to the south of Buckley Highway, east of 218th Avenue East.

A historical marker notes the location of the pioneer's defensive position of Fort Henness, west of Interstate 5, east of the town of Rochester.

There are stretches of these rivers still wild, suggesting the beauty of the country, and the ruggedness endured by the combatants, but no markers denote the struggles. Not even a road-side sign marks the fight for this paradise.

The battlefields that mark the eastern part of the total war are better preserved. As one heads up Washington State Highway 14, historical sites are clearly marked. Near North Bonneville, an Army Corps of Engineers park commemorates Fort Cascades. A little further on, a road-side sign shows where Fort Rains was located. Within the town of Stevenson is the location of Bradford's warehouse, which withstood the siege of Indians, but not of time.

Having traversed the Columbia Gorge, the jumping off point is The Dalles, just as many of the troops used Fort (The) Dalles. To the north and east are signs of three forts. One of the best preserved is Fort Simcoe, within the Yakama Indian reservation. Used only briefly, many of the original buildings still stand. Near this fort are the sites where A.J. Bolon was killed, the Haller battlefield, and the engagements of Toppenish Creek. Fort Na-chess was erected to interfere with the movement of the Indians where that creek flows into the Yakima River.

Near Interstate 84, within the town of Echo, is a replica of a bastion of Fort Henrietta. Nearby are ruts of the Oregon Trail and a commemoration of one of the earliest Catholic missions, which served the Cayuse, Walla Walla, and Umatilla Indians.

A little way north and east, on U.S. Highway 12, within the town of the same name, are remains of Fort Walla Walla. A replica of a bastion, a historic cemetery, and a museum mark the passage of time. To the west of town, and west of the Whitman Mission National Historic Site, a plaque marks the Frenchtown battle fought in the broad valley as it looked in 1855.

To the north of Walla Walla are two significant streams: The Touchet and Tucannon Rivers. The Touchet flows from north of Walla Walla to the west and joins the Walla Walla River at the town of Touchet, west of the Frenchtown fight. Due north of Walla Walla, near Waitsburg, one engagement was fought along the Touchet River. Much further north is the Tucannon River where numerous scraps and skirmishes were fought along. Fort Taylor was erected on the north bank of the Snake River near where the Tucannon flows in to protect the major river crossing there.

Fort Taylor was built to protect Colonel Wright's crossing as he marched north in 1858 to revenge the Steptoe loss. That battle started to the north of the small town of Rosalia, Washington, and ended on a hill within the south end of that town. An obelisk marks the site where Steptoe nearly made his last stand and gives a fine panorama of Pine Creek.

The surgeon's house at Fort The Dalles. Built in 1856, it is the only original structure from the fort remaining. It houses a museum. (*Author*)

To the north lay the sites of the two major engagements of Colonel Wright. Just south of Interstate 90, on Washington State Highway 904 is the community of Four Lakes, located on the site of the first of the two battles. A little further north, along U.S. Highway 2, is a stone pyramid, which is within the Spokane Plains Battlefield State Park. That battle ranged from there to the northeast and the Spokane River.

Finally, within northeastern Oregon are two sites of this long war. To the northeast of La Grande, is the valley of the Grande Ronde River, where the Shaw Massacre took place. Nothing commemorates this disgraceful battle, on par with Sand Creek in Colorado. The second site is less shameful. From the mouth of the John Day River, the Oregon Rangers chased some marauding Indians until they overtook them near the mouth of the Burnt River. It flows into the Snake River near Farewell Bend State Park, just off of Interstate 84.

A few of the significant sites of the Great Outbreak are marked, fewer still are preserved, and most have been lost. However, much of the country is still the same, and a traveler through this region will cover many of the same obstacles both warring parties faced. It is a travel through time.

Chapter 6

The Snake Indian
Wars

1858–1868

The successful completion of the wars known as The Great Outbreak had crushed the threat of hostile Indians west of the Cascades in both the Washington and Oregon territories. Further, it had curtailed, but not eliminated, the number of hostile Indians in the central parts of both territories. By the time of Colonel Wright's return to Fort Walla Walla after defeating the Spokane confederation in 1858, reports of attacks on wagon trains and settlers were already threatening the tenuous peace. However, the reports of Indian attacks were made from much further east in the Snake River drainage within the boundaries of what would become the State of Oregon and in Washington Territory (part of which became the Idaho Territory), and further south, along the region's lifelines, the Oregon and Applegate Trails.[1]

The Indians of the Snake River drainage had been among the most fierce and feared Indians encountered by any men, including the bold fur trappers. A number of different, Shoshonian-speaking tribes were called "Snakes," named in part for the area they lived in, and as an expression of contempt used by other Indians and whites. Indians from the many Paiute tribes, Shoshonis, Bannocks, and other, lesser tribes were all called Snake Indians at one time by ill-informed whites.

The number of settlers living in areas long considered Snake country expanded quickly after Brigadier General William S. Harney took com-

---

1. The numbers on the trail for the year 1858 was about 6,000. In 1859, about 8,000 moved into the Pacific Northwest, and stagecoaches first started to travel the trail on regularly scheduled routes.

Portions of the Oregon Trail can still be seen, such as these tracks at Massacre Rocks State Park, Idaho. (*Author*)

mand of the Columbia Department of the Pacific Division on September 13, 1858. Shortly after Wright's victory, Harney opened the eastern sections of the Columbia Department to formal white settlement. In response, marauding Indians renewed their attacks on travelers along the Oregon Trail and also menaced the scattered settlements of miners and ranchers in the area. Protecting the settlers were Fort Colville, in the mining region of the Upper Columbia, far removed from the Snake Indians; Fort Simcoe, guarding Kamiakin's home country (which would later be abandoned the following year, 1859); Fort Dalles, at the eastern end of the Columbia River Gorge; and Fort Walla Walla, home to Colonel Wright's command.

On February 14, 1859, Oregon achieved statehood and became an Edenic beacon to many who were willing to travel the well-established Oregon and Applegate Trails.

To protect the increased flow of emigrants, the 4th U.S. Infantry sent patrols out to guard the trail. Captain H.D. Wallen, who had built Fort Rains in 1855 to guard the Cascades of the Columbia, assumed command of the infantry's efforts to protect the travelers.[2] While most wagon

2. The soldiers were drawn from the contingent assigned to guard the Warm Springs Indian Reservation. The confederated tribes of the Warm Springs were the traditional enemies of the Paiutes. Once the troops were pulled to patrol the Oregon Trail, the Paiutes raided the Warm Springs. Freed in the raids were two Paiute chiefs, captured in earlier raids, Paulina and Wehveveh.

trains did make it through unscathed, there were enough attacks to give the general public the impression that the Indians were a constant threat.

On July 26, a wagon train was attacked near the Hudspeth Cutoff in Idaho, and the next day another train was attacked nearby, resulting in what was called the Shepherd Massacre, in which five white men lost their lives. The Army responded by increasing patrols. The 1st U.S. Dragoons intercepted and followed the trail of hostiles, resulting in a two-day skirmish against Shoshoni Indians in Box Elder Canyon, Utah.

But, this did not stop the Indian attacks. Two more trains were attacked in August, one of which resulted in the Miltimore Massacre, near present-day American Falls, Idaho. The entire seven-member Miltimore family was killed, as well as another white man.[3]

An extreme measure had to be taken on the Oregon Trail. As the wagons arrived at Fort Hall, they were held until an extremely large train was created. Once gathered, Major John Reynolds, with two companies of the 3rd U.S. Artillery, started to march in the van of the train. Guarding the rear and able to act as a quick reaction force, Captain Wallen rode with two companies of dragoons. While this stopped the attacks, it was an impractical solution.

The public demanded greater protection in 1860. From the Utah territory, troops patrolled the region where the trail divided—one path leading to Oregon, and the other to California. The Columbia Department also provided more troops. Captain Grier's Company I, 1st Dragoons, from Fort Walla Walla, patrolled the trail as far east as Salmon Falls, Idaho. Two more companies of dragoons patrolled in Central Oregon. Major Enoch Steen led one half of his force in a column to the west while Captain Andrew Jackson Smith, of Rogue Indian Wars fame, patrolled to the east.

On June 27, 1860, Captain Smith's command repelled an Indian attack by an estimated 150 Indians north of the Malheur River, near

---

3. As the majority of the emigrants traveled the Oregon Trail, the focus was to protect that road. The Applegate Trail also suffered attacks by Paiutes or Modocs. In September 1858, the Felix Scott wagon train was attacked near Goose Lake, California, resulting in the death of eight pioneers, including Scott. In June of 1859, Bloody Point, California maintained its reputation when another train was attacked; all the men and women were killed, and the children captured. These innocent captives were killed when a larger wagon train overtook the fleeing Indians, who killed the captives to speed their escape.

Harney Lake in eastern Oregon.[4] The battle lasted for nearly six hours, finally ending when Smith's troops held off the attacks until nightfall. Steen reunited his command, and he and Smith searched for hostile Snakes for the rest of the summer.

Colonel Wright, fearing a repeat the past war's lack of concentration of force, ordered Captain (Brevet Major) George Andrews to reinforce Major Steen with three companies of the 3rd U.S. Artillery acting as infantry. Having found evidence of marauding Indians in a miner's camp in which the inhabitants had been killed, they failed to bring the Indians into a fight, capturing a total of three warriors and some women and children.

This was not because the Indians were idle. At least five wagon trains were attacked between late August and mid-October, 1860. Two of the attacks would be awarded the press label of massacres.

On September 9 and 10, one Idaho train was repeatedly attacked. In the Utter family, eight of twelve family members were killed, as were several other pioneer sojourners; many of the killed were women and children. The Army sent out a rescue column under the command of Captain Frederick Dent, but it failed to stop the attacks.[5]

From October 16 through the 18, another wagon train was attacked just west of the Snake River in Oregon. The Van Ornum family was wiped out; some were killed, others were captured. The public demand for protection from the Snakes grew as the press wrote of little children being killed or carried off into captivity.

Two factors complicated the Army's response. The first was that the attacks were not conducted by a single tribe. Captain Smith's battle was probably with a group from the Northern Paiute, while the Utter Massacre could have been Bannocks. Evidence suggests that the Shoshonis slaughtered the Van Ornums. Either tribe could hit and run, traveling to regions they each new well. Pursuit was, at best, difficult in the dry deserts of Eastern Oregon and Southern Idaho.

National politics was the second factor that ensured the Army's response inadequate. The 1860 election resulted in Abraham Lincoln's

4. Movius dates the battle as June 30, 1860.

5. Included in the command was a young Second Lieutenant of dragoons, Marcus A. Reno who was in command of Company J, First Dragoons. After the Civil War, Marcus Reno hit the apex of his career as a major with the Seventh U.S. Cavalry, and fighting at the Battle of the Little Big Horn.

victory, and the consequence was the threatened division of the union. Even as far west as Oregon, many Southern sympathizers advocated the secession of Oregon into the Pacific Republic as an independent country.

War in the east would draw most Army regulars out of the Oregon Country, many officers being called to assume field command. Others left to join the Confederate Army, as did Oregon Militia General John Lamerick, of the Rogue Indian War. Others from Oregon were recalled or volunteered east to the Union cause. Major John Reynolds would die a major general and a corps commander at the Battle of Gettysburg. Marion County resident Joseph Hooker would eventually command the entire Army of the Potomac. The commander of the Department of the Pacific in 1860 was Colonel (Brevet Brigadier General) Albert Sidney Johnston, destined to die at the Battle of Shiloh in 1862 for the Confederate cause. A divided country made any military response to the Snakes almost impossible until replacement troops were found.

The responsibility for command in the Pacific Division was ultimately given to Brigadier General George Wright, formerly of the 9th U.S. Infantry.[6] The Department of the Columbia was assigned to former paymaster, Brigadier General Benjamin Alvord. In accordance with President Lincoln's call for state troops, General Wright requisitioned the states and territories in his division to supply troops.

In 1861, after political infighting, Oregon called for the creation of the 1st Oregon Cavalry, under the command of Colonel Thomas R. Cornelius. This was a good appointment which gave great credibility to the regiment. Cornelius had started as a private then quickly promoted to sergeant in the Oregon Rifles of the Cayuse war, and had commanded the Oregon Mounted Volunteers in the wars of the mid-1850s. But, even with Cornelius' credibility, recruiting was slow, and the constantly understaffed regiment would not take the field until 1862.

Washington Territory also responded to the call. The unit created was the 1st Washington Territorial Infantry, commanded by Colonel Justin Sternberger. Colonel Sternberger had trouble recruiting enough troops, and only six companies of the ten authorized in standard regiments were recruited from Washington or Oregon. Subsequently, four additional companies were recruited exclusively in California.

---

6. Brigadier General Edwin Vose Sumner took command on April 25, 1861. However, desirous to serve on the East Coast during the Civil War, he quickly recommended Colonel Wright, his brother-in-law, for the command.

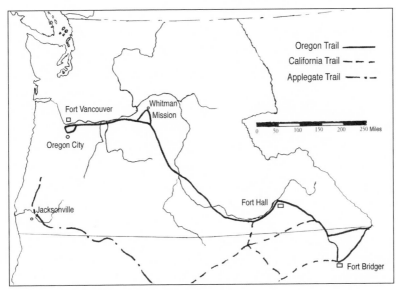

Map Trails to the Oregon Country. *(Author)*

Recognizing the shortfall of needed troops for the Department of the Columbia, General Wright deployed two California regiments to the Northwest, the 2nd California Infantry Regiment and the 4th California Infantry Regiment. The 2nd deployed Companies A, B, C, D and E to the District of Oregon in the fall of 1861. Various companies of the 2nd California would serve in the Northwest until June 1862, at such posts as Forts Dalles, Vancouver, Hoskins, and Colville. None of the 2nd would see combat in the Oregon Country. The 4th deployed Companies A, B, C, D, and E at such posts as Forts Walla Walla, Vancouver, Dalles, Yamhill, and Steilacoom. Most were withdrawn by late 1862. Only Company D remained at Fort Yamhill until March 1863, and was the last of the California companies to serve in the Northwest. Like the 2nd, the 4th saw no action during its tour of duty in the Northwest.

This was not true for the four other regiments that soldiered during the Civil War period in the Oregon Country. The 9th U.S. Infantry stayed active in the Northwest and was buttressed by the 1st Washington Territorial Infantry, the 1st Oregon Cavalry, and, eventually, the 1st Oregon Infantry Regiment. The year 1861 was spent in transition from a professional army garrisoning the Oregon Country to one of a force of volunteers once again protecting the Far West. But, it was not without incident.

As word reached southern Oregon in 1861 of attacks on wagon trains along the Applegate Trail, the special agent to the Indians of the Lakes Region, Lindsay Applegate,[7] believed it was his responsibility to protect whites from the Indians in his charge. Raising a company of forty-three volunteers, Applegate started to patrol the Applegate Trail. Word reached him on the march of an attack on a wagon train on August 27, near Goose Lake, California. Spurring their mounts harder, Applegate reached Bloody Point, California in time to find a group of wagons circled and hard pressed by the Modocs. Having more firepower, the Applegate's volunteers quickly drove off the Indians, saving the wagon train. Applegates' efforts throughout 1861 helped to prevent the loss of life of emigrants; but over 900 head of cattle and other livestock were successfully raided from the passing trains by the Indians of southern Oregon and northern California.

In 1862, the number of emigrants crossing to Oregon grew to more than 10,000. As the numbers swelled, so did conflicts with the Indians. To forestall trouble, elements of the 1st Oregon Cavalry actively patrolled the Oregon Trail in Idaho. Under Colonel Reuben F. Maury's leadership (Colonel Cornelius having resigned), the Oregon cavalrymen from Companies A, B, and D covered more than three thousand miles back and forth along the Snake River. To add further protection, elements of the 1st Washington Territorial Infantry joined the horse soldiers.

Despite their best efforts, Indian attacks persisted. In one two-day period, August 9 and 10, 1862, the Shoshonis attacked five different wagon trains, killing ten whites, west of Pocatello, Idaho. On both the Oregon and California Trails, just south of the old Oregon Country border in Utah, Snake Indians savaged wagon trains. Even with the increased Army patrols, the Indians still fought the invasion of their homeland.

Bear Hunter, a Shoshoni chief, continued to lead his warriors in attacks on the Oregon Trail. Information was gathered that surviving children of the Van Ornum family were still being held captive by Bear Hunter's tribe. In an effort to stop continuation of the 1862 problems in his district, Colonel P. Edward Connor ordered a column to search for the Indian village. Major Edward McGarry did find some hostile Indians. Surrounding the village, located in Cache Valley, near present-day

7. One of the leaders of the exploring party that created the trail named for them.

Indian encampment at The Dalles photographed in May 1860. (*Library of Congress*)

Weston, Idaho, McGarry made a surprise attack at dawn, capturing some women and children, and one warrior, but reported more than twenty were killed while attempting to escape. Some of the captives identified Bear Hunter's village as being near present day Preston, Idaho. Further information gathered by a relative of the captive Van Ornum children, Zachias Van Ornum, suggested they were still alive, and Major McGarry followed the leads.

On November 23, 1862, Major McGarry, leading the 2nd California Cavalry, captured Bear Hunter, and held him captive until one of the Van Ornum captives was released. Believing that the other Van Ornum captives might still be alive (they were not), Colonel Connor ordered his forces into the field for a winter campaign.

Bear Hunter was on somewhat friendly terms with the white settlers in the area. When he visited a nearby Mormon community in Franklin, Idaho, he was warned that the troops were coming. He returned to his village, not to flee, but to prepare.

Bear Hunter's village contained about 300 warriors who surrounded the settlement with twelve-foot earthen revetments. The village became almost a fort, and certainly was a very strong defensive position. Bear Hunter had located his village in a valley along the Bear River, protected by timbered slopes of the steep mountains forming the boundary, and near hot springs, which made the camp an ideal wintering location. On the valley floor, away from the forested slopes, the ground was clear, providing a killing zone of an unobstructed field of fire.

Fearing the escape of Bear Hunter's warriors, Colonel Connor marched during the night on January 27, 1863, to surprise the Shoshonis. Instead, Connor found the Indians had not fled and were ready to fight. It was to be a fight between nearly identical-sized forces, and the largest battle since the Battle of Spokane Plains.

Arrayed against the Indians, Connor had almost 300—parts of the 3rd California Infantry and the 2nd California Cavalry. After fording an ice covered stream, in twenty-three-degree temperature weather, Colonel Connor had his cavalry make a frontal attack. Slowed by the deep snow, the cavalry under the command of Major McGarry were easy targets for the Indians. The Indians yelled taunts at the mounted Californians, "Fours right, fours left, come on you Californian sons of bitches!" Finally forced to dismount, the whites tried to advance on foot, but the Indians' intense fire threw back McGarry's force with heavy casualties. The cavalry now acted as skirmishers, while Connor surrounded the Indian fort with his infantry and opened with a cross-fire. The Shoshonis fought back with determination, but were trapped. The rest of the morning was consumed with the intensity of the battle, which slowly diminished as the Indians suffered heavy loses.

The Battle of Bear River resulted in 224 Indians killed,[8] all at least reported to be warriors, 160 women and children captured, seventy lodges destroyed, and 175 horses, the life blood of the Shoshonis, captured. Among the killed were three chiefs, including Bear Hunter. The Californians suffered, including those who eventually died of their wounds, twenty-four dead, forty-four wounded, and seventy-nine frost-bite casualties. For his victory, Colonel Connor was promoted to brigadier general.

Part of the American's problem was that the closest fort to the areas of operation was Fort Walla Walla. While useful in subduing the Cayuse Indians, it failed to meet the emerging threats. New forts were needed. Fort Lapwai, the first of these bases, was built in Nez Perce lands in November 1862, to help keep those traditionally friendly Indians at peace. Now to insure peace in the area he just subdued, the new general established Camp Connor, which he named for himself, in May 1863, near present-day Soda Springs, Idaho.

8. The official number of Indians killed was 224, though other sources put the estimate as high as 400.

The site of Camp Connor. (*Author*)

In June 1863, a new treaty was signed with the Nez Perce. In return for more unfulfilled promises, the 1863 treaty seized further Nez Perce lands promised in the 1855 treaty. Nevertheless, the treaty insured that the Nez Perce would remain at peace during the Snake Indian Wars.

In July 1863, Fort Boise was erected to protect the emigrant trail. Major Pinkney Lugenbeel ordered it built using four companies of Washington Territorial Infantry. Companies D, G, I, joined H Company from Fort Walla Walla in the mission to protect the Oregon Trail. With the hard work of the three companies of Oregon Cavalry plus the efforts of California Cavalry operating on the California Trail in Utah, 1863 saw the fewest Indian problems then recorded along the Oregon Trail.

The active efforts of all the troops forced the Indians of southern Idaho to either remain peaceful or flee. Those Indians still intent on open warfare, fled to southern Oregon and northern Nevada.

This area had already been a problem. Klamath Indians, sometimes erroneously identified as Snakes, would frequently cross the Cascade Mountains and raid the Rogue River Valley. To stop the raids, a company of the Oregon Cavalry, Company C, built Fort Klamath in 1863. The combination of a strong military force, plus the founding of a reservation as a result of a treaty in 1864 with the Klamath and Modoc Indians, helped to establish peace in the immediate area.

While the periphery of the state was being secured, the heart of the Oregon desert was still wild and open to the Indians. This was changing as miners entered the area in greater numbers hungry for mineral wealth. Stagecoaches, wagon trains, isolated travelers, and ranches were all attacked. To counter the Snake Indians, the authorities conceived a summer campaign. Oregon Cavalry started patrolling from Forts Klamath, Dalles, and Boise, as well as units of the Nevada Cavalry from Fort Churchill.

At the 1864 peace treaty, one of the most war-like chiefs, Chief Paulina of the Paiutes, had failed to show. As the Indian Superintendent, J.W.P. Huntington was returning from the conference at Fort Klamath, he and his cavalrymen escort came upon Paulina's camp on the Deschutes River. The troopers immediately attacked; three Indian warriors were killed, and three women and two children were taken hostage, one of whom was Paulina's wife. Paulina was not in the camp at the time of the ambush.

Seeking his wife's return, Paulina went to Fort Klamath. At first he pledged his good conduct, but changed his tact by leading a surprise attack on the troopers at the fort. Paulina and his warriors were repulsed, leaving fourteen dead on the field. This marked one of the few incidents in western history when an army fort was actually attacked by Indians.[9]

Whites saw Paulina as one of the principle war leaders and efforts were made to seek him out. On May 18, 1864, Captain John Drake, of Fort Dalles, led Oregon Cavalry Company B in an attack against Paulina on the Crooked River near Maury Creek. Making their approach at night, they timed their charge for dawn. Captain Drake, remaining with the main force, divided his attacking force into three elements to insure the capture or destruction of the Paiutes. On the left flank was Lieutenant John M. McCall; the center was led by Lieutenant Stephen Watson, while the right was an attack by Warm Spring Indian scouts. Watson sprang his attack before McCall was in place. The Indians retreated to a natural redoubt on top of a hill. Fearing the Indians were escaping, and without waiting for all the command, Lieutenant Watson ordered a charge. Three cavalrymen, including Watson, were killed, and five were wounded. The Paiute easily moved off.

But Paulina was not the only Paiute war chief. His brother, Wahveveh, was also marauding. Using intelligence about attacks along the John Day River, Lieutenant James A. Waymire followed a civilian force in hot pursuit of the Paiute raiding party. Joining near Harney Lake, the two forces found the Indians in the Alvord valley.

On April 7, 1864, Lieutenant Waymire found the Northern Paiute grazing horses stolen from various ranchers or miners. He ordered the

9. According to Braly, page 39.

The valley outside of the Fort Klamath Site, looking southwest toward the Cascade Mountains. Mount McLoughlin is visible in the far right background. (*Author*)

troopers to attack, but it turned out to be a trap and a fierce battle took place. Breaking out of the trap, Waymire retreated to where the civilians had remained, but nearly 300 Indians followed. The civilians panicked, and it was only the steady rear-guard action by the regulars that prevented a rout. The Indians fled, but with casualties and the loss of their stolen horses. The whites suffered three soldiers killed as well as one rancher wounded.

The spring battles convinced General Alvord of the need for more aggressive tactics. Oregon Cavalry engaged in a two-pronged campaign. First, they chased the Indians without let-up and engaged them whenever the opportunity arose. Small battles were waged throughout the region: June 2, 1864 on the Owyhee River (Company D); June 24, 1864, near Fort Klamath (Company I); July 13, 1864, south of the John Day River, southwest of Camp Watson (Companies G and H); August 8, 1864 on the Malheur River (Company A); and September 23, 1864, Companies G and H.

The plan of the second half of the campaign was to build outposts through the region to further disrupt the Indian's annual subsistence cycle lifestyle, a proven tactic. Military camps established in the affected areas were named Camps Watson (Wheeler County), Dahlgren (Crook County), Alvord (Malheur County), Gibbs (Crook County), Henderson (Malheur County), Lincoln (Grant County), Maury (Crook County), and Logan (Grant County)—all in Oregon; while Camp Lyon was established in the Idaho Territory, which had been carved out from the Washington Territory in 1863.

Most of these camps were not elaborate or built with any sense of permanence. For example, when the Camp Alvord site was first occupied by Lieutenant J.A. Waymire and a troop of Oregon Cavalry, it consisted of some rifle pits built during an Indian attack. In June 1864, Captain

George Curry was again operating in the area and found the rifle pits. He had his Oregon cavalry troopers and Washington infantry put up star-shaped earthworks to connect the rifle pits, and used the camp all summer during the campaign. He abandoned the camp in September, but it was soon reoccupied by Captain Borland of the Oregon Infantry.

Camp Alvord was maintained until June 1866. The infantry then moved twenty-five miles southeast to a spot better sited to interdict Indian movement, and built a new camp, Camp C.F. Smith.

The Army quickly abandoned many of the 1864 camps and built new ones throughout 1865 and 1866 as they sought to control the shifting Snakes.

General Alvord recognized the need for more troops to man all of these forts and camps. In order to meet the Army's demands, Governor Addison C. Gibbs ordered the 1st Oregon Infantry Regiment raised in October 1864. He gave command to former captain of Company E of the 1st Oregon Cavalry, George B. Curry, one of the officers of the Oregon Cavalry. Needing experienced officers, John Drake was drawn from the cavalry and made Lieutenant Colonel. Although the infantry was never used offensively and fought only one serious engagement, they freed up other troops in 1865 by garrisoning, in part, Forts Vancouver, Klamath, Yamhill, Steilacoom, Dalles, Walla Walla, Colville, Hoskins, and Boise, as well as some of the camps. They would remain in service until July 1867.

During the summer of 1865, the Army sought to engage the Snakes whenever possible. However, the Snake Indians proved elusive, and only three significant engagements were fought. The first was on July 9, 1865, when Lieutenant Charles Hobart, along with Oregon Cavalry Companies A, B, and D on the trail of the Indians, was ambushed on the Malheur River. The battle was settled when Hobart unlimbered his howitzer, and fired several rounds. One Paiute was found dead, but it was believed others might have been carried off, while Hobart's soldiers had two wounded.

On July 17, on the south fork of the Owyhee River, Sergeant Wallace caught some Paiutes exposed, and attacked, killing four, wounding an undetermined number, and all without any loss to his command of the 1st Oregon Cavalry.

Another engagement was fought in August by Captain L.L. Williams and Company H, near Harney Lake. As the battle raged, the Indians set fire to the grass which forced the troopers to retreat to a knoll where they

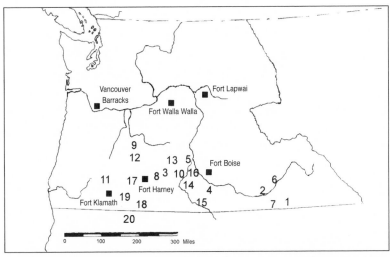

Snake Indian Wars Overview. 1. Shepherd Family Massacre. 2. Miltmore Massacre. 3. Battle of Malhuer River. 4. Utter Massacre. 5. Van Ornum Massacre. 6. Five wagon trains attacked near present-day Pocatello, Idaho. 7. Bear Hunter's camp attacked. 8. Battle of Harney Valley. 9. Battle of Maury Creek. 10. Battle of Owyhee River. 11. Battle of Klamath Creek. 12. First and Second Battles of Camp Watson. 13. First and Second Battles of Malhuer River. 14. Battle of the South Fork, Owyhee River. 15. Chinese wagon train wiped out. 16. Battle of Owyhee River. 17. Battle of Steen Mountain. 18. Battle of Pueblo Mountain. 19. Battle of Silver Lake. 20. Battle of Infernal Caverns. (*Author*)

fended off their attackers. Unable to get back to their camp, the soldiers were forced on an evasive march of nearly forty-five miles. Williams lost one killed and two wounded, but the troopers believed they had killed fifteen of the Paiute.

The fourth battle broke out as a company of Oregon Cavalry was returning to Camp Watson, under the command of Lieutenant Oliver. C. Applegate. Chief Wahveveh attacked and pinned the cavalrymen down. The Indians then burned Camp Watson, destroying supplies and equipment.

While no combat was initially involved, Captain F.B. Sprague, of the 1st Oregon Infantry, found a major Paiute trail, indicating how they were moving in and out of the country. His few cavalry attached to his infantry were not able to trail the Indians, adding to Sprague's sense of impotence in forcing combat with the Indians. This inability to bring the Snakes to decisive combat frustrated the Oregon infantry. The Regulars would soon share the frustration as they began to replace the volunteers.

The final act of the campaign also involved Captain Sprague. On October 31, 1865, near Warner Lake, in an effort to locate where the Indian trail he had discovered led to, the 1st Oregon Infantry unit was ambushed by 125 Paiute Indians. Caught between two forces of Indians, at first Sprague merely returned fire. However, it soon became obvious that the Indians had concentrated their warriors with rifles to the front, while those to the rear had mostly bows and arrows. Finding that weakness, Sprague broke through and charged without loss of life.

With the end of the Civil War, regular U.S. Army forces started to return west. One of the first moves by Army leaders was to have Brigadier General George Wright resume command of the Columbia Department after General U.S. Grant ordered General Alvord relieved.[10] But, while en route to assume his new command, General Wright was drowned in a shipwreck off of Crescent City, California on July 30, 1865. This left Colonel Curry as the ranking officer in charge. He immediately started planning in late August for a winter campaign.

Supplies and troops were delivered to Camp Polk near the mouth of the Crooked River; Camp Logan along the John Day River; Camp Lyon in the Jordan Valley near the Oregon-Idaho Valley; Camp Alvord, a temporary camp on a creek flowing into the Malheur River; Camp Colfax on the road between Canyon City and Boise; Camp Lander near the old Fort Hall; and Camp Reed near Salmon Falls. As soon as was possible after the first major snowfall, the troops would begin their operations against Indian winter camps.

Even as the troops moved to their designated spots, they came upon Indians and attacked. They destroyed twenty-three Indian camps, plus precious winter supplies. The Oregon volunteers killed sixty Indian warriors. However, as Colonel Curry prepared to take command in the field, he was intercepted by a telegram from the War Department. He was ordered not to take to the field, instructed to muster out the remaining volunteers, and was, himself, ordered mustered out on October 14, 1865.

10. One of the strange contradictions of Grant's life was that he did not like military life. This, coupled with the dislike of his first commanding officer after graduating from West Point, explains Alvord's dismissal. In 1843, Grant reported to duty at his first posting, Jefferson Barracks, Missouri, and reported to I Company, 4th U.S. Infantry, commanded by First Lieutenant Benjamin Alvord. As an interim district commander, Colonel Reuben F. Maury of the First Oregon Cavalry assumed the leadership after Alvord was recalled.

Other than the minor engagements that occurred while en route to the jump-off points, the winter campaign of 1865 was stopped before it began. Instead of war, peace was made with the Shoshonis through a treaty in December 1865, securing southeastern Idaho, which been the impetus for stopping the winter campaign in Oregon. The treaty had been signed as a result of efforts made within Utah.

Even though the Oregon troops' campaign was ended before it began, the final battles closed one chapter in Oregon Country history. Volunteer troops created at the state or territorial level had fought their last battles as the sole protectors of the Oregon Country.

Washington Territory's 1st Infantry was mustered out on December 11, 1865; the 1st Oregon Cavalry was mustered out officially on November 20, 1866; while the 1st Oregon Infantry lasted until July 19, 1867, when the regiment's service was officially ended.[11]

While militia would be called out again for service outside of Oregon or local units raised for defense, no longer would the states call out troops into state-created military forces. From this point on, the wars in the Oregon Country would be fought exclusively by United States Army regulars with minor assistance by militia and local volunteers with a very limited function.

The 1st U.S. Cavalry and the 14th U.S. Infantry replaced the Oregon troops. In 1866, the Regular Army tried to subdue the still hostile Snakes, but without significant success. Lieutenant Reuben F. Bernard led a troop of 1st U.S. Cavalry from the rebuilt Camp Watson across the Crooked River and throughout southeastern Oregon, covering more than 630 miles in twenty-six days. He engaged the Indians twice in combat and destroyed several Indian villages. Despite Bernard's efforts, 1866 became a bloody year for citizens entering the Oregon Country. In just one case, a wagon train of Chinese miners was attacked near Battle Creek, Idaho, on May 19. Over one hundred Chinese were killed, and only one survivor was discovered.

As a result of the Chinese massacre, Major Louis H. Marshall took to the field from Fort Boise. With Captains David Perry's and James C. Hunt's 1st U.S. Cavalry troops, and Captain Patrick Collins' 14th U.S. Infantry Company, Marshall located nearly two-hundred-fifty Paiutes on the Owyhee River at the extreme southeastern corner of Oregon. In the

11. Company I, 1st Oregon Infantry, was one of the very last Civil War volunteer units to be mustered out.

June engagement lasting half a day, the Paiute succeed in killing ten soldiers, while losing only seven themselves. The press reported the battle as an Indian victory.

Not trusting the Army, volunteers from Silver City, Idaho, had also moved out and located the same Indians (from indications found later) that Marshall engaged. The thirty-six miners were surrounded on June 23 by the same sized party of Indians (250), and were besieged for twenty-four hours, until the word of troops arriving from Camp Lyons caused the Paiute to break off their attack. The miners reported one killed and two wounded, but in typical white bravado, reported they had killed thirty-five Paiute.

The Army continued to hunt the hostile Indians. Warm Springs Indians,[12] acting as Army scouts, found a camp of Paulina's Paiute on Dry Creek near Prineville. In a dawn surprise attack by the Warm Springs, thirty-two Paiute were killed. Later that summer, near Harney Lake, Paulina and his brother Wahveveh were discovered and attacked by First Cavalry troopers. The majority of the Indians escaped, but Chief Wahveveh was killed.

Another cavalry pursuit, this time by Captain Walker from Camp C.F. Smith, found a camp on Steen Mountain. On July 20, 1866, the cavalry attacked, killing three Paiute and wounding five others, while only suffering one wounded trooper. However, as was seen as typical by civilians, the soldiers did not pursue the fleeing Indians.

Criticism was often made against the U.S. Army for their apparent lack of energy and zeal in pursuing Indians, such as the attack near Lake Harney, which stopped after the initial onslaught, or on Steen Mountain, when surprise was complete. A change of command would remedy the Army's will to fight and pursue.

In December 1866, a new district commander arrived at Fort Boise. His assessment of the district was succinct and accurate. As the new commander would later recall,

> They were accused of all manner of things. One thing was certain: they had not, nor were they, making headway against the hostile Indians. There was much dissipation amongst a good many officers, and there seemed to be a general apathy amongst them, and indifference to the proper discharge of duty. (Utley, 1973, 178)

12. A generic name for the many tribes residing on the Warm Springs reservation, such as the Wasco, Tygh, Deschutes, and others.

All of the conditions described would be changed by the energy and leadership of Lieutenant Colonel (Brevet Major General) George Crook, of the newly formed 23rd U.S. Infantry.

Crook, who had fought Indians in Oregon before the Civil War, had new tactics he wished to employ. Within one week of his arrival, the Indians attacked a miner's camp near the mouth of the Boise River. Colonel Crook took one company, F Troop, Captain David Perry commanding, of 1st Cavalry to the field. In the Battle of Owyhee River, on December 18, 1866, Crook attacked the Indians in their winter homes. Starting with subterfuge, he dismounted the troops, had the horses hidden in a ravine, and started his approach as if he had infantry. The more mobile Paiutes feared the infantry less, and charged out at the foot soldiers. The cavalry men simulated panic (probably easy to do as over a hundred warriors streamed out of the camp), and ran, but only to where their horses were held. Mounting, the 1st Cavalry troopers charged, catching the Paiute out in the open, and then swept through the village, killing thirty Indians, and capturing their much needed livestock. Sergeant O'Toole was mortally wounded as he rode through the village.

For the next two years, Crook reenergized and redirected the troops in his district. Once on the trail of a hostile band, he would pursue relentlessly, without leaving the field, until the Indians were killed or captured. He led over a dozen forays, which resulted in combat six times. As would be his trademark, he employed Indian scouts to act as troops. Of the forty engagements his troops fought in, fourteen were waged by regular troops augmented by Indian scouts while four engagements were fought exclusively by Indian against Indian, with the leadership provided by white officers.[13]

Crook led troops in several engagements, with some being very memorable. Continuing his winter campaign of 1866-67, Company M of the 1st Cavalry joined Crook as he hounded the Indians in their once-safe winter sanctuaries.

13. Most of the engagements were very small. For example, Captain E. M. Baker led I Troop, 1st U.S. Cavalry, on a patrol in July 1867. On July 8, he fought a small band on the Malheur River, killing two, and capturing fourteen, mostly women and children. Continuing his patrol, On July 19, further up the Malheur basin, two more Indians were killed and eight more captured. In neither engagement did Captain Baker report any loses of his own.

On January 30, 1867, near Steen Mountain, Crook charged into another Indian village. The Battle of Steen Mountain resulted in the killing of sixty Paiute, and the capture of all the remaining Indians, except one warrior and two women. The losses suffered by Crook were one civilian scout killed, one wounded, and three troopers wounded.

Chasing the other bands of Paiute, H Troop joined M Troop and marched out of Camp C.F. Smith in late February of 1867. High in the Pueblo Mountains southeast of Steen Mountain, the two troops struggled through thigh-deep snow to attack another village. On February 28, 1867, the two troops surrounded another village, pouring in rifle fire. The Battle of Pueblo Mountains netted two Indian warriors dead and the capture of the entire village, all without a loss to the troopers of George Crook.

But, Crook was not always so fortunate. Chasing a band of Indians south from Camp Warner, near Hart Mountain, in September of 1867, he led his troops into California. Along the Pit River, near present-day Alturas, California, the command found the Indians dug in behind a natural fort, a cascade of fallen rocks between canyon walls. On September 26, Crook ordered his troops, Company D of the 23rd Infantry, and Troop H of the 1st Calvary, to charge the Indian fortifications. Captain William Parnell[14] charged with his H Troop command, and recalled the climb. "We commenced climbing up the steep mountainside, over rocks and huge boulders, down through a deep ravine, and up again through rocks and juniper trees, when the Indians opened a heavy fire upon us." (Cozzens, 14)

The Indians fired into the advancing cavalry, then retreated deeper into the rocks. The fighting lasted until sundown, when half the command retired to care for the wounded, and to eat and rest while the other half kept the Indians contained. Later, they exchanged places, keeping a vigilant watch.

14. William Parnell is a character of interest. Originally from Ireland, he served with the British Army during the Crimean War as a member of the Light Cavalry Brigade, made famous by Tennyson's poem, "The Charge of the Light Brigade." As an enlisted man in the 4th New York Cavalry in the Civil War, his talents were recognized where he was commissioned and eventually promoted to lieutenant colonel. After the war, he accepted a first lieutenant's commission in the 1st U.S. Cavalry in early 1866, in time to be sent west.

As Crook planned for a renewal of the fighting, the weary troopers sat about thinking of the day and the next yet to come. Captain Parnell was called to deal with his second in command, Lieutenant John Madigan, who he found shaking. "I did and said all I could to cheer him up, but he evidently had a premonition of death, and nothing I could say or do had any effect whatever." (Cozzens, 14)

As first light broke, Crook ordered another charge. Sweeping the rock walls, Parnell took the position, but at the loss of two killed and two wounded. As the troopers attacked, they had to claw their way around or over the boulders. Sometimes the troopers had to crawl into the caverns. On one such occasion, Sergeant Michael Meara led his men forward, into a hole, shouting, "Here they are boys!" and was instantly shot in the face. Creating a breach, the soldiers fought with pistols and rifles used as clubs.

Crook ordered his Indian scouts around to one side, and then had his infantry move up the right flank toward the pinning force of scouts. On the left flank were the cavalry troopers. Crooks' instructions were that at his command of "Forward! . . . they should rise up quick, go with a yell and keep yelling and never think of stopping until they crossed the ditch, scaled the wall, and broke through the breastworks, and the faster the better."[15] As the command was yelled, the troops jumped up and charged where they were met with a volley of rifle slugs and arrows, and Lieutenant John Madigan was struck down at the front of his yelling men.

As noon approached, word came that the Indians had rallied and counter-attacked; they had recaptured their "fort." The cavalry troopers charged again and retook the position. An Indian woman was captured, and reported about one hundred Indian warriors had started the fight; but sixteen were dead and nine were wounded.

As both companies of men moved forward, they chased a vanishing enemy. The Indians had escaped into the caverns throughout the valley and canyon walls. Bullets would zing out of a crevice, dropping a soldier, but the Indian marksmen were never seen. By the afternoon, all that could be done was to create a picket line around the Indian position.

Early the next morning, an Indian woman came out to say the warriors had escaped in the night. Taking the women and children captive, the Battle of the Infernal Caverns had cost Crook eight killed and ten

15. Joseph Wasson, *Owyhee Avalanche* newspaper, November 2, 1867.

wounded. Approximately seventy-five Paiute, thirty Pit River Indians, and a few Modoc were killed.

Besides the constant pursuit of the hostile Indians, further interdiction was created by placing more camps throughout the Indian's territory as well as the establishment of Fort Harney on August 10, 1867. The pressure on the Indians was constant, but not only by the U.S. Army. On April 25, 1867, some cowboys discovered Paulina in a camp on Trout Creek near Maupin's stage station, and attacked, killing the war chief.

In accordance with Crook's directive to never let the pressure ease, cavalry and infantry troops ranged throughout the deserts of southeastern Oregon. Crook had his troops seek out the villages of the Snake Indians, forcing them to seek peace.

Colonel J.J. Coppinger led a patrol of his 14th Infantry, mounted into the southeastern corner of Oregon. On August 12, he surprised a band of Paiute and killed all ten. His own Indian scouts reported another village nearby. The next morning, at two A.M., his infantrymen charged into the village, killing twenty Paiute, taking some prisoners, and destroying much needed supplies.

In another engagement, on September 2, 1867, A Troop, 1st U.S. Cavalry, Lieutenant John F. Smith commanding, found a village on Silver Lake. He ordered his fifty-one troopers and ten Klamath Indian scouts to encircle, then charge the village. Two of his men and one scout were killed. Twenty-four Indian warriors were also killed, and ten women and children were captured.[16] Crook's inspired leadership kept the troops in the field, and the pressure constant.

With both Paulina and Wahveveh dead, there were fewer chiefs willing to wage war against the whites. This was true, in part, to Crook's aggressive campaign, which had claimed 329 Indians killed, twenty wounded, and 225 captured.

By the summer of 1868, only one prominent war chief remained, Old Weawea. On July 1, 1868, Old Weawea and eight hundred of his followers came to Fort Harney for a peace conference with George Crook. As Parnell assessed Crook's campaign, he concluded, "The con-

16. Crook would promote Smith to captain for his leadership in this patrol.

stant harassing, winter and summer, day and night, by the regular troops since their arrival from scenes of war in the East had so demoralized the Indians, by destroying their provisions and lodges, capturing their women and children, and killing many of their chiefs and braves, that nothing was left them but to surrender and beg for clemency." (Cozzens, 30)

It would be here that Colonel Crook first tried the negotiation tactics that would become his trademark. He would tell the Indians he was sorry they wanted peace. "I was in hopes that you would continue the war." Crook promised he could easily replace his fallen troops while the Paiute could not raise a warrior so quickly. "In this way it would not be very long before we would have you all killed off, and then the government would have no more trouble with you." (Utley, 1973, 180) It was with the greatest of reluctance, he said, that George Crook would let the Indians seek peace. Chief Weawea summed up the Indian dilemma in the negotiations.

> Your great white people are like the grass; the more you cut it down the more it grows and the more numerous its blades. We kill your white soldiers, and ten more come for every one that is killed; but when you kill one of our warriors, or one of our people, no more come to replace them. We are weak and can not recuperate. (Cozzens, 31)

Crook finally accepted the Paiute pleas for peace and allowed them to stay near Fort Harney. Eventually, their own reservation was created on the Malheur River.

The summer of 1868 ended the Snake Indian Wars. While small bands of hostiles caused minor problems, the next phase of Indian problems moved southwest to the Klamath and Modoc Indian region of the Oregon-California border.

~

The precipitating events of this era were the Indian attacks on wagon trains along the Oregon Trail, often labeled massacres. The first of these was the Shepherd Massacre in 1859, which occurred near Montpellier, Idaho, at the extreme southeastern corner of the state. The town has an excellent museum on the Oregon Trail in that town, which fully details the area's history.

Also in 1859, was the Miltimore Massacre, near American Falls, Idaho. The Massacre Rocks State Park is located along Interstate 86.

Parts of the original Oregon Trail can be seen, and information regarding the attack by Indians is at the park.

The Van Ornum Massacre, much publicized because of the children being taken captive, occurred in 1860, just west of the Snake River in Oregon, near the community of Huntington, along Interstate 84. Nearby is the Oregon State Park called Farewell Bend, which also explains the history of the Oregon Trail through the region.

As a result of these attacks, the Civil War Army created several posts. The four most significant are Forts Lapwai, Klamath and Boise, and Camp Harney, (which later became Fort Harney). Fort Lapwai was established near the old Spalding Mission within the Nez Perce Indian Reservation. Now within the community of Lapwai, on U.S. Highway 95, one original building still stands. Nearby is the museum at the Nez Perce National Historical Park near the junction of U.S. Highways 95 and 12.

Fort Boise is not well preserved. The old fort grounds are now part of a city park, a Veteran's Administration hospital, and an Army Reserve station named for Fort Boise's founder, Pinkney Lugenbeel. An old cabin, dating from 1863, remains the only building from the early era of army activity.

Camp (Fort) Harney is marked by a roadside historical marker along U.S. Highway 20, east of Burns, Oregon. About three miles north is the actual site, with a sign denoting the lay-out of the camp.

Fort Klamath, southeast of Crater Lake National Park, on Oregon Highway 62, is now a park, and a small museum. Of note are the graves of Modoc Indians (see below) who were tried, executed, and buried at this post.

Many minor posts were created and abandoned; few are even marked. One post preserved for history if only by a sign is Camp Polk. Northeast of the town of Sisters, Oregon, the camp is accessed off of Camp Polk Road, onto Cemetery Road, following the road to a historical marker-wayside.

Significant camps have been lost, including Camp Watson, the sight of a battle. Minor posts, such as Camp McDowell, near Ukiah, Oregon, can only be imagined, as nothing remains, with even the memory of its location gone. Camp Warner was established and then moved. The old Camp Warner is south of the Hart Mountain Antelope Refuge headquarters, along county Route 3-12, for about 12 miles, eventually moving onto four-wheel drive tracks, located near the Blue Sky Hotel Camp, about two miles south-southeast of Warner Peak. The newer camp is accessed from Lakeview, east along Oregon Highway 140 to U.S. Forest Service Road 3615, and north for about sixteen miles and U.S. Forest Service Road 3720; then east for about three miles to 3720B, and north for another three miles, and the camp's location.

None of the battlefields fought in this era are preserved, and almost none are even remembered by roadside signs. Near Preston, Idaho, on U.S. Highway 91, is a sign commemorating Colonel Conner's attack on Bear Hunter's village. The sign, entitled Bear River Battle, marks one of the largest battles of the entire region. As a result of the battle, Camp Connor was built near Soda Springs, Idaho, and the site is marked by a roadside historical marker along U.S. Highway 30.

Other battlefields are just areas to be visited to gain better understanding of the terrain within which the battles were fought. The Owyhee River, in the extreme southeastern part of Oregon, was the site of two major engagements. The country is wild and scenic, but the sites are not marked.

Steen Mountain is also beautiful, and the site of two skirmishes, one along the Dunder and Blitzen Creek. Neither are noted beyond the citation that they occurred and that men died. South of Steen Mountain is Pueblo Mountain, another battle site of George Crook.

In the central Oregon mountains, near where the minor post Camp Watson was, can be seen the general area of another battle. South and east of Prineville, Oregon, along the Paulina Highway, named for the great chief, near Camp Creek Road, is the site of the post and the battle. Still another battle took place less than five miles west, near Maury Creek. The country here has little changed since the time it was fought over.

Chapter 7

Flight from Paradise

The Modoc and Nez Perce Wars

T he next two wars are significant and similar for two reasons. First, they started in the Oregon Country but the military operations quickly moved out of our area of study. The narration of the wars will follow the movement of the Indians, however, just as the military followed the Indians out of the Oregon Country. Second, they both engaged the national press to a much larger degree than ever before, with a further difference of increasingly sympathetic coverage of the Indian plight.

Journalists accompanied Army command into the field, posting dispatches via telegraph very much in the modern sense of near real-time journalism. As each war spread beyond the borders of Oregon, public interest in the conflicts grew. As never before, the press slanted the news to portray the Indians sympathetically, as merely trying to preserve their way of life. Public sentiment was remolded from "a good Indian is a dead Indian" to the new image of the Noble Savage.[1]

The Modoc War

The Modoc War started during the Civil War when the 1st Oregon Cavalry established Fort Klamath as part of an effort to subdue the Indians of the south-central and southeastern sections of the State of Oregon. A treaty was signed in 1864 which established a reservation near Fort Klamath for members of the Snake (Northern Paiute), Klamath, and Modoc Indian tribes. Signing for the Modoc tribe was a chief named Kientpoos. The Modoc, although noted for attacking white settlers and

---

1. In the case of the Modoc, this was true until the death of General Canby.

travelers, had also established a working relationship with the miners in nearby Yreka, California. The Yreka miners, unable to pronounce Modoc names such as Kientpoos, quickly coined new names for the Indians. Kientpoos was given the name which history has kept: Captain Jack.

Captain Jack's tribe's dislike of the Klamath Indian Reservation was based upon a historical truth—their homeland was really on the Lost River and Tule Lake, straddling the Oregon-California Border. The location of the reservation was a convenience for the whites, not a just establishment of Modoc rights.

Another reason for Modoc displeasure was the dominance of the warlike people with whom they were forced to share the reservation, the Klamath Indians. Furthermore, the Snakes, some of whom were placed on the Klamath reservation, and Modocs were hostile to each other.

With the desire to go back to their Lost River home added to the desire to remove themselves from their enemies, the Modocs left the reservation in 1865. Indian Superintendent Alfred B. Meacham was sympathetic to the Modocs' desire to create their own reservation, but had to make allowances for white settlers' fears of the Modocs as well. Pledging to help gain a separate reservation for the Modocs, Meacham persuaded the Indians to return to the reservation in late 1869. The return was tempestuous and the timing was poor.

The Klamath agency had for years agents sympathetic to the Indians in general, and the Modocs in particular. The Applegate family had a long history of working on the Klamath Reservation and they were trusted by the Indians.[2] Oliver Cromwell Applegate, son of Lindsay Applegate, a

2. One crucial exception to this was the case of Ivan Applegate, Lindsay's son, and Captain Jack. In the spring of 1871, Captain Jack's niece became ill, and with the Modoc shaman Curly Headed Doctor absent on a hunting trip, Jack turned to a Klamath Indian shaman for the ill child's treatment. The shaman could wait to be paid upon a successful treatment, or accept payment in advance if they guaranteed a cure. The Klamath shaman accepted payment in advance, but failed in curing the child. In accordance with Indian law, Captain Jack killed the disgraced shaman. Ivan Applegate, a sub-agent to the Klamaths, requested the Siskiyou County Sheriff to arrest Captain Jack, as stipulated by the treaty of 1864. After a warrant was issued, Lieutenant Moss, 1st Cavalry, led a detachment from Fort Klamath to arrest Jack, but failed to find him. Ultimately Indian Superintendent Meacham intervened on Captain Jack's behalf, and had General Canby recall any Army effort to arrest Captain Jack. Captain Jack hated Ivan Applegate as a result of his labeling Captain Jack as an indicted murderer.

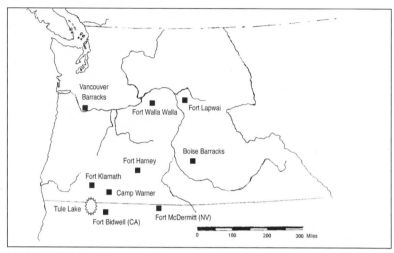

Modoc War Overview. (*Author*)

pioneer who created the Applegate Trail into southern Oregon, was particularly well known and trusted; he worked at the Yainax Annex of the
reservation.

In 1869, the national policy was changed, with Indian reservations
removed from the Department of the Interior, and reassigned to the War
Department's U.S. Army. In October, just as Captain Jack led his Modocs
back to the reservation, Captain O.C. Knapp assumed control of the
Klamath Reservation. Knapp was incompetent and a drunk.

Fed up with Knapp's inept and unfavorable treatment, within the first
few months of 1870, Captain Jack again led his band south to the Lost
River. In October 1870, Captain Knapp was removed, but it was too late
to offset the Modoc resentment.

Superintendent Meacham and then his successor, Thomas B.
Odeneal, wanted to forcibly return the Modocs to the reservation. Since
the reservation was located in the Department of the Columbia, while
the Modoc Indians had relocated to their home within the Department
of California, Odeneal turned to General Edward R.S. Canby for military
assistance. At first Canby refused, doing nothing more than try to keep
the peace. As a stop-gap effort, Canby had a 1st Cavalry detachment
under Major Elwell Otis make a temporary camp along the Lost River,
but did nothing more until some resolution was reached on the issue of
possibly creating a new reservation for the Modoc along the Lost River.

Despite Canby's reluctance to act since the question of a new reservation for the Modocs had not been settled, when the Indian Bureau ordered the Indians returned in 1872, General Canby ordered troops to move into northern California and return the Modocs to Oregon.

Coinciding with the orders to move the Modocs was an Indian religious revival. Many tribes were receptive to the Ghost Dance religion, which called for the destruction of the whites, and the return to the ways of the past. One Paiute Ghost Dancer, "Doctor George," held religious dances on the Klamath Reservation, and word was spread to the Lost River Modoc. Curley Headed Doctor quickly added the Ghost Dance to his shaman powers, promising to use his powers to keep the whites away.

Given responsibility for the removal was Lieutenant Colonel Frank Wheaton of the 21st Infantry, based at Camp Warner, Oregon.[3] To support Wheaton, Major John Green's 1st Cavalry, based at the closer Fort Klamath, Oregon, was also ordered to march. Recognizing the need for a swift and complete removal of the Modocs, Canby's orders stated that "the force employed should be so large as to secure the results at once and beyond peradventure." (Utley, 1973, 199-200) All that was needed was for Superintendent Odeneal to give the word.

Although authorized as early as July 1872, Odeneal did not request the military until November. He asked Major Green to come immediately, implying an imminent threat to the peace. Major Green, without consulting with field commander Colonel Wheaton, sent troopers. However, General Canby's admonition to use sufficient force had not made it through the chain of command from Canby through Wheaton to Green to the troop's commander. Instead, a solitary troop, B Troop, 1st U.S. Cavalry was dispatched. Captain James Jackson was sent to bring back the fierce Modocs with three officers and forty enlisted men.

From Fort Klamath, Captain Jackson's command, rode south to round up the Modocs. The original plan Jackson had decided upon was to divide his troops to make contact with the two villages located on each side of the Lost River. As the command neared the Modoc, Captain Jackson started to feel ill. He decided to keep the command unified, and

3. Wheaton had been a cavalry officer prior to the Civil War, and quickly rose in rank during that conflict. He obtained the rank of major general and was assigned the Sixth Corps at such battles as Fredericksburg, Gettysburg, and the Wilderness. His defense of Washington, D.C. against Jubal Early's raid explains why a suburb of Washington is named for him.

contact the most import camp, Captain Jack's first. Instead, he sent civilians, under Oliver Applegate, across the river to wait at Crawley's Ranch. Once Captain Jack was captured, the civilians could contact the other village of Hooker Jim's and have him follow Captain Jack back to the Klamath Reservation, all accomplished without bloodshed.

At dawn on November 29, 1872, the weather was cold with a heavy downpour of sleet. Not wishing to encumber his men, Captain Jackson stopped about a mile from the Indian village, and in the cold predawn darkness, ordered his men to adjust their saddles and to take off their overcoats. The men were very tired from their sixteen-hour ride, and now added the discomfort of freezing rain hitting them while in just their field clothes, consisting of slouch hats, shirt, pants, and long underwear. Remounted, the command moved forward.

Captain Jackson found Captain Jack's band of about seventy Indians camped on their beloved Lost River, just north of the border. With what seemed complete tactical surprise, the cavalrymen ordered the Indians to lay down their arms. Instead, the Indians quickly armed themselves and assumed a defensive position.

The day before, Winema, Captain Jack's cousin, had visited the camp.[4] Winema, also known as Tobey Riddle, was the wife of Frank Riddle, both employed by the Army as translators. She came to Captain Jack's camp to tell him of the Army's plan to forcibly remove the Modoc to the Klamath Reservation, and to warn them not to resist. Instead, many of the warriors prepared themselves for the cavalry's arrival. When the Army arrived, the tension was already felt by both sides and the seemingly inevitable conflict broke out.

The Indians provided one version of the start of the fighting: Lieutenant Frazier A. Boutelle, believing the Modocs were about to fire on the troopers, shot first. Ivan Applegate, who witnessed the event, described the start as the fault of the Indians. "At this, the captain

4. In addition, Ivan Applegate had visited the area prior to the Army. Ivan was the sub-agent to the Modoc on the Klamath Reservation, and wanted to protect his charges from Army attack. He asked the Modoc to return to the protection of the reservation, and conveyed word to Captain Jack of Superintendent Odeneal's desire to talk, but in Linkville (present-day Klamath Falls), Oregon. Partly because of Captain Jack's hatred of Ivan Applegate, this effort failed, and probably added to the Modoc's sense of impending action.

ordered Lieutenant Boutelle, who stood in advance of the line, to take four men and arrest the two Indians who had guns in their hands. As Boutelle stepped forward with the four men, the two Indians fired." (Cozzens, 112) Regardless of which side fired first, a general fire fight ensued.

> Then all was din and commotion; men were falling in the line, the riderless horses were dashing here and there. The attack was so sudden and desperate, the Modocs rushing onto us with demonlike yells, that the men were forced back a step or two, and it seemed for a moment that the thinned line would yield and break. But immediately came the order 'Forward!' and it was like an inspiration. The men sprang forward under the leadership of brave Boutelle, delivering a deadly fire, and the Indians were forced back. (Cozzens, 112)

In the confusion, the Indians broke into separate bands and fled; some into the countryside, while Captain Jack crossed nearby Tule Lake to escape and hid in the the lava fields south of the lake. The Indians suffered one killed and one wounded. The troopers had one killed outright, with seven wounded, one of whom later died as a result of his wounds. No effort was made to pursue Captain Jack's band. Many cavalry horses had bolted at the first sound of gunfire as the green troops responsible had not held onto the mounts, ducking for cover when the shots rang out.

This was only half the Battle of Lost River. The ranchers, seeing the cavalry attack Captain Jack, joined in and jumped on the nearby camp of Hooker Jim, another Modoc chief. They were easily repulsed, with two killed and one wounded, but not without inflicting losses on the Modoc. Fleeing as the Modocs attacked, a rancher discharged his shotgun. The buckshot hit a mother and child, killing the child, an act which enraged the Modoc of Hooker Jim's village.

As the whites ran, they were forced to take refuge in the cabin at Crawley's Ranch. Hooker Jim's band moved to the south by way of the east shore of the lake. As they made good their escape, they killed fourteen unsuspecting settlers. According to one Indian account, the reason the settlers were killed is that when Winema had warned the Modoc, they had visited their white neighbors, asking them to refrain from fighting them. The whites reassured the Modoc that all were their friends, and they would not join the soldiers. The Modoc felt betrayed and they also sought revenge for the murder of the child. The war had changed from one of words and coercion to one of weapons and death.

Captain Jackson sent a galloper to Fort Klamath with word of his failure to capture the Modocs. Word also reached the fort of several attacks on white settlers by fleeing Modoc. With the death of sixteen white settlers, demands for Army protection were heard from the Presidio of San Francisco to Vancouver Barracks, Department of the Columbia.

Colonel Wheaton tramped south and took field command on December 21, 1872; he reached Crawley's Ranch on Christmas day. He ordered additional troops from nearby posts, and mustered in two companies of Oregon Volunteers, Companies A and B,[5] Colonel John Ross, commanding, and one from California, ordered into the field by their states' respective governors.

On the same day Colonel Wheaton assumed field command, the Modocs made a foray. Their scouts had reported a supply wagon train carrying, among other supplies, much needed rifle ammunition, headed toward them that was lightly guarded by five troopers of a corporal's guard. Slipping out of their redoubt, the Modocs attacked the wagons and the five cavalry troopers providing an escort. In the surprise attack, two troopers and five horses were killed. The corporal and the two other privates gave cover fire, holding off the Modocs until Captain Reuben F. Bernard arrived with more men, driving the Modocs off. Despite being within a half mile of G Troop's camp, Privates Sydney Smith and William Donahue died of their wounds.[6]

On January 5, 1873, another skirmish took place between Captain Kelley's Oregon Volunteers and about an equal number of Modoc. As Kelley marched around the lava on a reconnaissance, the Modoc attacked, but quickly retreated, without loss to either side. While Wheaton dismissed the attacks' aggressiveness at the Battle of Land's Ranch and against Kelley, believing they were signs of the Modocs' attempt to evade his trap, he gathered his forces to overrun the Indians.

5. Company A was under the command of Captain Oliver Applegate. One of his first assignments was to talk with the Modoc who were still on the Klamath Reservation's Yainax sub-agency. He succeeded in persuading the Modoc to remain on the reservation and uninvolved. Company A did not join the troops on Tule Lake until January 5, 1873.

6. Private Smith was found naked, scalped, and his ears cut off. He had bullet wounds in his head, abdomen, and leg.

It was not hard to find the Modocs. Word was quickly obtained that the Indians had retreated to their traditional stronghold, the lava beds immediately south of Tule Lake.

By the evening of January 15, Colonel Wheaton had deployed his force on the edge of the natural Modoc redoubt with the plans drawn.[7] From the north, he would use his two howitzers to shell the Indian position while Major Green moved in from the west.[8] From the east, another 1st Cavalry command, under the leadership of Captain Reuben F. Bernard, planned to advance. The two forces would converge to the south, cutting off any possibility of retreat to the surrounded Modocs. From the north, two companies of infantry were to advance. The militia, to act as a blocking force, was placed to prevent the Indians' escape.

No one had actually reconnoitered the next day's field of battle. Captain Bernard, wanting to get a clearer understanding, advanced his force one day early to make a reconnaissance-in-force.[9] As the morning of January 16 broke, the jagged lava was covered by a dense, cold fog. Bernard ordered one of his troops, Troop B, still under the command of Captain Jackson, forward. Covering it was his other cavalry troop, his own Troop G, under the command of Lieutenant J. Kyle. Each advanced taking turns to alternate cover for the other. The fog was so dense that even by noon the visibility was only fifty yards.

With his men deployed at twenty-five yard intervals, Bernard slowly moved forward. As they did so, the fog lifted sufficiently for the troopers

7. By January, Wheaton had mustered in about 350 men to join the regular troops. His force consisted of 1st U.S. Cavalry: F Troop, Captain Perry, with 46 troopers; B Troop, Captain Jackson, with 42 men; G Troop, Captain Bernard, and 47 cavalrymen; H Troop, Lieutenant Adams, and 16 troopers; 21st Infantry-B Company, Lieutenant Ross, with 38 foot soldiers; and C Company, Captain Burton, with fifty-seven infantrymen. Oregon Militia: Seven field officers, Colonel Ross, commanding; A Company, Captain O. Applegate, with 56 men; and B Company, Captain Kelly and his 46 men; California militia, Captain Fairchild and twenty-five men; and twenty Indian scouts, led by head scout, Dave Hill.

8. On January 16, Captain Perry's men had been ordered to clear the heights, now known as Gillem's Bluff, to the west of the Stronghold of any Modoc sentries. In the fog, the Indians surprised the dismounted cavalry, and retreated to give warning of the approaching troops, forewarning the Modoc of the impending attack.

9. He had been ordered to send out a patrol to capture any canoes on the shore to prevent the Modoc from using the lake as an avenue of escape. He changed the patrol to a reconnaissance-in-force.

A view of the Modoc stronghold in the lava beds. (*Author*)

to see the Modocs. As his force probed the lava beds, they suddenly came under rifle fire from the Modocs in the stronghold. Having made his reconnaissance, Bernard attempted to withdraw, but the fire only increased. To provide cover fire, Bernard ordered a retreat by companies, each company in turn moving back fifty yards and then turning to give cover fire to the next company. First B Troop moved back followed by G Troop.

The Modocs surged forward to their left to outflank the retreating cavalry troopers. Fearing his men would soon be successfully flanked, Bernard personally led a charge that drove the Modoc back into their redoubt. The two troops then retreated with only ineffective, long distance Modoc rifle fire hindering the movement. Once the two troops had retreated, they cared for their three wounded at a position soon to be known as Hospital Rock. The Modoc now knew that there were troops to the east and west readying to attack.

Bernard knew his men would have to advance across very rugged ground, torn by deep chasms, under the direct fire of the Modocs. While the main force was to be from the west, under Major Green, Bernard moved forward with his two troops, ready to attack on January 17 at sunrise.

Knowing the whites were about to attack, Curley Headed Doctor prepared for a Ghost Dance ceremony. He put up a medicine pole and stretched a red painted tule-braid rope completely around the Stronghold. The tule rope would prevent any white from ever crossing it.

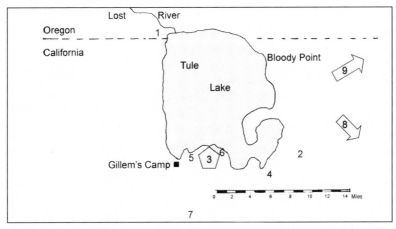

Modoc War: Tule Lake Area. 1. Battle of Lost River; 2. Battle of Land's Ranch; 3. The Stronghold; 4. Scorpion Point; 5. Peace Council site; 6. Hospital Point; 7. Thomas-Wright Battlefield; 8. Battle of Dry Lake; 9. Langell's Valley, Oregon. (*Author*)

On pain of his own death as a shaman, Curley Headed Doctor promised, that if the Modoc would believe in the Ghost Dance, none would be harmed in the coming battle.

Bugles sounded revelry at four, insuring the Modoc of further warning. After a brief breakfast, more bugles sounded, east and west, and the soldiers moved forward. As dawn came, the light was defused as dense fog, even thicker than the day before, covered the lava fields. Bernard had his two troops return to the position from which they had drawn the Modocs' fire the day before. All they need do was wait until the designated time to attack.

As his watch marked the moment, Bernard ordered his men to attack by shouting, "Charge!" The Modocs immediately opened fire in an even more intense display of rifle fire than the day before. Lieutenant Kyle was hit while leading G Troop and Captain Jackson sent Lieutenant Boutelle over to assume command.

Advance was impossible across the lava strewn field against a well fortified enemy giving good effect with rifle fire. Bernard halted his advance; he now had one killed and five more wounded.

From the west, Major Green had started forward with his larger force. He began his attack with Troop F, Captain David Perry commanding, making a charge to sweep around to the southwest of the Modocs. But, the ground was ill-suited for cavalry (the horses had been left in camp).

At a deep ravine, Perry's command was halted where they found themselves trapped, neither able to advance nor retreat. Green then ordered his infantry forward, which rescued the trapped cavalry, and prepared for the next advance.

Instead of moving his strong force forward to connect with Bernard's (which had been ordered to move south for an attack from the southeast), Green's command had advanced little and was still a long way from penetrating the Modoc lines. Rather than attack frontally, Green ordered his infantry to move to the left, towards Tule Lake, to find an easier way into the Modocs' lines. All the while Green had his howitzers firing.

Bernard's forces were making a flanking movement, too. With his two companies now formed at five-yard intervals in the thick fog, Bernard advanced left. He made three hundred yards and attacked from the southeast, but encountered the same deep ravine that had halted Perry's advance. The ravine cut nearly three-fourths of the way around the Modocs, creating a very effective dry moat, through which the troopers could not advance, but over which the Indians could fire.

Worse, due to the fog, much of the howitzer fire was conducted blindly, frequently going completely over the Indian camp. The result was that a great deal of Bernard's advance was made under an artillery barrage. Between the artillery fire and the deep ravine, Bernard was unable to advance further and retreated to his original jump-off point.

Within an hour of sunset, the fog finally lifted. One result was the immediate ability of Major Green to communicate with Captain Bernard. Not only could signal flags be used, but runners could find a safe passage between the separated commands. With word exchanged, the howitzer fire was redirected. This allowed Bernard to probe the Modocs again. Major Green supported the action by making a major infantry push north to connect with Bernard. At first naturally hesitant, the infantry moved forward, once given encouragement by Major Green.

Major Green led by example. Respected by his troops, "Uncle Johnny" Green, as he was referred, jumped up on a rock and exposed himself to Modoc rifle fire. He yelled at his men that they had nothing to fear since the Modocs could not hit him standing out in the open. Moving out to be in front of the timid infantry, Green called on his men to follow him as he stood exposed to Modoc fire. He personally led the charge, for which he was awarded the Medal of Honor.

But the Modocs quickly redirected more of their fire against the advancing 21st Infantry companies. Some of the infantry broke through

A U.S. Army picket station in the Lava Beds. (*National Archives*)

to Bernard, but most were hit so hard that the infantrymen simply went to ground until darkness allowed them to retreat. As they retreated, the Modoc went out among the dead and took the Army's Spencer carbines, Henry and Winchester repeating rifles, hand guns, and much needed ammunition.

Wheaton's attack at the First Battle of the Stronghold had been a disaster. No Indians could be reported killed as none had even been seen, so effective was the cover of their defensive positions. However, the U.S. Army had suffered sixteen killed, all enlisted men, and fifty-three wounded, nine of whom were officers. Most of the casualties were experienced by the 21st Infantry.

The troops felt dispirited. The California riflemen went home. Colonel Ross lead his two companies of Oregon Volunteers home (the Volunteers had received two killed and nine wounded, two of whom would die before they could get home). The troops of the regular Army who were forced to stay faced a bleak winter; snow covered their exposed winter camps and the Modocs were still there, adding to their misery.

Inside the Modoc camp, Curley Headed Doctor took credit for the victory. No Modoc had been hurt, and the shaman claimed it was because of his powers and the Ghost Dance ceremony. If the Modoc would be true to the religion, claimed Curley Headed Doctor, victory would be theirs.

The news of the failed attack spread quickly. Despite the army loses, the press was sympathetic to the Modoc. The *New York Herald's* reporter, Edward Fox, kept the world informed of the unfolding drama at Tule

Lake providing the news in a manner much different from previous reporting on Indian wars.

> February 12: "There is, however, little doubt that the Indians have been badly treated, and if the whites had kept faith with them, there would have been no disturbance at all." (Cozzens, 169)

> February 25: "If the peace commissioners expect them to give up the Indians that killed the settlers, they need not for one moment flatter themselves of obtaining such a result, as the Indians will fight to the last man, believing they have done no wrong. They are, however, willing to go on a reservation, and if the whites only keep faith with them and the Indian agents do not rob them of their supplies, for which the government pays, they will remain quiet like the rest of their tribe and give no further trouble." (Cozzens, 193)

> March 1: "I feel satisfied that these Indians have been badly treated and forced into a war which they appear perfectly able to sustain." (Cozzens, 194)

With major papers supplying such a favorable view on the Modoc, pressure built to find a different solution than the typical one of bloodshed.

When word reached Washington, D.C., it coincided with President Grant's inauguration for his second term of office. Grant had campaigned on, among other planks, a platform of a Peace Policy with the Indians. Present in Washington, as a presidential elector from Oregon, was Alfred Meacham. Still considering himself an advocate for the Modocs, Meacham went to Secretary of the Interior, Columbus Delano, with the idea that a peace council could achieve with the Modocs what Colonel Wheaton had failed with his troopers. A peace commission was soon appointed with Meacham as its head. They then headed for Tule Lake.

The Army had not been idle during the interim. Wheaton was relieved of field command and replaced with Colonel Alvin C. Gillem[10], the 1st Cavalry's colonel. General Canby also arrived, to determine what had gone wrong. There, he received word that the peace commission had been ordered. Canby wired his superiors that a peace commission had little chance of success so immediately after a stunning Indian victory. Canby was told to keep the troops on the defensive and to give peace a chance. In keeping with his orders, Canby had Colonel Gillem pulled his camp back about two miles to the southern base of a steep ridge (now called Gillem's Bluff) at the extreme southwestern edge of Tule Lake. On the east, he ordered Captain Bernard's forces back about nine miles to the Applegate Ranch. On January 20, Bernard reached the ranch, which at least provided greater comfort to the wounded.

General Edward R. S. Canby. (*Library of Congress*)

On January 22, the Modocs made another raid to the south and east, near Scorpion Point. This time it was against two wagons carrying grain to the Applegate Ranch. The escort fled, and as the Indians plundered the wagons, Captain Bernard arrived with a portion of G Troop, killing one Modoc, wounding an undetermined number of others, who were carried off with the raiding party, finally chasing the Indians back into the lava beds.

While the peace commission gathered, so did more soldiers. Troop K, 1st Cavalry arrived, as did Company I of the 21st Infantry. In addition, two other regiments took the field, at least in part. The 4th U.S. Artillery arrived with Batteries A, E, K, and M. No longer would the howitzers be manned by either cavalry troopers or infantrymen, but by professional gunners. In addition to howitzers, a unit of Coehorn mortars was brought to the field. The balance of the 4th Artillery acted as infantry support. Further support was gained when two companies, E and G, of the 12th Infantry arrived.

Despite the huge increase in manpower, the Army gave the peace commission every opportunity to succeed. After a month of nothing but words, Interior Secretary Delano took the unusual step of putting General Canby in charge of the peace efforts.

10. Gillem was a Tennessean, and owed much of his success in the Army to his friend and benefactor, former President Andrew Johnson. His promotions in the Civil War had been made not for military talent, but to show that there were loyal men from the Confederate South. He was not well respected by the other officers, partly because he had served in the Marine Corps as a political appointee, and many openly showed contempt. Worse, Gillem became ill shortly after taking field command. While never relinquishing command, he never fully recovered from his illness, and was dead within two years as a result of his protracted disease.

March 24 marked Canby's first effort at direct negotiations with the Modocs. But, he believed the Modocs would not come to the peace table as willing supplicants of peace while still victorious. The Modocs must feel the Army's strength. General Canby ordered Colonel Gillem to increase the pressure on the Modocs by moving the army closer. On the east, Hospital Rock was reoccupied with Major Edwin C. Mason, 21st Infantry, commanding, and patrols were directed to push right to the edge of the lava redoubt. The pressure helped to clarify both side's demands, but the talks dragged on.

In a tent placed about one mile from Gillem's camp and two miles from the Modoc stronghold, Canby and the peace commissioners met with Captain Jack and the other Modoc leaders. The Modocs asked for a reservation on the Lost River and forgiveness for any acts done by Captain Jack's people as a result of the war. General Canby's reply was unconditional surrender.

Between the demand for unconditional surrender and the pressure of Colonel Gillem's tactics, Modoc dissension increased. Urging the killing of the white peace council was the war-bent shaman, Curley Headed Doctor. Through ridicule and by shaming him, Curley Headed Doctor overcame Captain Jack's resistance to continue the war. Curley Headed Doctor called Jack womanly, pointing out the strength of his medicine, which had kept the whites out of the Stronghold. The shaman said that if the Indians killed the white leaders, the soldiers would go away. The result was that the Modocs planned to kill the peace commissioners and as many of the white leaders as they could at their next meeting.

Winema, also known as Tobey Riddle, the Modoc wife of Canby's interpreter learned of the plan, and warned General Canby who refused to believe the Indians would violate the terms of the peace meetings. On Good Friday, April 11, 1873, General Canby and the six members of his party went to the peace tent.[11] As per the Modoc plan, in the midst of the talks, after General Canby rejected the Modoc peace plan yet again, Captain Jack drew a pistol and shot General Canby in the face, killing him instantly. The other Modocs opened fire; a commissioner was killed and a second, Alfred Meacham, was severally wounded. General Canby became the first and only serving general officer ever killed in an Indian war. His death transformed the campaign into one of purposeful, if inept, annihilation.

Further, at nearly the same instant as the peace talks started with General Canby, another group of Modocs approached Major Mason's camp and asked to speak with him. The duty officers, First Lieutenants William L. Sherwood and W. Boyle, both of the 21st Infantry, went out to talk to the Modocs, unaware of any of the events unfolding three miles away. Sherwood refused to call Major Mason and, unless the Indians were willing to enter the camp unarmed and under escort, there would be no further conversation. At that juncture, the Indians opened fire, killing several soldiers, including Lieutenant Sherwood.

Winema, left, Captain Jack's cousin and wife of General Canby's interpreter. (*Library of Congress*)

Washington appointed a new commander for the Department of the Columbia, Colonel Jefferson C. Davis, of the 23rd Infantry. Until Davis's arrival, Colonel Gillem assumed command. Making sure the Modoc had not fled, he sent out search parties to scout around the Stronghold.

On April 12, Lieutenant Edward Theller led Company I of the 21st Infantry to the south and east, making contact with the Modoc, and insuring that they were still in the Stronghold. This was the only action taken for over forty-eight hours.

The quiet of the soldiers strengthened Curley Headed Doctor's claim to leadership of the Modoc. He had convinced the Modoc to kill Canby and the other white leaders, promising that the whites would not attack them if they did. As no attack came, the shaman knew the Ghost Dance powers were very strong and he seemed to be all powerful. As the whites waited, the Modoc danced more Ghost Dances. Finally, on April 15, Gillem ordered the Modocs attacked.

11. Colonel Gillem was scheduled to be another member, but begged off because of his continuing illness. Interestingly, they were accompanied by two Modoc from the Stronghold. During the talks, the Indians were allowed to visit the Army camps without objection. Boston Charley and Bogus Charley arrived in the Army camp the night before, fully armed. The next morning, as Canby led his team to the Peace Tent, unarmed, Boston Charley and Bogus accompanied them, openly displaying their weapons. Both would take a part in the unfolding attack of Canby's peace party.

Gillem's plan mirrored Colonel Wheaton's first attack, but with a much stronger force—four batteries of artillery, five companies of infantry, four troops of cavalry, and seventy-two Warm Springs Indian scouts.[12] For three days, the Army advanced. Again the main thrust was from the west, with Major Green commanding.

Green advanced, under the supporting fire of the mortars, with two troops of 1st Cavalry[13] (dismounted), three batteries of 4th Artillery[14] acting as infantry, and two companies of 12th Infantry.[15] As they advanced, the Army took casualties, mostly in the head and upper body, as the troops peeked above the lava to get a shot.

From the east, under the command of Major Mason, the advance was to be made by four companies[16] of 21st Infantry, supported by Captain Bernard's squadron[17] of two troops of the 1st Cavalry, G[18] and B Troops. Mason's advance was supported by howitzer fire.[19]

At the end of the first day, the Modocs still held out. The Army troops, however, did not retreat as they usually did at night. Instead, they held

12. They had arrived on Saturday, 12, under the leadership of Donald McKay, a step-grandson of John McLoughlin.

13. Part of K Troop was on the extreme left, under the command of Lieutenant Charles C. Cresson; the balance of K Troop was held as a reserve, under the command of Captain Joel Trimble. Next in line was F Troop, Captain David Perry commanding.

14. Battery A, under Captain Evan Thomas, supported with the mortars. Batteries M (Captain Charles Throckmorton), K (Lieutenant George Harris), and E (First Lieutenant Peter Leary) advanced as infantry. Captain Marcus P. Miller was in overall command of the artillery/infantry.

15. Attacking in the middle were First Lieutenant Charles Eagan's Company G, and First Lieutenant Thomas Wright's Company E.

16. On the extreme right were Company C (Second Lieutenant Edward Rheem), Company F (First Sergeant John McNamara commanding), Company B (First Lieutenant John Rose), and Company I (First Lieutenant Edward Theller). All were under the command of Captain George H. Burton.

17. Besides his cavalry, Bernard was responsible for Donald McKay's Warm Spring Scouts.

18. G Troop was under Lieutenant John Kyle; B Troop was under Captain James Jackson.

19. Battery A's howitzers were under the command of Second Lieutenant Edwin Chapman.

their positions. The soldiers built breastworks by piling chunks of lava, until a group of soldiers would each have their own fort. Supplies were brought up to them and mortars kept dropping shells into the Modoc redoubt.

Slowly the soldiers advanced, from position of cover to position of cover. To the north, the two forces joined on the shores of Tule Lake, thus depriving the Modocs of their water source. Again, as night fell, the soldiers dug in and mortars lobbed their shells into the Modoc camp.

By the night of April 16, Colonel Gillem was convinced he had the Modocs surrounded. However, the next day, the Army moved into the now-abandoned camp and found eleven dead Modocs, eight of whom were women. The rest of the Modocs had escaped to another lava bed further south. Their flight had been made possible because an officer failed to obey orders. Major Edwin. C. Mason had dug his troops in, instead of advancing as ordered. He left a gap to the east in the surrounding forces, which the Modocs exploited[20] to make good their escape.[21]

The Second Battle of the Stronghold had ended differently than the first, but equally a failure. The only real positive result was discrediting the shaman Curley Headed Doctor. As the troops crossed the red painted tule rope, his powers seemed to have completely failed in the eyes of the Modoc.

With the Modocs out from the Army's grip, the problems became evident. While they were inside the stronghold, they were hard to get, but at least the Army knew where they were. Having forced them out, the Army had no idea where the Modocs had gone. Colonel Gillem had to find the Modocs if he was to fight them.

Sending out scouts, Gillem also sent out a reconnaissance in force. Sixty-four soldiers marched out on April 26, under the command of Captain Evan Thomas. Captain Thomas was of the 4th Artillery, which

20. The Modoc exploited the gap by staging a diversionary attack on Gillem's camp. Led by Hooker Jim, it helped to allow the Modoc to escape. As Hooker Jim retired, he captured two reporters and one sixteen-year-old boy. The reporters fled, but the boy was killed and mutilated. He was the only casualty in Hooker Jim's raid.

21. Mason's report on his failure to advance was summed up as, "I did not however follow them, as it was no part of my plan to expose anyone unnecessarily." (Murray, 211)

had two batteries[22] of artillerymen acting as infantry. Accompanying him was Company E of the 12th Infantry, under the command of Lieutenant Thomas Forster Wright.[23]

As the force marched south, they displayed their limited experience fighting Indians. While Captain Thomas ordered out flankers, he failed to correct their behavior as they kept creeping in so as to be almost walking next to the main column. When the column halted for lunch, few sentries were set, and they were not very attentive. Wright prophetically warned Thomas that the time to worry about Indians was when you could not see any; a civilian packer wagered that they were "not within fifteen miles of Jack's camp."

The Modoc camp was not fifteen miles away, and neither were the Indians. Looking down on the resting troops, the Modocs crawled very close to the sprawling soldiers, then sprang a complete surprise attack. Half the command panicked and fled toward Colonel Gillem's camp four miles to the north. Captain Thomas organized his remaining soldiers into a defensive perimeter and then ordered Lieutenant Wright to take some men to charge the ring of Modocs. Thomas' plan was to have Wright force an opening toward the northwest to allow the command to retreat toward Gillem's camp. As one observer wrote:

> At the first fire, the troops were so demoralized that officers could do nothing with them. [Brevet] Captain Wright was ordered with his company to take possession of a bluff, which would effectively secure their retreat, but Captain Wright was severely wounded on

22. Thomas' Battery A, and Battery K, commanded by Lieutenant Albion Howe.

23. Thomas Wright was the son of General George Wright, famous for the Spokane Indian War of 1858. He had been admitted to the U.S. Military Academy at West Point in 1848, but was dismissed the following year, to his father's great disappointment. He soon took to a life of adventure, joining William Walker's attempt to create a Central American empire, starting in Nicaragua. After that failure, he seemed to settle down, and during the Civil War, was given a commission first in the 2nd California Infantry, and later, in the 6th California Infantry. In the latter regiment, he reached the rank of colonel. In 1865, Wright was given command of the U.S. Army post of the Presidio, at San Francisco, and was awarded the position of a brevetted brigadier general. With his muster out of volunteer service in 1866, Wright still longed for a life of adventure, and obtained a commission as a first lieutenant in the 32nd U.S. Infantry, that same year. In 1870, he transferred to the 12th U.S. infantry, in which he served until his death.

The remains of Colonel Gillem's camp can still be seen. The piles of stones were not primarily defensive works but were built to provide weather protection and to keep the troopers' tents from blowing away. (*Author*)

the way to the heights, and his company, with one or two exceptions, deserted him and fled like a pack of sheep; then the slaughter began. (Rickey, 280)

But as Wright attacked, he was killed and the rest of the 12th Infantrymen retreated back to Thomas' defensive stand. Trying to move to Wright's defense, a column led by Lieutenant Arthur Cranston, was turned back when Cranston and five soldiers were killed. Rallying the few soldiers still alive, Thomas moved into a slight hollow and said, "This is as good a place as any to die." (Murray, 231)

The Modocs wiped out the remaining command, resulting in twenty-five killed, including all of the officers[24] and sixteen men wounded. It was not until the next day that Lieutenant Boutelle of the 1st U.S. Cavalry arrived on the field to find the command slaughtered.

Colonel Davis arrived at his new command on May 2, to find that this latest disaster had again caused morale to plummet. After evaluating his command, he advised General Schofield, in San Francisco, "a great many

---

24. Lieutenant Gregg Harris was found alive, but severely wounded. He was manhandled back to Gillem's camp, in unrelenting pain, and died sixteen days later. Initial reports of his surviving, although severely wounded, reached his mother in Philadelphia. She made a cross-country rail and stage trip to reach Gillem's camp twenty-four hours after her son's death. Harris was twenty-seven at the time of his death, having graduated from West Point in 1868.

of the enlisted men here are utterly unfit for Indian fighting of this kind." What was needed was the dash of cavalry.[25] Shortly after taking command, he ordered his cavalry to act as beaters and drive the Modocs out.

Warm Springs scouts tracked some Modoc to the south and east of Tule Lake. The trail became hot when on May 7 a supply train was attacked near Scorpion Point. While being able to drive off the attacking Modoc long enough to retreat, the train's escort had three soldiers wounded. However, more importantly, the Second Battle of Scorpion Point provided much needed supplies to the Modoc from the abandoned Army supply wagons.

On May 9, Captain Henry Hasbrouck, 4th Artillery, took command of one battery of artillery, mounted to act as cavalry, parts of Bernard's and Jackson's 1st Cavalry troops, and Indian scouts from the Warm Springs Indian Reservation. Working south and east, Hasbrouck camped on Dry Lake, a major water supply point for the Modocs. Early the next morning, the Modocs attempted another surprise attack. The first sign of danger was when a mule skinner's dog started to growl in the dawn's light. Warning the troops that Indians were near, the packer, Charley Larengel, told the officer of the guard to report the dog's warning. Instead, just as Wright's warning had been ignored two weeks prior by Thomas, the officer told Larengel to go back to bed. Larengel ignored Thomas, and the officer of the watch went to tell Captain Hasbrouck. Just as the warning was conveyed, the fighting broke out.

Seen leading the attack was Captain Jack, clearly wearing General Canby's field jacket. Initially, the ambush worked as it had with Captain Thomas' command. Private Charles Hardin of G Troop, 1st Cavalry, described the initial attack.

> We became very much alive and full of action, But, this action was poorly directed, as it consisted only of men bobbing about from place to place, vainly seeking better shelter than was afforded by

25. Other authorities agreed that more "dash" was needed. Disgusted at the continued failure of the Army, Oregon Governor Grover ordered out three more companies of Oregon Volunteers. Arriving unwelcomed by the Army shortly after Colonel Davis' arrival were Company C, Captain Joseph H. Hyzer commanding; Company D, Thomas Mullholland commanding; and company E, with George R. Rogers as captain. Newly promoted, General John Ross was once again put in command of the Oregon Volunteers.

their saddles, with some firing of carbines at nothing. Meanwhile, the Modocs were pouring in a hot fire. The situation was becoming serious. The men were milling like frightened animals. It began to look like the prelude of a stampede. (Cozzens, 277)

Another participant noted the impending break-down of control, and how it was averted.

I saw a line of Modocs pop up their heads and fire a volley. This caused some confusion. Men rolled over behind saddles and bundles of blankets-no covering however small being ignored, fastening on belts and pulling on boots under a hail of bullets. There was a possibility of a panic, but this was happily averted by Sergeant Thomas Kelly of our troop [Captain Bernard's G Troop], who sprang up and shouted, 'God damn it, let's charge!' (Rickey, 287)

Captain Henry C. Hasbrouck rallied his men and counterattacked. The artillerymen marched from their camp to the sound of the fighting in the cavalry camp. Meanwhile, the Warm Spring scouts made two sweeping raids behind the Modoc, while the cavalry charged the warriors. The cavalry kept the Modoc fighters occupied, allowing the Warm Spring scouts to raid the Modoc women, who were with the Indians' supplies. Thus, the attack captured much of the Modocs' supplies, including most of their horses and almost all of their ammunition.

Unable to fight without supplies, the Modocs broke into small groups and scattered. As the bands dispersed, the First Cavalry troopers doggedly pursued. On May 18, just south of Lower Klamath Lake, Captain Hasbrouck's troopers found and attacked a group of Chief Hooker Jim's Modocs. He had been one of the chiefs who had taunted Captain Jack into the slaying of General Canby. After having several of his band killed, Hooker Jim fled, with the cavalry pursuing, and on May 22, he led his band into General Davis' camp where they surrendered.

Hooker Jim offered to trade Captain Jack's band for amnesty for himself and his band. The betrayal was quickly accepted, and on May 28 Hooker Jim found Captain Jack's band on Willow Creek, a tributary of the beloved Lost River. Hooker Jim urged the surrender of Jack's band, but Captain Jack refused, sensing the betrayal. The next morning, Major Green led two squadrons of 1st Cavalry in a surprise attack on Captain Jack's camp in Langell's Valley, in Oregon. One arm of the attack was lead by Captain Hasbrouck and the other was lead by Captain Jackson.

The graves of Captain Jack (far left) and three other Modoc Indians at the Fort Klamath site. (*Author*)

Suffering more casualties, Captain Jack's party scattered, broken even further into smaller units, but all were determinedly pursued. On June 3, 1873, Captain David Perry's command found Captain Jack, now only accompanied by his family, hiding in a cave. Realizing it meant certain death, Captain Jack nevertheless surrendered.[26]

The end of the Modoc war came with a whimper. Upon return to Fort Klamath, a court-martial was held in early July and found six Modoc leaders guilty of murder. As a reward for his treachery Hooker Jim, despite clear evidence of his part in the killing of civilians, was not even tried. The six leaders were found guilty and were sentenced to death. President Grant commuted the sentence of two to life in prison and the other four, still led by Captain Jack, were hung at Fort Klamath on October 3, 1873. The rest of the warring Modocs were sent to Indian Territory in Oklahoma.[27]

26. The last of the Modoc were captured by Oregon Volunteers. General Ross wired the governor of Oregon with the immodest message, "The Modoc War was ended by the Oregon Volunteers at 12 o'clock last night. [Murray, 272]" At first Ross refused to turn the Modoc over to the Army, which wished to treat them as prisoners of war. The desire of the Oregonians was to hang them as common murderers, but calmer heads prevailed, avoiding a conflict between white authorities. Ross surrendered his prisoners to the Army.

27. Other Modocs had never left the Klamath reservation and had remained on it throughout the fighting. They were allowed to continue living on the reservation without disruption.

While most of the battles took place in California, the start and end of the war was really at Fort Klamath. The army forces involved were all from the Department of the Columbia and Oregon, except for a few California militia. It was a fight for paradise, one side fighting for a lost cause along the Lost River of Oregon.

The Nez Perce Flight from Paradise

From the first contact with Europeans, the Nez Perce had been notable for their willingness to accommodate the white men who entered their country. It had been the Nez Perce who had come to Lewis and Clark's salvation in 1805 after they had crossed the Rockies. In the Cayuse Indian War, as well as the period of resistance led by Kamiakin, the Nez Perce had remained friendly to the whites. Their reward had been the constant diminution of their homeland, starting with the Treaty of 1855.

During the height of the Snake Indian War, the Nez Perce were given a new treaty and had a fort, Lapwai, established to protect them (or secure the northern front, depending on the interpretation). The 1863 treaty again reduced the size of the Nez Perce reservation. The Nez Perce home land outside the new reservation was now principally in two areas. The first was the lower Salmon River area of north-central Idaho, where the "non-treaty" Nez Perce were led by Chiefs White Bird and Toohoolhoolzote. The second area was the Wallowa Valley of northeastern Oregon. There, the Nez Perce were led by Old Joseph (Wellamotkin) until his death in 1871. His son, Young Joseph (Tooyalaket), would lead the tribe during the ensuing crisis.

Recognizing the historical accuracy of the Nez Perce's claim to the Wallowa Valley, in 1873, President Grant created a reservation for the tribe in the valley. This seemed to settle the Nez Perce's single largest objection to the Treaty of 1863.

It was into this status quo that the new commander of the Army's Department of the Columbia arrived in Portland in September, 1874. Brigadier General Oliver Otis Howard, of antebellum abolitionist tendencies, brought more than his military experience as a Civil War corps commander. He had been in charge of the Freedmen's Bureau after the war and helped to establish Howard University in Washington, D.C., which is named for him.

A religious man convinced that he understood the Indians better than most whites, General Howard was genuinely concerned for the Indians, but knew little of their beliefs or their culture. Upon assuming his command, Howard was subjected to the same pressure President Grant was feeling for the removal of the Nez Perce from the Wallowa Valley. It came as no surprise that the order to create a Nez Perce reservation in the Wallowa Valley was rescinded in 1875. The betrayed Nez Perce were angry.

The non-treaty Nez Perce leaders, Eagle from the Light, White Bird, Looking Glass, Toohoolhoolzote, and Joseph (the younger Tooyalaket), met to discuss their options. With their Wallowa Valley reservation rescinded, the Nez Perce were left with only two options: either abide with the white treachery and live in peace, or war. It was decided that peace was the best option, and the Indians continued to quietly live near the whites.

Tensions remained high when the whites killed a Nez Perce outside of the established reservation. War seemed a very real possibility. A five-man Peace Commission was created in October, 1876 to resolve the lingering Nez Perce problem. General Howard had himself appointed to the commission and, while not officially the head of the commission, quickly assumed effective leadership. General Howard's proposed solution was for the Nez Perce to be compensated for their loss by buying their ancestral rights to the Wallowa Valley. The Peace Commission met with the non-treaty Nez Perce at the Lapwai's area church on November 13, 1876.

When the whites proposed that the Nez Perce sell their homelands, the Indians attempted to explain their deep attachment to the land. The Indians explained their love of the valley in terms of their religious beliefs. Unable or unwilling to understand, the Peace Commission confused the Nez Perce's religion with another Indian religious movement, the Dreamer religion,[28] sweeping the Columbia Valley which called for the removal or death of the whites. When the Nez Perce absolutely refused to sell their land rights, citing the Treaty of 1855, the Peace Commission rejected their arguments and recommended their removal, by force if necessary.

28. "Christian expansion among the Interior Indians was paralleled by a revival of the Dreamer religion. A messianic form of the old Ghost Dance faith, it swept through the mass of non-Christian Indians, especially along the Columbia River and in Nez Perce Territory." (Burns, 365)

General Oliver Otis Howard, left, and Chief Joseph (*Library of Congress*)

The situation remained in a tense status quo over the winter. On March 7, 1877, the Department of the Interior's Indian Bureau requested the Army's help in removing the Nez Perce from their valley. General Howard asked for a meeting with the Wallowa Valley and other non-reservation Nez Perce in an attempt to resolve the crisis.

General Howard and Chief Joseph, with other chiefs met in May. This time their meeting was held at a slightly different and ominous location. Instead of the Lapwai church, the two met in an Army tent at Fort Lapwai, surrounded by troops. A clear message was sent to the Nez Perce.

Despite the implied threat of force, Chief Joseph pled for justice and their ancestral home. General Howard said he wanted to hear the words of the Nez Perce that he was there to listen. Toohoolhoolzote rose to speak, saying "The Great Spirit chief made the world as it is and as He wanted it, and He made a part of it for us to live upon. I do not see where you get the authority to say that we should not live where He placed us." (Glassley, 209) The challenge to his authority and his religion angered General Howard.

According to his written account, General Howard wanted to divide the Nez Perce to stop the protests. He demanded, "Then you do not propose to comply with the orders of the government?" When Toohoolhoolzote responded, "The Indians may do what they like, but I am not going on the reservation," Howard took immediate action. Despite Howard's assurance to the Nez Perce that he was there to listen, he had Toohoolhoolzote arrested. Chief Joseph, responded, "I am going to talk now. I don't care whether you arrest me or not. The arrest of Too-hul-hul-sute [an alternate spelling] was wrong, but we will not resent the insult. We were invited to this council to express our hearts and we have done so." (Glassley, 209)

Even as General Howard ignored Chief Joseph's protest, word arrived among the Indians that the 1st Cavalry troops from Fort Walla Walla had entered their Valley. Faced with a fait accompli, all of the non-treaty Indians decided they had no choice and agreed to move to the reservation surrounding Fort Lapwai. Their acquiescence had the positive result of Toohoolhoolzote's release.

However much the Nez Perce wished to avoid war by moving to the reservation, conditions hampered their compliance. Regional rivers were swollen with spring run-off making the crossings extremely difficult and dangerous. It was not until mid-June that the Nez Perce could make real progress toward the reservation. As they moved closer, resentment built. To some, it was the tribe's destruction. Within White Bird's group, some got drunk to deal with their sorrow, and three of the drunken braves went on a revenge mission.[29] On June 13, four white settlers were killed.

General Howard was awaiting the Nez Perce's arrival at Fort Lapwai when word arrived of the killings. He immediately alerted his command, ordering a concentration of troops to the area. However, feeling quick intervention[30] would prevent further killings, Howard ordered Captain

29. An Indian had been killed by a white, years prior, and his son, Wah-Lit-Its, sought revenge. He and his two drunk cousins went searching for the white, but not finding him, killed an elderly white settler who had a history of mis-treating Indians. Not satisfied, they continued their revenge raid, killing three more and wounding three others.

30. Another aim of Howard's quick intervention was his decision, a short time later, to send a command north to impress and contain other tribes that had expressed discontent. Colonel Frank Wheaton led troops north to the Spokane area to restrain restless tribes in northeastern Washington, northern Idaho, and northwest Montana. On August 10, 1877, he held a council with the tribes in question. Wheaton estimated "some nine thousand" Indians, but other sources estimated a third of that number. One result of the meeting was the creation of a new military district, with Wheaton in command, centered on the area of his council.

David Perry to take over one hundred 1st Cavalry troopers to bring White Bird's clan in to the reservation immediately to prevent further bloodshed.

As Captain Perry arrived in the area of White Bird's village on the Camas Prairie, he learned he had arrived too late to prevent further bloodshed. Fifteen more whites had been killed. Despite covering the seventy miles in just two days, his exhausting efforts were late. Scouts reported the Nez Perce had moved south a few miles, to White Bird Creek.

Approaching White Bird Canyon, where the Nez Perce were camped, Captain Perry had picked up eleven Mount Idaho volunteers[31] who had assembled to protect the settlers. Nez Perce scouts intercepted the white column as it crossed the treeless hills and reported back to the camp, alerting the Indians to the approaching danger. As Lieutenant William Parnell noted, "Almost immediately the cry of a coyote was heard on the hills above us—a long, howling cry, winding up, however, in a very peculiar way not characteristic of the coyote. Little heed was paid to it at the time, yet it was a fatal cry to the command. It was made by an Indian picket on the watch for the soldiers." (Cozzens, 348)

The Nez Perce, warned of the cavalry's approach, decided they would first seek peace with the cavalrymen, but fight if necessary. The cavalry became less willing to tolerate the Indians when at three A.M., they found a woman and child[32] hiding along their march. She was the wife of a murdered rancher, and was holding her four-year-old daughter in her arms, crying with a broken arm. Both were cold, hungry, and very much afraid the Nez Perce would find them. The volunteers, many of whom knew the family, urged greater violence against the Nez Perce. As Sergeant John P. Schoor (F Troop, 1st Cavalry) reported, "Perry, once in the field, was swayed by the ever-voluble Ad Chapman [a volunteer] and others who urged him to follow up the 'cowardly Injuns' and administer a crushing defeat." (McWhorter, 2001, 232)

Leading the troopers in were the Idaho volunteers, who were more familiar with the area. Keeping them under military control, Captain Perry put Lieutenant Edward R. Theller, 21st Infantry, in command. Theller saw a party of Nez Perce move out from their camp under a white

31. Under the command of George Shearer, a former major in the Confederate Army.

32. McWhorter reported the survivors as a mother and two children (2001, 235).

flag of truce. The first battle of the Nez Perce War would start under a cloth of peace, with both sides claiming the other fired first. Captain Perry's report concluded the Nez Perce fired first in treachery. Nez Perce Chief Yellow Wolf's description of the opening shot was completely different.

> Five warriors, led by Wettiwetti Houlis. . . had been sent out from the other side of the valley as a peace party to meet the soldiers. These warriors had instructions from the chiefs not to fire unless fired upon. Of course, they carried a white flag. Peace might be made without fighting. From the north echoed a rifle report and right away a white man on a white horse came riding swiftly south. . . . He did not look like a soldier. . . he was dressed more like a citizen. . . . Now he was the first enemy we see. Charged, and trying to kill each other. It was he who had fired the first shot we had just heard. Fired on our peace party. (McWhorter, 1995, 55-56)

As the Battle of White Bird Canyon started, Theller led his volunteers to a knoll on the left to anchor a flank. Captain Perry lined up his tired troopers for a charge to break the Indian line. Before Perry had a chance to order the charge, the Nez Perce attacked the volunteers, probably in accordance to Yellow Wolf's description, believing the civilian volunteer had attacked them first. The volunteers collapsed under the attack and scattered, leaving Perry's left flank exposed. The Nez Perce quickly took advantage and attacked Perry from slightly behind him and from this flank. Parnell described the attack: "In the meantime, the Indians had driven a band of some 500 ponies through the line, and scattered in among the ponies were some sixty or seventy of their men, which so thoroughly demoralized the troops, many of whom were recruits, that it became utterly impossible to control them." (Cozzens, 350) The poorly trained cavalry troopers broke and a rout ensued.

The army officers attempted to convert the rout into an ordered retreat, but Perry's bugler had lost his horn and the shouted commands could not be heard. Captain Joel Trimble, commanding H Troop, tried to rally his men, but they continued to run under pressure from the Nez Perce. Lieutenant Theller gathered eighteen troopers and assumed a defensive position to cover the withdrawal; all were killed. Another officer, Lieutenant William R. Parnell, gathered a force that successfully made a fighting withdrawal, giving Captain Perry time to gather his

White Bird Canyon. (*Author*)

remaining troopers, approximately half, into a strong defensive position. During the covering withdrawal, Lieutenant Parnell turned and charged the attacking Nez Perce in an effort to allow others to rescue a trooper whose horse had been killed from underneath him. For his display of gallantry, Lieutenant Parnell received the Medal of Honor.

First Sergeant Michael McCarthy, Troop H, 1st Cavalry also received the Medal of Honor that same day. He and six men were part of the squad assigned to provide cover for the retreating troopers. They did so, but Sergeant McCarthy was cut off. Surrounded, he fought his way through to others of his command and led another holding action. During these actions, Sergeant McCarthy had two horses shot out from beneath him. Again, holding his position as long as possible to give his comrades an opportunity to escape, Sergeant McCarthy held his position until he was captured. Being placed in the rear, he escaped at his first opportunity, and hid among the angry Indians for three days until he was able to complete his escape and rejoin his command.

Unwilling to take huge casualties to overcome the defensive redoubt of Captain Perry, the Nez Perce retired to cover the village's movement. The Battle of White Bird Canyon was a lopsided Nez Perce victory. Thirty-four whites[33] had been killed and three Nez Perce were wounded.

After word of this loss reached Fort Lapwai, General Howard decided to take the field himself. With the new concentrated command, General Howard left the fort on June 29, 1877, with four troops of 1st

---

33. Sixty-three rifles were recovered from the battlefield by the Nez Perce.

Cavalry, six companies of 21st Infantry, and five companies of 4th Artillery acting as infantry.

In a war distinguished by U.S. Army blundering, the second major blunder occurred. As the non-treaty Indians now headed into the wilderness of Idaho to escape the Army, Howard believed the neutral Chief Looking Glass would join White Bird and Joseph as they retreated. Howard wanted to prevent the concentration of Nez Perce forces, and ordered Captain Stephen G. Whipple to take two companies of 1st Cavalry and two Gatling guns to compel Looking Glass to bring his village to Fort Lapwai. Captain Whipple took some white settlers with him.

As the army arrived, Looking Glass sent word saying, "Leave us alone. We are living here peacefully and want no trouble." (McWhorter, 2001, 265) Seeking peace, Looking Glass raised a white flag, and sent an emissary to express the villages' desire for peace. As the Indian ambassador Peopeo Tholekt recalled, "But these soldiers would not listen. The same one again struck his gun against me and said to the interpreter, 'I know this Injun is Looking Glass! I shall kill him now!'" (McWhorter, 2001, 267)

The talks quickly broke down and the tensions built. Failing to control the white volunteers with him, Captain Whipple allowed them to precipitate a fight, forcing him to deploy his Gatling guns.

On July 1, Whipple's Gatling guns decidedly pushed Looking Glass into the hostile camp by opening fire indiscriminately into the camp. The Nez Perce returned a covering fire to allow time for retreat, losing 750 horses and their village. Looking Glass's people joined the exodus of White Bird and Joseph.

Tensions increased. As Captain Whipple returned empty-handed to the main column, he was attacked in an ambush and had a brief skirmish at Camas Prairie on July 2.

On July 3, a reconnaissance party of eleven, under Lieutenant Sevier McClellan Rains, was ambushed and destroyed by the Nez Perce. The next day another army party was attacked to the south of the town of Cottonwood, but drove off the Nez Perce by the use of their Gatling guns.

On July 5, seventeen Mount Idaho volunteers, Captain Darius Randall, commanding, were surrounded until 1st Cavalry troopers rode to their relief; three were killed, including Captain Randall, and two were wounded in the hand-to-hand fighting.

The Nez Perce were soon further reinforced. Two of the Indians' most notable warriors, Five Wounds and Rainbow, returned from Montana where they had been peaceably hunting buffalo. They brought news that there were no troubles on the other side of Lolo Pass. They also brought needed experience in combat.

As General Howard moved to capture or destroy the Nez Perce, now in total open warfare, his column was provided a diversion.

Looking Glass. (*National Archives*)

On July 9, Mount Idaho volunteers, under the command of Colonel Edward McConville, were again attacked and surrounded on a small hill. Digging rifle pits for protection, they were kept under siege into the following day, in what became known as the Battle of Mount Misery.[34] This diversion was ended when General Howard attacked the retreating Nez Perce in their village on the banks of Clearwater on July 11.

With nearly six hundred troops supported by artillery and Gatling guns, Howard ordered an advance into the camp. The Nez Perce, under Toohoolhoolzote, crossed the river and from prepared rifle pits successfully defended a hill over-looking the army. Albert Forse, a 1st Cavalry officer described the battlefield.

> The position. . . was well selected. The ground at the head of the larger canyon was higher than that occupied by the troops and commanded all the mesa, or tableland, from the bluffs to the heavy timber beyond our left. This ground had been chosen in advance, and General Howard forced to fight on it. This was proven by the breastworks of logs which were thrown up at the river to protect [the Indians'] retreat in case of defeat. (Cozzens, 334)

34. The Nez Perce were led by Ollokot, Joseph's brother.

This stopped Howard's advance. The whites were forced to retire to their own defensive position on the hills overlooking the Clearwater valley. During his retreat, Howard's command abandoned the precious Gatling guns and one of their howitzers, but First Lieutenant Charles F. Humphrey, 4th Artillery, led a party of artillerymen directly into the Nez Perce lines and retrieved the invaluable weapons.

Howard's recovered artillery and Gatling guns prevented the Nez Perce from charging the whites while the strong rifle-pit defensive line successfully prevented the army from charging the Indian village.

Throughout the day, the stalemate provided time for the Nez Perce to prepare their village to move again. As the stalemate continued into the following day, the tactical situation changed when reinforcements arrived. Captain James B. Jackson's 1st Cavalry troop rode in from Fort Klamath, as part of Howard's original order to concentrate forces. The new troops allowed Captain Marcus P. Miller to organize 4th Artillery men into an infantry charge, forcing its way into the now nearly abandoned Nez Perce village. While the majority of the Indians managed to flee, many of their supplies were captured. At the end of the Battle of the Clearwater, the U.S. Army had lost thirteen dead and twenty-seven wounded to the Nez Perce's four dead and six wounded.

One reason given to account for the poor showing of the Army was made by Lieutenant Harry Bailey, Company B, of the 21st Infantry. "At this era of our army, we had had almost no target practice, . . and so. . . sent most of our shots too high." (Cozzens, 416) Once again, despite odds of better than six to one, the Army had failed to defeat the Nez Perce.

The Indian chiefs met and conferred at Kamiah, the legendary place of creation of the Nez Perce. Now it was evident that they could not merely retreat into the wilderness of the Bitterroots. While some[35] wished to stay and fight for their homeland, Looking Glass and Toohoolhoolzote argued that their one salvation would lie in crossing the Rockies into Montana. The Nez Perce hoped to leave their tormentors behind after nearly two weeks of continuous fighting. As they marched, they at first hoped to make a circle, and return to their reservation. As events unfolded, they soon recognized that their only salvation was to flee the United States by turning north, to Canada.

35. Led by Joseph, who had promised his father that he would never give up the beloved Wallowa Valley.

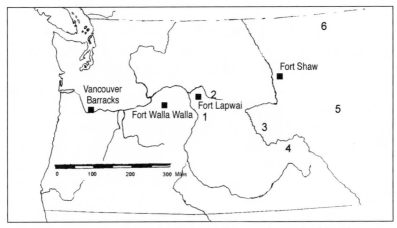

Nez Perce War Overview. 1. Battle of White Bird Canyon; 2. Battle of the Clearwater; 3. Battle of the Big Hole; 4. Battle of Camas Meadow; 5. Battle of Canyon Creek; 6. Bear Paw Battlefield. *(Author)*

In another army blunder, while awaiting more troops, General Howard decided not to pursue the Nez Perce, and so gave them a needed respite. After two weeks of rest, Howard had assembled an even larger force. Allowing Captain Perry's tired command to rest in garrison duty, Howard had reinforcements sent from Fort Boise and other posts from throughout the west.[36] He resumed his pursuit with four troops of 1st Cavalry, six companies of 21st Infantry, one company of 8th Infantry, another of 12th Infantry and seven companies of 4th Artillery as infantry. The squadron of cavalry was lead by Major George Bliss Sanford. Using Bannock Indians under Chief Buffalo Horn, the 1st U.S. Cavalry led the pursuit. Scouts[37] reported the Nez Perce had crossed Lolo Pass into Montana.

By crossing Lolo Pass, not only had the Nez Perce entered a separate territory, but they had fled from the Army's Division of the Pacific into the Division of the Missouri, another general's department, the Department of the Dakota under the command of Brevet Major General Alfred H. Terry. While Terry would order more troops concentrated against the

36. As well as two companies of Washington Territory Mounted Volunteers.

37. The scouts pushed ahead, under the command of Major Edwin Mason. On July 17, near Weippe Prairie, a minor skirmish occurred when the Nez Perce ambushed their followers, killing three.

weary Nez Perce, thus adding to the pressure General Howard maintained, it would take time. Almost all of his forces were stationed in the far eastern portion of Montana, fearing a renewal of a war with the Sioux.

Once through the pass, the Indians easily by-passed a futile white defensive fortification. Hearing of the Nez Perce's flight to Montana, Captain Charles C. Rawn lead two companies of the 7th U.S. Infantry to Lolo Pass in an attempt to block the Indian's flight. He erected a weak redoubt, sent two reconnaissance forces[38] out, and was joined by nearly 200 Montana Volunteers. As the Indians approached, they attempted to talk. Captain Rawn believed it was his duty to stop the Indians. His report detailed the problem. "I had a talk with Chiefs Joseph, White Bird, and Looking Glass, who proposed, if allowed to pass unmolested, to march peaceably through the Bitter Root Valley, but I refused to allow them to pass unless they complied with my stipulations as to the surrender of their arms." (McWhorter, 2001, 349)

The Indians refused and Captain Rawn attempted to buy time for General Howard's column. However, hearing the proposal, the Montanans believed it was their duty to protect their families. Reaching a separate peace, the Montanans agreed not to oppose the Nez Perce if they agreed not to attack the citizens in the valley ahead. The Nez Perce[39] agreed and the Montana Volunteers left Rawn's command. Rawn's under-manned command could do nothing to stop the Nez Perce. As a result of the fort's failure to prevent the Nez Perce from entering into the Montana region, it was appropriately named Fort Fizzle by the Montana citizens.

One result of their deal with the Montana volunteers was the Nez Perce's peaceful trading with the citizens of the Bitterroot River Valley. Believing they had escaped Army pursuit, the Nez Perce knew they were very tired. As they headed south, the exhausted Indians longed for rest.

38. Second Lieutenant Francis Woodridge led one and First Lieutenant C.A. College led the other. Crossing over the Lolo Pass, the two joined after finding the Nez Perce. The combined forces sent a courier to Captain Rawn, then retired to help man the fortifications at the pass.

39. The valley was the home of the Flathead Indians, a traditional ally of the Nez Perce. One reason the whites made an agreement with the Nez Perce was for fear that the Flatheads would join the war. If they had, the two tribes would have easily overwhelmed any white resistance.

The site of the Battle of Clear Water. (*Author*)

Their chiefs were divided. Some urged they push on for the protection of the Sioux under Sitting Bull, now in Canada; others, particularly Looking Glass, urged rest.

Looking Glass had been brought into the war reluctantly and was never a willing participant. The need for respite overwhelmed the sense of urgency and flight, and the Nez Perce dallied in a beautiful valley along the Big Hole River. Between their agreement with the Montana Volunteers, their ability to trade with the local whites, and the knowledge that General Howard's command only covered west of the Rockies, the Nez Perce started to believe that they were now safe.

Tough and tested, Colonel John Gibbon's 7th Infantry commanded the military district in which the Indians now rested. Assembling what parts of the Seventh he could at Fort Shaw[40], on August 2, Gibbons marched[41] with 150 infantry, eleven members of L Troop, 2nd Cavalry, and was later joined by 45 Montana volunteers. The infantry was comprised of six under strength and poorly trained companies. This represented approximately a quarter of the regiment's authorized manpower. With such limited resources, Colonel Gibbon decided his only hope lay in surprise.

40. He marched with the following companies: A, D, F, G, I, and K, plus one mountain howitzer.
41. Gibbons' command covered 150 miles, on foot, in seven days.

At dawn on August 9, the 7th Infantry rushed from the timbered hills into the peaceful village on the valley floor. One of the infantry's officers, Lieutenant Charles Woodruff, described the opening moments.

> At last the eastern sky begins to take on the rosy hue of the coming day; one by one the tops of the lodges come into view above the blackness of the valley. The hour had come. Quickly the whispered order is given for the two skirmish lines to "forward, guide center." The men tighten the grasp on their rifles as they give a trial glance along their sights. While they are silently moving forward, a solitary Indian going out to look at the herd approached the volunteers. He leans forward on his horse to try to make out in the dim light what is before him. Two rifle shots ring out; the Indian falls dead. The battle is on: "Charge!" (Cozzens, 427)

From the village, the opening moments were perceived differently as recalled by Yellow Wolf.

> It must have been about three o'clock in the morning, just before daylight, when I heard it—a gun-two guns! . . . Maybe I was dreaming? I did not think what to do! Then I was awake. I heard rapidly about four gunshots across there to the west. . . . This gunfire made me wide awake. Then came three volleys from many rifles, followed by shouting of soldiers. (McWhorter, 1995, 115)

In less than a half hour, Colonel Gibbon had seized most of the upper camp. The lower portion of the camp had not been captured; that mission had been detailed to the volunteers, under Lieutenant James H. Bradley. Swinging around the perimeter, the volunteers charged; Bradley was killed. Without leadership, the volunteers did not press their attack, leaving the lower half of the village as a rallying point for the Nez Perce.

It was from that portion of the village that Five Wounds, Rainbow, White Bird, and Looking Glass rallied the warriors, and quickly turned the surprise attack into a counter coup. Joseph related what happened. "He charged upon us while some of my people were still asleep. We had a hard fight. Some of my men crept around and attacked the soldiers from the rear." (Cozzens, 310) The infantry was on the valley floor and completely surrounded by hostile Indians, and they received the same murderous fire they had recently inflicted on the Nez Perce. Colonel Gibbon was shot through the thigh. Realizing that his command was too

A U.S. Army 12-pound mountain howitzer preserved at Fort Laramie Wyoming, the standard artillery piece used during the wars against the Indians in the Pacific Northwest. (*Author*)

small, he ordered his men to retreat. So as to deprive the Indians of their supplies, he ordered the village burned.

Unbeknownst to the colonel, many of the Nez Perce children were hidden within the tepees, resulting in some being burned alive. Adding to the smoke of the gunfire, the soldiers prepared to retreat under the cover of a burning village. Seemingly lost in the din of gunfire were the cries of the wounded and the pleas for help from the children trapped within the burning village. Captured in the memory of both whites and Nez Perce participants was an image that summed up the brutality of this battle. An Indian mother lay dead, on her back. On her naked chest was her infant, still alive, crying in pain, as it held one arm up, flaying helplessly since the arm had been broken by a bullet.

Covering the main body's movement to the wooded hillside, Gibbon ordered Captain Rawn's I Company to cover the men. One corporal, Charles Loynes, related what happened. "Then the discipline of the regular soldier showed itself, for the company formed under fire and advanced toward the Indians. On they went, over dead and wounded soldiers and Indians. The move was simply to cover the retreat of the main body, who were to fall back, cross the creek, and fortify as best they could on the side of the hill." (Cozzens, 436)

Once on the hill, the Nez Perce kept them under siege that day and all the next. The mountain howitzer was brought up, but fired only two ineffective rounds before the Nez Perce captured and destroyed it. Snipers kept deadly fire[42] pouring into the hastily dug rifle pits.

That afternoon, the Indians tried to burn the soldiers out, but the grass was too damp to burn rapidly, merely smoldering slowly along, adding more smoke to the hellish environment of the field. Many, including Colonel Gibbon, thought during the battle that the regiment was in serious trouble, and the number seven must be an unlucky regiment number. "I tell you, Major Clark, that we hadn't been in that fight but a short time when I thought it would be another Custer massacre." (Haines, 113)

While keeping the infantry pinned down until dark, on August 10, the Nez Perce gathered their people and fled further south and now east.

The Battle of Big Hole was another army defeat. Colonel Gibbons' command suffered thirty-two dead and thirty-seven wounded. Of the seventeen officers in the command, fourteen were killed or wounded. The Nez Perce also suffered heavy casualties. Eighty-nine Nez Perce were killed, many of them women and children killed in the initial attack.[43] Among the leaders slain were Five Wounds and Rainbow.

On the morning of August 11, General Howard's scout elements rode into the valley, only to find another decimated command. On August 12, the rest of Howard's forces gathered and resumed their pursuit the next day.

42. One interesting feature of the rifle fire was that the Nez Perce used exploding bullets against the soldiers, apparently captured while raiding settlers' cabins. "In addition to being commercially available, such particularly lethal bullets could be made by boring a hole of the right size to accept a .22 caliber shell in the blunt nose of a large-caliber bullet. The base of the rim-fire .22 cartridge, upon striking something solid, like bones of a charging grizzly bear, blew up the larger bullet with frightful effect. Without a Geneva Convention to restrict them, the Nez Perce used whatever came to hand." (Haines, 88)

43. One of the Montana volunteers, John Catlin, provided his explanation for the women and children killed. "You may ask why did we kill the women and children. We answer that when we came up on the second charge, we found that the women were using the Winchesters with as much skill and as bravely as did the bucks. As to the children, though many were killed, we do not think a citizen or soldier killed a child on purpose." (Cozzens, 446) Contrasting that is Yellow Wolf's account of the women and children killed. "This tepee here was standing and silent. Inside we found the two women lying in their blankets dead; both had been shot. The mother had her newborn baby in her arms. Its head was smashed, as by a gun breech or boot heel. The mother had two other children, both killed, in another tepee. Some soldiers acted with crazy minds." (McWhorter, 1995, 132)

Moving southeasterly toward Idaho's Lemhi Valley, the Nez Perce raided for lost supplies. They seized 250 horses and killed four whites. In Idaho, they attacked a freight wagon train, killing another five whites. Howard's indecision caused needless delay, and when he crossed into Idaho he was a full day's march behind the Indians.

On August 19, Howard camped on Camas Meadows, where the Nez Perce had been that morning. Using the best rested cavalry mounts, Major Sanford sent forty troopers under Lieutenant George Bacon to scout for the Nez Perce.

Yellow Wolf (*Library of Congress*)

The scouts need not have left. As the tired command slept that night, two hundred Nez Perce attacked in the hopes of seizing, or at least running off, the pursuing army's mounts. Displaying their superior ability to use sound military tactics, the Nez Perce had about forty Indians ride slowly into the army camp by riding in fours abreast,[44] as if they were the returning cavalry under Lieutenant Bacon. The sentries never even challenged the disciplined Indians. Having gained the camp, the forty Nez Perce made their raid while the rest of the Indians created a diversion. Unable to run off the cavalry horses, the Nez Perce captured 150 mules needed to transport army supplies. Yellow Wolf's description sums up the first round of the battle.

> The soldier camp was alarmed. The bugle sounded quickly. The
> warriors were yelling and shooting fast. They had circled the sol-

44. McWhorter's interview of the Nez Perce discounts the "Four Abreast" tactic as white justification for inattention by the tired sentries. Peopeo Tholekt, one of those selected to infiltrate the herd, said, "We rode the Indian way, in three different bunches." Another Nez Perce, Wottolen, said, "Indians do not ride like that. We were divided into three companies and rode in Indian style." (McWhorter, 2001, 416-417)

diers' horses, stampeding them. The soldiers were now also firing in every direction. Some young men had gone in to cut loose the horse tied, and I, Yellow Wolf, was one of them. I found three horses staked on long ropes. I cut them loose. At this time the Indians were driving the horse herd rapidly away. Mounting, I followed silently as I could with my three captured horses. After traveling a little way, driving our captured horses, sun broke. We could begin to see our prize. Getting more light, we looked. Eeh! Nothing but mules—all mules! Only my three horses among them. (McWhorter, 1995, 167-168)

On August 20, Major George B. Sanford, from Fort Halleck, Nevada, led three troops of 1st Cavalry in pursuit. Finding the herd, Sanford ordered this command to split into three, with one troop following the trail, while the other two troops swung around each side to trap the Indians in a flanking attack. The central column, led by Captain Randolph Norwood, came upon the Indians and dismounted to form a firing line. The firing became intense, but believing his flanks were protected by the two other troops, Norwood stood his ground. The two flanking troops managed to recapture some of the mules. Now encumbered with a herd of mules, the cavalry was exposed and the Nez Perce counter-attacked.

The attack was so fierce, Sanford ordered "Recall." Two of the troops, under Captains James Jackson and Camillo C. Carr, fell back, while one, Norwood's, was cut off and isolated. In the melee, Norwood found the tactical situation completely reversed as had been planned. Instead of the cavalry out-flanking the Indians, Norwood was being out-flanked. Retreating to a small wooded area, Norwood set his troop up to defend against the charging Nez Perce.

Elsewhere on the battlefield, fighting was as fierce. Captain Jackson, 1st Cavalry, saw his trumpeter shot from his saddle. Rather than abandon him to his fate, Captain Jackson dismounted in the midst of the charging Nez Perce and, with the help of another trooper, rescued the wounded trooper. For his conspicuous display of courage, Captain Jackson was awarded the Medal of Honor.

Norwood's isolated troop held up in their defensive position until Howard led a relief column to the rescue. Once again, at the Battle of Camas Meadows, the last battle fought by the Nez Perce in the Oregon

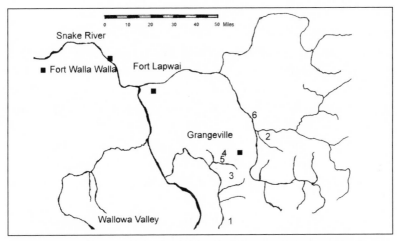

Nez Perce War Close-up. 1. Battle of White Bird Canyon. 2. Looking Glass's camp attacked. 3. Battle of Camas Prairie. 4. Lieutenant Rains attacked. 5. Skirmishes near Cottonwood, including Mount Misery. 6. Battle of Clearwater. (*Author*)

Country, the Indians had soundly beaten the U.S. Army. While casualties were relatively light, two killed and seven wounded, the defeat stopped Howard again. Worse, in not pursuing, Howard left a blocking force at Targhee Pass unsupported and uninformed. Those soldiers assumed the Nez Perce must not have tried their pass and abandoned their blocking action.

On August 22, the Nez Perce used Targhee Pass to enter Yellowstone National Park, crossing the Continental Divide, thus finally leaving the Oregon Country.

Howard's troops were now exhausted and needed supplies from the nearest towns after losing much from Nez Perce raids. Both his commanders and his medical staff declared his troops unfit for further efforts until given plenty of rest. As the Nez Perce raided through Yellowstone, killing two hapless tourists, Howard called for his command to rest beside Henry's Lake, in Idaho, and then rode to Virginia City, Montana to buy supplies and confer, via telegraph, with higher command.

Ironically, a recent tourist to Yellowstone National Park was Howard's commanding General of the Army, William Tecumseh Sherman. While still in Helena, General Sherman received General Howard's telegraph on August 24, proposing that General Terry's command (Terry was absent on assignment in the east) take over, and that the Department of the Columbia troops slowly retire to Fort Boise, the nearest fort within Howard's department. This proposal was met with scorn and ridicule. Sherman replied, "That force of yours should pursue the Nez Perce to the death, lead where they may. . . . If you are tired, give command to some young energetic officer." (Utley, 1973, 309)

With these and other critical words from Howard's division commander, General Irvin McDowell, Howard promised his renewed efforts and, on August 28, the Department of the Columbia forces resumed the chase.

General Sheridan, commanding the Division of the Missouri, of which Terry's Department of the Dakota was a portion, ordered two cavalry units to move to block the Nez Perce's escape from the Yellowstone Region onto the plains of Montana. Colonel Wesley Merritt led a squadron of 5th Cavalry to block the Nez Perce's escape from the park via the Shoshone River, then called the Stinking Water River. The Clark Fork River was ordered guarded by elements of the 7th Cavalry, with six troops under the command of Samuel D. Sturgis. But, Merritt could not reach his assignment right away so the 7th Cavalry had to cover both exits.

As the 7th Cavalry was stretched thin, the Nez Perce used a ploy to draw the cavalry off. In an effort to confuse the cavalrymen, the Indians had some warriors ride to the south, dragging brush behind their horse to simulate a larger number of Indians.

On September 8, a 7th Cavalry patrol spotted what was taken as the fleeing Nez Perce heading south and Sturgis immediately ordered his troopers to concentrate and attack the fleeing Nez Perce. As the 7th Cavalry prepared to attack, the truth became apparent that the Nez Perce had out-soldiered the Army again. The Nez Perce had marched along the unguarded Clark Fork to the north and east of Yellowstone Park and escaped onto the plains north of Yellowstone. Sturgis had been deceived so far south that Howard had time to exit the park in pursuit of the Nez Perce before the 7th Cavalry could catch up, combining both forces on September 11.

As the Nez Perce raided the countryside, killing some white settlers, Sturgis proposed he ride hard and overtake the Nez Perce. Howard's tired command was unable to proceed any faster and he agreed to allow

Sturgis, reinforced by Major Sanford's 1st Cavalry, to hasten his pursuit of the Nez Perce.

Along the Yellowstone River, on September 13, Sturgis found the Nez Perce with a captured stagecoach. Fording the river, Sturgis deployed his cavalry for the attack. Retreating up a gap in the canyon that forms the north bank of the river, the Nez Perce fought a delaying action to allow the women and children to escape. Forced to follow the Indians up the gulley, without the ability to maneuver his cavalry, Sturgis failed, as had every previous commander. Because of the terrain, Sturgis was forced to fight with his cavalry largely dismounted, as infantry, advancing for over eight miles against well-concealed Nez Perce.

The Indians held the high ground, and fired with great effect at the slowly advancing troopers. Sturgis believed his one hope was to send a squadron of troopers to the southwest, gain the heights elsewhere, and sweep back toward the mouth of the canyon. Toward that end, Captain Frederick W. Benteen led his men in the sweeping cavalry charge, only to find the hills were already occupied by Nez Perce sharpshooters. Twice Benteen charged, only to be repulsed.

Unable to out flank the Nez Perce, Sturgis was faced, at best, with another stalemate siege. The Battle of Canyon Creek ended as all previous battles: the Nez Perce escaped, leaving the whites to bury the dead (three) and tend the wounded (eleven). Three Nez Perce warriors were wounded.

It became apparent to Howard that the Nez Perce were pacing themselves to his advance. If he attempted to hasten his advance, the Nez Perce hurried. If Howard slowed, the Indians relaxed a little to rest their own weary people. Using this information, Howard proposed he would slow his march to about a dozen miles a day, thus slowing the Nez Perce, and providing time for another force to march ahead to intercept the fleeing Indians. This interception force was created by Colonel Nelson A. Miles. He was able to gather a force of over 400 men using four companies of 5th Infantry (mounted), three troops of 2nd Cavalry, three troops of 7th Cavalry, and about thirty Indian scouts. Colonel Miles quickly rode northwest to intercept.

On September 23, the Nez Perce crossed the Missouri River near the Musselshell River, and discovered an army supply dump. At first, the Nez Perce asked for supplies; Sergeant William Moelchert of Company B, 7th U.S. Infantry, commanding, refused. Pleading for the women and children, the Nez Perce were given a side of bacon and some hardtack. This did not appease their hunger, so the Nez Perce attacked the eleven-man squad guarding the dump.

Throughout the night, gunfire was exchanged. Keeping the soldiers pinned down behind their barricade; the Nez Perce raided the supply dump for the much needed food and ammunition. According to Peopeo Tholekt, "We took whatever we needed, flour, sugar, coffee, bacon, and beans. Anything whoever we wanted it. Some took pans and pots for cooking. We figured it was soldiers supplies, so set fire to what we did not take. We had privileges to do this. It was in the war." (McWhorter, 2001, 471) One warrior was hit and two civilian teamsters were wounded in the fight.

Resupplied, the Nez Perce then proceeded north at a reduced pace, believing they had out-marched Howard's command, and resting as much as they could. Major Guido Ilges reached the ransacked supply dump the morning after the attack. Following the slow moving Nez Perce, he was able to report on their location to the fast moving Miles column.

On September 29, near the Bear Paw Mountains and on Snake Creek, the Nez Perce camped. The next morning, Miles deployed his troops to attack the Nez Perce village.

The order of battle had two squadrons of cavalry move to the left. Captain George H. Tyler led the 2nd Cavalry to the left and attacked the pony herd to deny the Nez Perce their needed mounts. Meanwhile, also from the left, Captain Owen Hale led the squadron from the 7th Cavalry in a charge directly at the Nez Perce village. Supporting the 7th Cavalry was Captain Simon Snyder, leading the mounted elements of the 5th Infantry.

Upon hearing the attack, the Nez Perce assumed a strong defensive position in the coulees feeding into the Snake Creek basin. Unable to defend the ponies, the Nez Perce repulsed the 7th Cavalry, forcing them to dismount to take cover from the deadly rifle fire that had marked all of the battles with the Nez Perce. The 7th Cavalry remained pinned down until the 5th Infantry came up and took the ridge. This forced the Nez Perce to retreat to protect their village.

The damage had been severe to the 7th Cavalry. Thirty men had been killed and thirty-eight wounded. More significantly, the Nez Perce had concentrated their fire on the men leading the 7th's charge. Only one

The Canyon Creek battlefield located north of Laurel, Montana. (*Author*)

officer in the 7th Cavalry was left unhurt; all of the first sergeants had been killed. With the 7th largely leaderless, Miles ordered no more charges and instituted a siege. He ordered his howitzer to open fire and sharpshooters to pin the Indians down.

The Nez Perce were trapped. They had no ponies, many were dead, including Chief Toohoolhoolzote, and the weather worsened, with five inches of snow falling on their trapped encampment. Miles took advantage of their misery and advanced under a white flag to ask for their surrender. Looking Glass and White Bird urged resistance, but Joseph agreed to talk.

As the talks progressed, it became apparent that there would be no Nez Perce surrender. Colonel Miles then broke his own truce and captured Chief Joseph. The plan failed when an officer, believing peace was at hand, came too close to the Nez Perce and was captured, forcing an exchange of prisoners. Miles' treachery strengthened the Nez Perce's resistance.

For the next four days the siege continued. Random shots were fired by both side's sharpshooters, shooting at anything or anyone who moved.

On October 5, Howard arrived with an advance party. Until now, the Nez Perce's hope had been that Chief Sitting Bull would respond to their messengers' pleas for help and ride to their relief. With Howard's arrival, it became apparent that the additional soldiers had eliminated all hope. The Nez Perce chiefs met in council again. Joseph argued for surrender while White Bird and Looking Glass wanted to try to flee for Canada. Before any decision could be reached, a sharpshooter saw the movement within the Indian camp and fired. Looking Glass was killed instantly by a bullet to his forehead.

Chief Joseph handing rifle to General Nelson Miles as a gesture of surrender. (*Frank Leslie's illustrated newspaper, November 3, 1877; Library of Congress*)

Chief Joseph met with Colonel Miles and agreed to surrender under the terms that they would be returned to Idaho the following spring. Four hundred Nez Perce followed Chief Joseph into surrender. Remarkably, another three-hundred Nez Perce escaped under White Bird's leadership and reached Sitting Bull's camp in Canada. Within a month, the federal government broke the terms of the surrender, forcing the Nez Perce onto a reservation in Kansas then transferring them to the Indian Territory. The Nez Perce would not be allowed to return to the Oregon Country until 1885. Chief Joseph would die on the Colville Indian Reservation in northern Washington, never allowed to return to the Nez Perce reservation.

The Nez Perce fought the greatest fighting retreat in American Indian history. They covered over 1,700 miles of some of the most rugged terrain of North America. They fought seven major engagements and many skirmishes, out-fighting the army[45] every time, until overwhelmed by fatigue, weather, and a numerically superior force. They lost approximately 120 members of their tribe, of which half were women and children. The whites had about 180 dead and 150 wounded, the vast majority of whom were soldiers. The Nez Perce cause was just and helped persuade the general public of the need for greater protection of Indian rights.

45. They out-fought an army led by battle tested, experienced soldiers. Most of the field commanders including Howard, Gibbon, Miles and Sturgis had been corps commanders in the Civil War, and others held general rank as well.

The press recognized and helped promote the Indian cause. As the *New York Times* noted in its editorial of October 15, 1877, "We freely express the opinion that the Nez Perce War was, on the part of our government, an unpardonable and frightful blunder. . . . A crime whose victims are. . . the peaceful bands who were goaded by injustice and wrong to take the war path." (Haines, 119) It is a fitting epitaph for a war that never should have been fought.

~

The Modoc War was fought in a very small geographical area and is one of the better preserved wars of the Northwest. All the sights are within one day's drive of each other. To linger at each site would make for a longer stay, and well worth it.

The place to start is at Fort Klamath. It was from here that the cavalry went to get the Modoc, and it was here that the Modoc were brought, at the end of the war. A small county park and museum occupies the old post parade grounds southeast of Crater Lake National Park, on Oregon Highway 62. Also at the park are the graves of the four Modoc hung at the post, as a result of their acts of murder.

Heading south, the next stop should be at Klamath Falls, known at the time as Linkville. The county museum is located downtown and is an excellent place to gain more information about the entire region, as well as the fighting during the war.

Continuing southeasterly on Oregon Highway 39, which becomes California 139 at the border, the road follows the Lost River. While the river has been tamed and controlled for agricultural, it stills acts as an oasis in the arid valley.

Once in California, several sights beckon the visitor. A drive south from Lakeview will take you to the Fort Bidwell Indian Reservation where Fort Bidwell had once been; it is located northeast of Alturas, California, off of U.S. Highway 395. If the drive south is from Klamath Falls, then continue south on California 139, past the town of Tule Lake; follow the signs to the Tule Lake National Wildlife Refuge and Lava Beds National Monument. From the northeast, the road will skirt the southern edge of the lake and enter the National Park Service's preservation of the historical sights.

The first of these is Hospital Rock. It provides a scenic overview of the lake and commemorates the site where Lieutenant Sherwood was killed. A short drive takes you to Captain Jack's Stronghold. Two trails lead into the stronghold, transporting the visitor back into time. It is easy to see how so few Indians could hold off so many troops in the rugged abyss of lava, caves, and sage brush.

Next on the park's road is Canby's Cross. The interpretive sight explains well what happened on Good Friday at the location of the peace tent. Just another short drive is Gillem's Camp and an opportunity to see the conditions the troops stayed in for the long siege.

Driving south, toward the park's headquarters, a wayside marks the trail to the Thomas-Wright Battlefield. The walk is worth the time spent; from there it is another ten minutes drive to the Lava Beds visitor's center.

Outside of the National Monument, to the southeast, again along California Highway 139, are three sites. First, near the junction of county road 114 with 139 is the site of the Battle of Lands Ranch. Further to the southwest, to the west of Casuse Mountain, on jeep tracks, near country road 128, is the site of the two battles of Scorpion Point. Finally, there is the site of the Battle of Dry Lake located at the northeast corner of the lake. It is accessible via a jeep road (four wheel drive) from the intersection of Highway 139, and county road 136 (the jeep track leads to the southwest).

Few Indian wars are as close geographically, and few have so many of the major locations well preserved and marked. The Nez Perce War has many sites well preserved, but to visit each would require several days, since the locations are scattered in four different states. From the west, the best place to start is within Oregon's extreme northeast corner. The Wallowa Valley is still a scenic draw, and south of the town of Joseph, is Old Joseph's grave. The removal of the Nez Perce from their historic homeland was the impetus for war.

From near Lewiston, Idaho, the historic trail leads to many of the sites mentioned. Not necessarily in chronological order, the sites are mentioned in the rough order of approach. An excellent place to start is the visitor's center of the Nez Perce National Historical Park near the junction of U.S. Highways 12 and 95. The National Park Services efforts help to explain the history of the Nez Perce people and provide important information for finding the historical sites.

The Wallowa Valley. (*Author*)

If you proceed south on U.S. 95, the two major sites to visit are Fort Lapwai and the battlefield of Cottonwood. The old army post still has one original building on the old post's parade grounds. It was from here that Captain Perry rode hard to the south and his defeat at White Bird Canyon. Further south, near mile post 252, is a state of Idaho roadside historical marker explaining the fight at Cottonwood. South of the town of Cottonwood is a National Park Service sign that also documents the Cottonwood skirmishes.

If from the visitor's center you had proceeded east on Highway 12, the highway would eventually take you to Lolo Pass and the Nez Perce's first crossing of the Continental Divide. Prior to leaving the immediate area, proceed south on Idaho 13 toward Grangeville. South of the town of Stites is the site of the Clearwater Battlefield. Near mile post 21 is an Idaho State roadside marker, and nearby is a National Park sign helping to explain the events of July 11th and 12, 1877.

From where Idaho 13 joins U.S. 95, head south. A short drive out of Grangeville is the site of the Camas Prairie, the location where the first settlers were killed. It is marked by a roadside sign (near mile post 233) placed by the State of Idaho, and another sign nearby placed by the National Park Service. Just over the pass is the White Bird Battlefield. An auto tour guide is available and helps bring the battle in to clear explanation.

Just as the Nez Perce fled over the mountains into Montana, so does the historical trail. South of Missoula, on Montana Highway 43, is the Big Hole National Battlefield, part of the National Park Service. The park preserves the surprise attack by the 7th Infantry and helps to interpret the success of the Nez Perce in routing the Army.

The Battle of Camas Meadows is marked along Interstate 15 at the Dubois Rest Area, mile post 167, by the State of Idaho. The actual location of the battle is nearer to Kilgore, Idaho, on Clark County road A2. From there the trail leads to Henry's Lake, U.S. Highway 20, and the Targhee Pass, by which the Nez Perce left the Oregon Country for the last time. From West Yellowstone the Nez Perce entered Yellowstone National Park. On the road to Old Faithful is a roadside historical marker detailing what happened within the park.

The Nez Perce fled the park to the northeast. Just to the west of Billings is the commemorative marker for the Battle of Canyon Creek. Little more than a stone marker is to be found on Montana 532, north from the town of Laurel, but the country is little changed. It is easy to visualize the fighting as the Nez Perce covered their retreat up the canyon. The final site is Bear Paw Battlefield National Historical Park. The National Park Service has a unit located south of Chinook on U.S. Highway 2.

To visit the sites of the Nez Perce War is a long drive and a long journey, just as it was for the Indians. However, with many of the important locations marked, and many with rich interpretative restorations, the ability to capture not only the history, but the feel and texture of the war, makes the trip a worthwhile vacation.

Chapter 8

The Last Wars

The Bannock (1878) and Sheepeaters (1879) Wars

T he last two wars the Army fought within the Oregon Country were with tribes related to each other. They could almost be said to be episodes of the same war, fought over the course of two years. Both were most likely started by the actions of Bannocks and were fought by Bannocks or allied Indian tribes.

In 1877, the Bannock Indians were centered on two reservations, both in southeastern Idaho Territory. About six hundred Bannocks lived at the Fort Hall Reservation, while on the Lemhi Reservation, the mixture of Bannocks, Shoshonis, and Sheepeaters numbered about nine hundred.

The Sheepeaters were a tribe of mixed heritage, including many intermarried Bannocks and Shoshonis. Two traditional allies of the Bannocks were the Paiutes and Western Shoshonis, with the three tribes collectively referred to as Snake Indians. The Paiutes and Western Shoshonis tribes numbered about 8,000 Indians living mostly in northern Nevada, southern Idaho, and southeastern Oregon. The Bannocks had signed a peace treaty at Fort Bridger in 1867,[1] ending their limited part in the earlier Snake Indian War. Besides the two reservations, they had been ceded a traditional camas plant harvesting area about ninety miles northeast of Boise known as the Camas Prairie. Unfortunately, a government secretary had transcribed the treaty inaccurately providing for the Bannock's (and other tribes) continual access to the "Kansas Prairie" of Idaho, a place which did not exist.

1. General C.C. Augur negotiated the treaty with the principal leaders of the Bannock, Chiefs Taghee and Waskakie.

Despite this problem, the Indians and the whites at first lived peacefully together with each using the Camas Prairie. However, as the number of whites increased, so did their use of the prairie for grazing. Not only did the whites over-graze the prairie, they let their hogs dig for insects, which destroyed the camas bulbs.

The Bannock War

The leader of the Bannocks from the Lemhi Reservation was known as Buffalo Horn.[2] Whites and Indians respected him as a warrior. He had scouted for the Army against the Sioux and again when the army pursued the Nez Perce. One lesson learned from his Army service was contempt for the whites as warriors, particularly after the Nez Perce War.

As the Indians gathered, as they did each spring on the Camas Prairie, there was interaction not only with the Bannocks under Buffalo Horn, but Paiutes from Chief Winnemucca's people from the upper Owyhee River and Chief Egan's Paiutes from the Malheur Agency. Indians from as far away as the Umatilla Reservation, in northeastern Oregon, gathered on the prairie. As the Indians spoke, they pronounced not only their contempt of the whites, but anger at the destruction of their life, as witnessed on the Camas Prairie. War fervor swept through the traditional war societies of the area Indians.

Tensions had already been running high. In August 1877, Indians from the Fort Hall Reservation killed two whites. In seeking out the culprits, the Indian agents had increased disquiet to the point that Colonel John E. Smith had led three companies of the 14th Infantry from Camp Douglas, Utah, to the reservation, and had temporarily arrested fifty-three of the Bannock instigators. One chief, Tambiago, was executed, while his father and two brothers were exiled to Omaha Barracks. This incident added to the resentment of the Indians, voiced by Tambiago prior to his hanging. When asked why they had killed the whites, Tambiago gave several reasons, two of which were stark warning. He said that his people were being mistreated by the agent (and missionary) at Fort Hall Reservation, and the continuous destruction of the Camas

2. Chief Taghee, the most respected and influential of the Bannock chiefs, had died in 1871, leaving a leadership void until the emergence of Buffalo Horn, in 1876. General Howard described Buffalo Horn as a "handsome young Indian covered with plumage and dressed in skins." (Cozzens, 606)

An illustration of Bannock Indians in the July 6, 1878, issue of Harpers Weekly as part of a report on the Bannock War titled, "Indian Troubles." (*Library of Congress*)

Prairie by whites. Further, Tambiago said that Chief Buffalo Horn was planning to lead a war party to avenge the insults and damage done to the Bannock. No action was taken, either on the complaints or on the warning on impending war.

Other reservation agents had voiced warnings of war. Agent William V. Rhinehart,[3] formerly a major with the 1st Oregon Cavalry at Fort Klamath, reported talk of war by the Paiutes at the Malheur Reservation as well as Bannock showing up around the nearby settlement of Burns, Oregon. But the remoteness of the reservation delayed the arrival of Rhinehart's message until events elsewhere had already proved his warning to be accurate.

As the Indians gathered on the Camas Prairie the next spring, they found that more whites had come and, consequently, were destroying their precious food, the camas root, or bulb. The pressure on their whole traditional life came to a head. As the whites' animals, particularly pigs, destroyed the camas plants, the Bannocks, under Buffalo Horn, attacked three whites grazing stock on the prairie. Two were wounded on May 30, 1878 and all escaped to tell of the attack.

3. While serving with the 1st Oregon Cavalry, Rhinehart had earned a reputation of cruelty to both the Indians and his troopers. As one source points out, a principle reason for the Paiute's willingness to think of joining the Bannock in war was in no small measure to Rhinehart's lack of integrity and ineffectiveness as an Indian agent.

Buffalo Horn had decided that now was the time for a war party. Leading about two hundred warriors of his Bannocks, plus some Paiutes and Umatillas, Buffalo Horn raided across southern Idaho.

On May 31, from nearby Boise Barracks, came veteran Indian campaigner Captain Reuben F. Bernard and his troop of 1st Cavalry to track Buffalo Horn's war party. At first, the trail headed east toward the craggy lava strewn landscape of today's Craters of the Moon National Monument. Fearing another lava redoubt, such as Bernard knew too well from fighting the Modoc, the cavalry increased its pace. Arriving at a recently abandoned camp, G Troop knew its pace was putting pressure on Buffalo Horn. From the camp, the trail turned south and west toward the Snake River. At the King Hill stagecoach station, the evidence was clear that the wranglers manning the station had fled at the sight of the war party. The Indians had paused long enough to loot the station.

From the stage trail, the Indians headed toward a crossing point on the Snake River, Glenn's Ferry. Bernard knew that if the Bannock made it across, they would have a large lead on the pursuers. G Troop spurred on their horses, now growing spent by the hundreds of miles of hard riding. The race went to the Bannocks.

Reaching Glenn's Ferry, the Bannocks burnt the station, used the ferry to cross the river, and then cast the ferry adrift. Having reached the south bank, the Bannock found new targets to plunder. A freight train of wagons was nearby and made an inviting target. From there the Bannock continued riding westward, toward the Oregon border.

As the Indians scoured the area, ten white settlers were killed. As Bernard followed, he found the evidence of the attacks, and often had to slow to tend to the wounded. At one stop, where a telegraph was available, Bernard wired General Howard to bring him up to date. The first thought for reinforcements was to send the infantry from Fort Boise.

Major Patrick Collins, 21st Infantry, started south with instructions to join Captain Bernard's cavalry. They joined up near Mundy's Ferry where Bernard had gone to make his crossing to receive reinforcements. There, the two forces followed the lead, heading southeast toward Silver City, Idaho. Meanwhile, Howard was ordering more forces out to defend the area. Not only was the Army throughout the region ordered to the alert, volunteers quickly gathered to protect their homes.

On June 8, 1878, twenty Idaho volunteers from Silver City, under Captain J.B. Harper, discovered Buffalo Horn's camp and attacked. On a creek named for the incident, the whites charged into the camp with complete surprise. Buffalo Horn quickly led a mounted counterattack, scattering the whites from Battle Creek; he was shot from his horse and killed in the short battle. With even more reason for war, the Indians sought new leadership and headed west to Steen Mountain and the leaders of the Paiute, Egan, Winnemucca, and a shaman named Oytes.

As the Indians fled west, they continued to raid. On one stagecoach captured, the Indians found two crates of Winchester rifles, and several boxes of ammunition. The rifles were greatly esteemed for the ability to fire without reloading after each shot.

With reports of other pillaging, Captain Bernard pursued. By June 12, Bernard's 1st Cavalry had reached Sheep Ranch, Oregon, on the Jordan River, near its confluence with the Owyhee River.

Fearing a repeat of the debacle of the Nez Perce War, General Howard took field command and ordered additional troops to the area. He planned a three-column advance to cut off the Indians. The right column was under the command of Major Joseph Stewart who had D and G Companies of his own 4th Artillery, as well as Companies B, D, G, H, and I of the 21st Infantry. The left column, reinforced and reequipped at Fort Harney, was organized under Captain Bernard, who had A, F, G, and L Troops, 1st Cavalry now under his command. The 1st Cavalry's Colonel, Cuvier Grover, commanded the center column. His cavalry, D, I and K Troops, was under Major Sanford, while he was supported as well by F Company, 2nd Infantry.

General Howard ordered additional forces as support for the engaged troops or to block an Indian escape. Captain Harry C. Egbert, 12th Infantry, had five companies of infantry acting as a reserve while two blocking forces were created. Captain John Egan, 4th Artillery, had two artillery companies as well as two companies of 12th U.S. Infantry stationed just below the Oregon-Nevada border at Camp McDermitt. Colonel Frank Wheaton lead his 2nd Infantry troops from Fort Walla Walla to patrol the Columbia River[4], thus containing the hostile Indians in Oregon.

---

4. Making sure the Indians could not cross the Columbia to flee to the north, or Indians wishing to cross to join the warring Indians in the south, General Howard commissioned three steamers as his "navy." The *Welcome*, *Northwest*, and *Spokane* were outfitted with howitzers and Gatling guns. One ship, the *Spokane* attacked a group of Indians on the Washington shore on July 8; one Indian was reported to have been wounded.

Having prevented the Indians from conducting a campaign such as the Nez Perce had, General Howard was reassured because of his troop numbers and their deployment; therefore, recognizing the Indians' legitimate claim to the Camas Prairie, Howard preferred a peaceful solution. He found a peace emissary in the person of Sarah Winnemucca, daughter of the chief. She went to the Indian camp at the base of Steen Mountain, but found the desire for war high. She barely escaped with a few Indians who sought peace, including her father, and returned to the Sheep Ranch on June 15, 1878.

With this overture a failure, Howard ordered the columns to advance. On June 23, Captain Bernard found the Indians had moved and were now camped on Silver Creek, northwest of Steen Mountain. At daybreak, Bernard had his scouts, under Orlando Robbins, attack from upstream, making as much noise as possible, but with instructions not to engage too closely. Robbins' mission was to scare the Indians downstream to the south and away from the hills. Waiting out on the flats was the rest of the command.

Bernard then formed his cavalry squadron into three lines abreast, downstream from the village, and ordered the first line to charge. The surprise was complete, and despite being out-numbered by about 800 Indians[5] to 220 cavalry, Bernard led two more charges into the camp. The Indians retired across the creek to the cliffs and assumed a defensive position far too strong for a frontal attack with an inferior force. All that day, long-range rifle fire sniped at both sides. During the night, the Indians escaped.

The battle had not been bloody, though Bernard's cavalry suffered three killed and three wounded.[6] The Indians suffered few casualties as well[7], but Chief Egan had been wounded in the fighting. Reportedly, Egan saw Orlando Robbins charging through the village and met him in a head-long attack. Each had fired—the chief riding from the side of his horse using it for cover, and Robbins upright. Robbins shot Egan off his

---

5. One source puts the village at 2,000 Indians, with half being warriors (Glassley, 231-232).

6. Glassley puts the troops' losses as five killed, "and several times that number wounded." (Ibid, 233)

7. Glassley lists the Indians as having over one hundred killed and an indeterminate number wounded. (Ibid, 233)

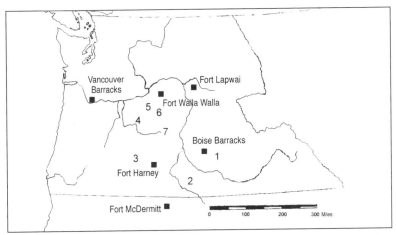

Bannock War Overview. 1 Camas Prairie 2. Battle of Battle Creek 3 Battle of Silver Creek 4. Battle of Birch Creek 5. Battle of Umanta Reservation 6. Skirmish at Meacham's 7. Skirmish on the John Day (*Author*)

horse by hitting him in the wrist, and then fired again when Egan stood to withstand Robbins' new charge. The next shot hit Egan in the chest. Worse for the Indians, a large portion of their supplies had been destroyed when they abandoned their camp. As they fled north, they killed white settlers in revenge.

Howard rode ahead of the center column and joined Bernard in his pursuit. Reinforced to a total strength of seven companies of 1st Cavalry, Bernard caught up with the fleeing Indians as they neared the Umatilla Reservation. On July 8, 1878, on Birch Creek near Pilot Butte, Bernard led another dawn attack against the Indians. Once again Bernard charged three times, renewing his attack each time the Indians retreated uphill and reformed a defensive line. Again the Indians fled, and again they lost their precious supplies. Bernard's command suffered one killed and five wounded.

As the Indians eluded the Army, they encountered a column of fifty white volunteers and on July 9, at Willow Springs, a fight occurred in which five volunteers were killed. The battle was insignificant except for the seemingly relentless pressure the Indians were now feeling. The fleeing Indians were being hemmed in. Behind them was Captain Bernard's 1st Cavalry. To the northeast was another 1st Cavalry force under Major George Sanford. Moving north from John Day was Captain Miles with mounted infantry. Hungry and harassed, the Indians needed respite and rode to the Umatilla Reservation. As the Indians reached part of the reservation, so did Captain Miles' column, now reinforced. Miles marched onto the reservation with seven companies of the 21st Infantry, two companies of the 4th Artillery, and one troop of the 1st Cavalry.

On July 13, Miles and the hostile Indians fought a battle lasting all day. With his large force, Miles ordered an advance, and literally swept the hostiles before him.

Significantly, the Umatillas, on their own reservation, remained neutral under a white flag. Fearing the destruction of their homes, the majority of the Umatillas now wanted nothing more to do with war. Wary of the consequences of the conflict that had spread to their own country, the Umatillas followed the retreating Bannocks and Paiutes and, pledging their alliance, instead betrayed their former friends by killing Chief Egan on July 14, 1878.

That same day, Colonel Wheaton arrived at the reservation from Fort Walla Walla with Lieutenant Colonel James Forsyth of the 1st Cavalry. Assuming command of the 1st Cavalry, Colonel Forsyth resumed the pursuit. The next day, Major Sanford's cavalry skirmished with the Indians near Meachem's Station, in the Blue Mountains. While not significant, the action kept pressure on the Indians.

Overtaking the Indians' rear-guard on July 20, a brief skirmish took place near the headwaters of the John Day River. Another 1st Cavalry trooper was killed and five wounded. To the Indians, the pursuit and pressure seemed relentless and they had nowhere to seek respite. By the end of July, the large war party was splitting up and small bands were either seeking surrender or escape. It must have seemed an omen to the defeated Indians when the stark landscape of the desert was darkened by a partial solar eclipse on July 31.

On August 12, the shaman Oytes surrendered with his Paiutes at the Malheur Agency. Others trickled in to other reservations or gave up to nearby Army units

Many fled east. Some fled into the wilderness of Idaho and joined their cousins, the Sheepeaters, while the more desperate sought the protection on the other side of the continental divide.

On August 25, near Henrys Lake, Wyoming, Bannock attacked a government survey party. In coming to the aid of the surveyors, Captain James Egan attacked a Bannock camp on August 27, still camped near the lake.

The site of the Battle of Birch Creek is located in Oregon's Battle Mountain State Park. (*Author*)

On September 6, Colonel Nelson Miles found some of the Bannocks east of Yellowstone National Park and attacked, driving them west again. At the Battle of Clark's Fork Pass, Colonel Miles attacked the Indians, inflicting eleven killed (although later reports said as many as twenty-eight were killed) to his loss of three killed including two Crow Indian scouts and Captain Andrew S. Bennett, and one wounded.

Finally, the last battle of the Bannock Indian War took place outside of the Oregon Country in the Wind River region when, on September 12, Lieutenant Hoel S. Bishop led a troop of 5th Cavalry in an attack at Dry Creek. One warrior was killed and five women were captured. Slowly, the rest of the Bannocks returned to their reservations.

The Bannock Indian War was the last war fought inside the State of Oregon proper. The total casualties were estimated at nine soldiers killed and fifteen wounded, with twenty-four civilians killed and thirty-four wounded. Against this the Bannocks and their allies lost much more than the seventy-eight killed and sixty-six wounded. Camas Prairie was lost forever and the Malheur Reservation was closed, with the warring Paiutes removed to the Yakama Indian Reservation. The Bannocks were forced to remain in the far eastern portion of Idaho, never to be allowed to return to their traditional hunting grounds in eastern Oregon. The "Indian problem" was nearly resolved.

Sheepeaters War

The last war to be fought in the Oregon Country was essentially a continuation of the Bannock resistance of 1878. Some of the Bannocks had dispersed to join their relatives in the remote mountains of central Idaho. There they were welcomed by the Sheepeaters, with whom they wintered over 1878-1879.

In May 1879, word reached military authority from the Lemhi Reservation that five Chinese miners had been killed during the winter in the mountains of Idaho. While it was unclear whether it was the Bannocks or the Sheepeaters who called the rugged mountains their home, a third year of Indian warfare within the Department of the Columbia had to be avoided. Three forces were gathered and headed into the rugged wilderness to fight what would be called the Sheepeaters War.

From Boise Barracks, Captain Bernard led his veteran 1st Cavalry. From Camp Howard, near Grangeville, Idaho, Lieutenant Henry Catley commanded fifty mounted 2nd Infantry. Ultimately, Lieutenants Edward S. Farrow, 21st U.S. Infantry, and William C. Brown, 1st U.S. Cavalry, would lead twenty Umatilla Scouts,[8] with seven soldiers as sharpshooters, into the wilderness.

Conditions were ideal for the Indians and almost impossible for the U.S. troops. The snow pack was particularly heavy and the snow did not clear the passes until July. The valleys were extremely steep, making travel difficult, and the streams encountered on the valley floors were swollen, making crossings challenging. If a trail was intersected it generally was cold. When an Indian camp was found, it had long since been abandoned.

Despite intense effort, the only consequence for almost all of June and July was that the Army troops simply wore themselves out. In late July, Lieutenant Catley's command crossed a fresh trail near the Middle Fork of the Salmon River, following it through the dense brush.

On July 29, Catley was ambushed and he retreated to his pack train. Still being harassed, he retreated to higher ground. On July 30, he was attacked again on a knob known as Vinegar Hill. The Sheepeaters set the dense underbrush on fire, trying to drive the soldiers off the hill. Lieutenant Catley, in his report of the engagement, credited First

---

8. Although from the Umatilla Indian Reservation, the Indians were Cayuse.

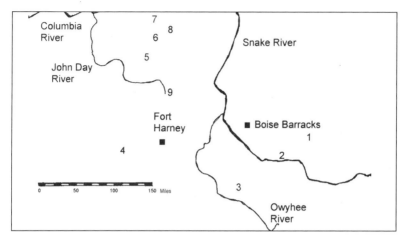

Bannock War Close-up. 1. Camas Prairie; 2. Glenn's Ferry; 3. Battle of Battle Creek; 4. Battle of Silver Creek; 5. Battle of Birch Creek/Battle Mountain; 6. Skirmish of Willow Springs; 7. Battle of Umatilla Reservation; 8. Skirmish at Meacham's Station; 9. Skirmish on the John Day River. (Author)

Sergeant John A. Sullivan, of Company C, with leading a party a short way in front of their lines, and starting a backfire, thus saving the command from being burned. Despite having a force of fifty men, Catley was successfully besieged by a force of fifteen Indians. Unable to overwhelm them, the Sheepeaters attempted to burn the whites off of the mountain. That night, abandoning their supplies, Catley's force escaped.

Disgusted with Catley's ineptness, Colonel Wheaton had him court-martialed.[9] Giving the body a new commander, Captain Albert G. Forse of 1st Cavalry and an additional twenty-five troopers, retook the field. Forse remained in better coordination with Bernard and with Farrow's Indian scouts, whose force had now taken the field.

On August 19, Bernard found an Indian camp that had to be abandoned quickly with the appearance of Army troops. Included in the camp were some of Catley's supplies lost during the July 30 battle. The Sheepeaters lost precious supplies to Bernard's cavalry.

9. Two officers in Catley's command testified against him. Lieutenant Muhlenberg stated that twice scouts reported to Catley that the Indians were near, but both reports were dismissed. Lieutenant Webster said that the night prior to the ambush, in light of the warnings, he recommended to Catley that a scouting patrol be sent out, but Catley denied Websters' request.

On August 20, as Bernard moved forward, the Sheepeaters made a surprise attack against his mule train but were driven off. In the fighting, Private Harry Eagan was hit by a bullet passing through both of his thighs. Pausing to treat the man, Private Eagan had both legs amputated. Despite the efforts of the surgeon, Eagan died and was buried at the site.[10]

Even with the overnight rest to treat private Eagan, the whole command was weary. Bernard's successes had worn out his troopers and mounts. Consequently, he brought his forces out of the mountains for refitting and returned to Boise Barracks.

By mid-September, Lieutenant Farrow was primed to resume his pursuit. As the Indians under Farrow and Brown moved through the mountains, they kept pressure on the Sheepeaters. On September 21, Farrow captured two women and two children. Hard on the Indian's trail, Farrow quickened the pace. The next morning Farrow and Brown charged into a Sheepeaters' camp only to find it had been abandoned as they neared. No one was killed but all the Indian's supplies were captured or destroyed.

Faced with unrelenting pressure, the Sheepeaters were willing to entertain peace overtures made by Farrow through the women he had captured. His offer to let the Sheepeaters surrender in peace was successful. On October 1 and 2, the remaining fifty-one fugitive Sheepeaters and a few Bannocks came to Farrow's camp and surrendered.[11] The Army oversaw the removal of the Indians to the Lemhi Reservation.

The last war was over. It was a war that did not need to be fought, and it was fought more against the elements and terrain than against Indians. However, it was a suitable ending to the struggles between the whites and the Indians. Not even the most remote areas of wilderness could offer refuge. All of the Oregon Country was now in the undisputed control of the U.S. Army.

10. In 1925, the 2nd Infantry erected a stone monument to private Eagan, in the middle of the wilderness where he was killed.

11. An interesting bit of history was just as the last Indian war was ending, former President U.S. Grant and his family were visiting Vancouver Barracks, where he had been assigned almost thirty years prior. The Grant family, accompanied by General William T. Sherman, was the guest of Major General Howard while at Vancouver Barracks.

~

M ost of the sites mentioned in the Bannock War are easily visited. Beginning where the fighting started, travel east from Boise Barracks in Boise, Idaho, as did G Troop of the 1st U.S. Cavalry, along present-day U.S. Highway 20. Near mile post 148, in the middle of the broad Camas Prairie, the State of Idaho has erected a roadside historical marker. Continue east until you reach the western edge of the rugged volcanic landscape near Carey, Idaho. A visit to the Craters of the Moon National Monument helps to understand this alien country.

The Bannock headed southwesterly, as does the time traveler. Near Interstate 84, between exits 120 and 121, is Glenn's Ferry. Here the Bannocks managed to inflict a naval victory by first crossing the Snake River on a ferry, and then burning it. Further, southwest of Murphy, on Idaho Highway 78, reached by taking gravel roads, is a ghost town. The once booming mining town of Silver City is where Buffalo Horn was killed.

Into Oregon the Bannock trail continues. Just north of Rome, Oregon, on U.S. 95, is where Sheep Ranch was, and a peace feeler was extended to the Paiute and Bannock, resting on Steen Mountain, thirty miles to the west. Along U.S. 95, near mile post 60, is a State of Oregon historical roadside marker providing detail on the Bannock's raid in the area.

From Burns Junction, take Oregon 78 to the northwest. At Crane, a road heads north, which would have been the route the cavalry would have taken as they headed to Fort Harney for fresh horses. Once the First U.S. Cavalry was resupplied, their path, as well as the history seekers, leads to the west. About fifty miles west of the junction of U.S. Highways 20 and 395, is another State of Oregon roadside marker relating the Battle of Silver Creek. A five-mile side trip up the paved road to the north finds the actual location of the battlefield, now private property.

Following the trail north, backtrack along U.S. Highway 395, through Burns, to the town of John Day. To the east, south of Prairie City, on the headwaters of the John Day River, the Army fought the fleeing Indians. The country is still as wild and scenic as when the trip could only be made on horseback.

Continuing north along U.S. Highway 395, the Battle of Birch Creek is commemorated by the State of Oregon at Battle Mountain State Park. The scenic picnic area overlooks the steep canyon the troops fought in, and is worth a stop.

A modern photograph of the Frank Church River of No Return Wilderness Area, Idaho, demonstrates that little has changed since the Battle of Vinegar Hill was fought in this area. (*Library of Congress*)

Two other sites are in Oregon. On the Umatilla Indian Reservation is a museum detailing the history of the tribes still residing on the reservation. From there, if you proceed east on Interstate 84, the small community of Meacham, a former stagecoach stop, was the site of a skirmish between the 1st U.S. Cavalry, and the fleeing Bannock.

Far more formidable is the effort to visit the sites of the Sheepeater's War. When the Army entered the mountains after the Indians, the commanders described the terrain as some of the steepest and most difficult in North America; it still is such a wilderness. The dominate feature of the war was the Salmon River, particularly the Middle Fork. None of the sites are marked.

The Battle of Vinegar Hill, which can be reached by a backpacker, is in the Frank Church River of No Return Wilderness Area, about fifteen miles east of Stibnite, an old mining ghost town on a gravel road. To the southeast of Vinegar Hill is Browns Valley, named for Lieutenant Brown. To the northeast is Farrow Mountain. All three of these features are to the west of the Middle Fork.

Also to the west, on Big Creek, is Soldier Bar Forest Service Camp, named for the area the soldiers camped on during the war. South of where Big Creek joins the Middle Fork and on that river, are Bernard's Bridge, and Bernard's U.S. Forest Service Camp. Both mark part of Captain Bernard's route into and out of the mountains as he sought the elusive Indians. This war is the least marked, and the sites are the most difficult to visit of all the wars for paradise.

Chapter 9

Sunset in Paradise

The Pacific Northwest from the Indian Wars to the End of World War II

*I*n the Pacific Northwest, after the Sheepeaters War, the fear of another Indian outbreak continued. This was particularly true as Indian wars continued in the Southwest and on the plains. No one could know that the 1891 Battle—also known as the Massacre—at Wounded Knee, would be the last.

The fear of an Indian war remained real, but faded as time passed. Every time an Indian committed an act of criminal violence, a cry of a possible Indian breakout was heard from excitable locals. Federal troops remained ready to respond, but slowly the threat diminished, as did the U.S. Army presence. Small army forts were closed or consolidated as the need for troops ready to suppress another Indian "uprising" was seen as a waste of taxpayer monies. The United States Army officially closed the Indian wars on January 11, 1905, and with it the fight for Paradise ended. The Pacific Northwest continued to participate in the defense of our country and, in fact, saw some of the only direct enemy action on the mainland during World War II, so it is appropriate to close with a short summary of the area's military contributions after the Indian Wars.

The U.S. Army in the Northwest slowly receded to a few primary military reservations. Immediately prior to World War I, Fort (Camp) Lewis became the dominant army base, but others were also used. Vancouver Barracks remained the headquarters of the Army in the Pacific Northwest; Boise Barracks, Fort Walla Walla, and numerous coastal forts continued to be of prime importance as well.

As the federal military changed, so did the states' militias. Since the creation of the United States, the chief resource during military emergencies rested with the states and the militias. Every war fought had required the states to raise troops. Although often ill-trained, the state militias were always ready to respond.

Toward the end of the Civil War, some states began renaming their militia units National Guard.[1] The name originated from Marquis de Lafayette's command of the "Garde Nationale" of the French Revolutionary era. Whatever the designation, the militia or national guard was solely a creation of the state and command authority rested solely with each state's governor.[2]

One reason for the surge in militia growth in the eastern half of the country was civil (racial) and labor unrest. In many states, Reconstruction had unintended consequences of fostering racial intolerance. Several states under reconstruction had black militia units, a continuation of the Civil War use of "colored" troops. While true of the east, blacks were not a major racial minority in the west, where Asians and Indians were often the focus of racial bigotry.

Labor unrest also stimulated the states' desire to have troops able to respond. Illinois State Militia restored order during Chicago's Haymarket riots.

Both of these trends were noted in the Pacific Northwest. While the desire to protect home and family from an attack by "savages" kept militia enlistments high, the governors of each state desired to have a force at their command. Oregon and Washington National Guards[3] were among those who demonstrated the new role for militias.

Racial prejudice incited violence not only in the South, but also in the Northwest, where bigotry was directed at the Chinese. Several Washington cities saw mob violence. The crisis climaxed on February 7, 1886.

1. The first "National Guard" was created prior to the Civil War when the New York State Militia changed its name.

2. During Reconstruction, the Southern states' right to establish a militia was suspended until the end of reconstruction in 1877, nearly coinciding with the end of the Indian wars in the Pacific Northwest.

3. The Washington Militia was renamed the Washington National Guard in 1884. The Oregon Militia was changed in 1887 to the Oregon National Guard by the Oregon Legislature's enactment of the Summers Law.

One bunch ranged throughout Seattle, demanding that the Chinese pack up, and be "deported" to San Francisco. At first, the King County sheriff tried to control the throng with his deputies, but the violence soon overwhelmed the local police forces.[4] As the threats of lynchings grew, the local authorities petitioned the governor for support. Washington Territorial Governor Squires called upon the Washington National Guard to support the sheriff. The "Seattle Rifles" quickly thwarted the mob by the threat of volleys of rifle fire, and once more the militia protected lives.

In April 1892, the sheriff of Malheur County, Oregon had two Asian prisoners in the Vale City jail. They were accused of murdering a prominent and popular local citizen. Crowd unrest continued, and cries for a lynching made the sheriff uneasy. Not believing he and his deputies could restrain the crowd, the sheriff requested state assistance. There was no state-wide police force yet, so the governor called upon the state militia. Company F, of the 3rd Oregon Infantry Regiment mustered in the fields outside of Baker, Oregon (now called Baker City), and entrained for Vale. Once they arrived, the infantry quickly restored the peace.

Labor unrest was another reason for the governors to use troops. In Astoria, salmon fishermen occasionally struck, demanding more money for their catch. Once again, in March 1896, over a thousand fishermen demanded that the canneries and packing houses pay them five cents a pound or all the fishermen would go on strike. This call was repeated in April, when over two thousand fishermen unanimously voted for the nickel per pound pay.

Across the river, the State of Washington National Guard had responded to the fishing villages of Chinook and Ilwaco, fearing an outbreak of striker violence. The troops were withdrawn from Chinook within two weeks of the fishing season opening, on April 10, but posted to the Columbia River's Sand Island, while other Washington troops remained quartered near the town of Ilwaco, Washington.

Astoria was the center of both the fishing industry and union activity. "Scabs," non-union workers who cross picket lines, started to undercut union solidarity. The June 9 edition of *The Daily Astorian* reported that several bodies had been recovered floating in the river, and most assumed

---

4. The City of Seattle Police actually sided with the rioters, and stood aside for the lawbreakers.

they were the scabs caught by union fishermen. Cannery owners reported additional threats on their property and their lives.

Union meetings called for the forceful seizure of fishing nets, retained
by the cannery owners, and the burning of packing houses. Violence
seemed imminent. In response to repeated calls for assistance, Governor
Lord ordered elements of the Oregon National Guard to Astoria.

From Portland, seven companies of the 1st Oregon Infantry Regiment
responded. Artillery and Gatling guns were set up to protect property and
nightly patrol boats, armed with a Gatling gun, prevented a water-borne
attack of owners' property. After successfully maintaining the peace,
within weeks, the 1st Oregon was no longer needed, as the strike ended
with an agreement.

Spanish-American War

The origins, causes, and outbreak of the Spanish-American War are
beyond the scope of this work. But, the war had a direct effect on the
military history of the Pacific Northwest.[5] As with all previous wars, at
the outset, the regular U.S. Army was woefully inadequate and small.
President McKinley needed an immediate source of troops, and turned
to the various states' militias. The president called for 125,000 volunteers, effectively tripling the size of the nation's land forces.

An obstacle to the troop increase was the president's uncertainty of
his ability to federalize state forces. Congress introduced a proposed bill
giving the president the authority to by-pass the states and directly order
the states' militias into the regular army. In the interest of states' rights,
this proposal was defeated and an alternative bill was passed, The
Mobilization Act of 1898. This law allowed the states' forces to create
"volunteer" regiments, which in turn would be incorporated into the regular army's command structure.

The majority of the regular army, reinforced by several states' national guards and militias formed into "volunteer" regiments, fought in the

---

5. One impact on the State of Oregon was the role its namesake battleship played
in the war. The *U.S.S. Oregon* had been stationed in the Pacific, and would make
a historic run around the tip of South America in time to fight in Cuba at the
Battle of Santiago, July 3, 1898. Later, during World War I, it was assigned to
guard the Pacific Coast, and was decommissioned in 1919.

Caribbean. But, the Spanish-American War was a two-ocean war, and troops were needed to fight in the Philippines. Three quarters of the troops assigned to fight in the islands were volunteer regiments. The five states that formed the old Oregon Country[6] all created volunteer regiments, mustering in between May 5 and May 18, 1898. The five states' volunteer regiments were Idaho 1st Volunteer Infantry Regiment, Montana 1st Volunteer Infantry Regiment, Oregon 2nd Volunteer Infantry Regiment, Washington 1st Volunteer Infantry Regiment,[7] and Wyoming 1st Volunteer Infantry Regiment.

As the troops were raised, they were sent over in "expeditions." Ultimately, the order of battle in the Philippines during the Spanish American War was as follows:

VIII Army Corps
(Major General Wesley Merritt, commanding)
2nd Division
(Brigadier General Thomas M. Anderson[8], commanding)
First Brigade
(Brigadier General Arthur MacArthur[9], commanding)
Second Brigade
(Brigadier General F. V. Greene, commanding)

Within the First Brigade were two Northwest regiments: the 1st Idaho Volunteer Infantry and the 1st Wyoming Volunteer Infantry. Within the Second Brigade was the 2nd Oregon Volunteer Infantry Regiment.

Oregon's regiment, with less than two weeks' training as a unit, departed in the First Philippine Expedition on May 24, 1898. At the end of June, Idaho and Wyoming's regiments were sent over in the Third Expedition. Montana's regiment was sent in the Fourth, at end of July,

6. The old Oregon Country contained all of Idaho, Oregon, and Washington, as well as a portion of Montana and Wyoming.

7. Washington also mustered the Washington Volunteer Infantry Battalion, but that unit remained as a reserve stationed at Vancouver Barracks.

8. General Anderson had another connection to the Pacific Northwest. As a colonel, he was the longest serving commander of Vancouver Barracks, serving there as the colonel of the 14th U.S. Infantry from November 1, 1886 to August 1, 1897. On his retirement from the Army, he would return to Portland.

9. Father of General Douglas MacArthur

and Washington's in the Fifth Philippine Expedition, in October 1898, but neither of these units saw combat in the war. Oregon and Idaho's regiments did arrive in time to fight. With the fall of Manila, an armistice was signed on August 13, 1898, and a final peace treaty was completed in Paris on December 10, 1898. No losses from any of the regiments were reported during the brief action in the Philippine Islands.

The Philippine-American War

At the outset to the Spanish-American War, Spain had already been combating Filipino freedom fighters. Initially, the Filipino irregulars welcomed the Americans as potential liberators. When Commodore George Dewy commenced combat operations against the Spanish on May 1, and he seized the Cavite Naval Yard, he was short of troops to protect the fleet. Thus, Commodore Dewey welcomed the Filipino Liberation Army (FLA) as allies. This step encouraged the Filipino belief that the Americans might be their liberators.

It quickly became apparent, though, that the Americans were conquerors. Officially, war against the FLA commenced on February 4, 1899, with the Americans referring to the event as the Philippine Insurrection. All of the Pacific Northwest regiments would see combat in this war.

In many ways, this new war was a continuation of the Indian wars. Unlike the war with Spain, the Philippine-American War was seen as just a continuation of the racial struggle against savages, such as the fights against the American Indian peoples.[10] An editorial in the March 14, 1899 *Oregonian* directly associated the Philippine "insurrection" with the "Indian problem" that the American people had so recently completed.

The Oregonian often presented the idea that the annexation of the Philippines would reenact the settlement of Oregon. The industrious Americans would simply take another step to the West. They would fend

10. Equally true was the racial struggle by African-Americans. After fighting in Cuba, the Black 24th U.S. Infantry Regiment needed a break, and was assigned to Vancouver Barracks before being sent onto the Philippine Islands. "There is little question that African-American had run into hostile attitudes in the Oregon Country, especially south of the Columbia River." (Shine, 196) While fighting in the Philippines, American troops often referred to the Filipinos as Indians or Blacks.

off claims from other European powers, subdue the indigenous inhabitants, and begin prospecting for minerals and harnessing the region's agricultural wealth. Eventually, they would remake this new land in the image of their own.

> Oregonians so often did not view Filipinos as foreign nationals or potential American citizens. Much like the Klamaths, Modocs, and Nez Perces in Oregon, the Filipinos were seen as people who inhabited the land but had no ultimate claim to it. (McEnroe, 31)

Not only did the troops of the Northwest see the issue as a racial struggle, but they fought it as they and their fathers had fought against the Indians. Their commanding officers were experienced Indian fighters, and their campaigns were fought as they had fought in the West. "Soldiers described the torture and execution of Filipino captives, the wholesale destruction of Philippine villages, and the displacement of citizens." (McEnroe, 24) Even the troops referred to the Filipinos as "Indians."

The Philippine-American War would be fought for almost seven years, but the states' volunteer regiments were of limited enlistments. Between the end of July and the first week of September, 1899, the five states' volunteer regiments left the Philippine Islands with battle streamers on their flags, but also with dead and wounded. Each regiment experienced the following losses:

State	Dead	
Idaho	22	(7 Killed in action)
Montana	37	(21 KIA)
Oregon	54	(15 KIA)
Washington	68	(26 KIA)
Wyoming	13	(3 KIA)

Interlude, Reform, and Preparation

The end of the states' troops participating in combat also stimulated a change in how the states' national guards would be called upon in future combat emergencies.

Three pieces of federal legislation changed how the national guard would be viewed and used. The first major change to the Militia Act of

1792 was the 1903 Militia Act. Once the militia reached Army standards, the militia would be federally funded and would be integrated into the regular army command structure.[11] Each state's governor retained control over his state's national guard's mobilization and limited federal duty to nine months' service. The 1908 amendment to the Militia Act removed the nine month limitation as well as the previous limit to overseas deployment. The third change occurred in 1916, with the enactment of the National Defense Act. This law changed the militia into a fully funded federal military reserve and directed all states to rename their forces as National Guard.

The states' armed forces reflected all the defense forces of the federal government. For example, during the Spanish-American War, Oregon created a Naval Militia, and in 1911, added to that by creating a Marine Militia. These units would use the U.S.S. *Boston* as a training ship starting in 1906, and then transition to the U.S.S. *Marblehead* in 1912. Washington had three companies of Naval Militia starting in 1911.

In other respects, the national guards of the five states reflected standard army order of arms: infantry, cavalry, and artillery. One distinction was made in Oregon and Washington. Because of the need for protection of the Pacific coast, a special element was created with the Coast Artillery Corps. This force manned the many forts at the mouth of the Columbia River and around Puget Sound.

All of this reform and reorganization was first tested in 1916. Mexico was suffering from one of its periodic civil wars and Mexican forces, under the command of Pancho Villa, had crossed into the United States, killing civilians. President Woodrow Wilson sent the U.S. Army into Mexico on a punitive expedition, and ordered 158,000 National Guard troops into

11. This was reflected by the joint maneuvers held near Tacoma starting July 1, 1904. While the Washington National Guard had used the American Lake area for training in 1892, 1894, and 1902, as a result of the 1903 Militia Act, Idaho, Oregon, and Washington National Guard troops held joint exercises with regular U.S. Army troops. Included with the regular Army troops were elements of the 9th U.S. Cavalry Regiment, part of the famous "Buffalo Soldiers" of the four regiments of African-American soldiers. This exercise was observed by the commander of the Division of the Pacific, General Arthur MacArthur. Additional joint maneuvers were held at American Lake in 1906, 1908, 1910, and 1912, until Camp Lewis (later Fort Lewis) was established in 1917, just before the start of World War I.

Panoramic view of Camp Lewis in 1917. (*Library of Congress*)

federal service along the border. None of the troops would be called upon to fight, but it was the first test of the National Guard after the reforms of the last fifteen years. Washington was the only state in the Northwest that could field a complete regiment meeting the new federal standards, while several Northwest states' smaller sized units participated.

World War I

On April 17, 1917, the U.S. Congress declared war against Germany and its allies. Using the 1916 law, President Wilson called upon 379,000 National Guard troops, including units trained during the Mexican crisis, to augment the regular forces of the United States. These troops were to form seventeen divisions, or forty percent of the strength of the American Expeditionary Force sent to Europe.

While the major contribution of the Pacific Northwest would be with its infantry, it should be noted that the last experiment of Naval and Marine militias served in the war. The naval companies of Oregon and Washington reported for service aboard the U.S.S. *South Dakota*. The Oregon Marine Militia was ordered to North Carolina, where it would join the 1st Marine Division, fighting in Europe.

The National Defense Act of 1916 required the states' National Guard to achieve the standards of the regular army. Having done so, they would become part of the regular army when federalized. The five states of the Pacific Northwest once more joined together to fight for the country. The National Guards of Idaho, Montana, Oregon, Washington, and Wyoming were ordered into the 20th Division, which was designated the 41st Division on July 18, 1917. The 41st Division was given a distinctive shoulder patch of a setting sun, and nicknamed The Sunset Division. This was the Sunset of Paradise, the division of the Pacific Northwest.

Regrettably, the 41st did not see combat in World War I as a division. Instead, prior to departure, the Sunset was informed it would be a replacement division. Nevertheless, it departed for Europe on November 26, 1917. Its only combat casualties as a division occurred en route to France. A German U-boat torpedoed a transport, the *Tuscania*, just off-shore of France[12], resulting in some loss of life, but miraculously, most of the troops on board were rescued.

Once in France, the 41st had its troops removed piecemeal as replacements, with troops from the Northwest serving with the 1st, 2nd, 32nd, and 42nd Divisions. All served with distinction.

Between the Wars

After World War I, the National Guard was recognized as a crucial part of the country's defense. The National Defense Act of 1920 fully integrated the Guard for future defense needs. One result was that the National Guard was organized into four cavalry and eighteen infantry divisions when called into federal service. The Sunset Division remained the Pacific Northwest's division.

Another change Army command recognized was the need for coastal defense. With the Army and Navy planning for a possible war with Japan, it was assumed that the United States could no longer depend on the ocean's vast distances to protect the country from enemy attack. Coastal defense became a new priority for the National Guard, and both Oregon and Washington had coast artillery units. Coastal defense forts around the mouth of the Columbia River and the Strait of Juan de Fuca/Puget Sound became critical. Forts Stevens, Canby, and Columbia protected the Columbia River while Forts Worden, Casey, Lawton, and Flagler in Washington protected the coast from enemy ships.[13]

12. February 5, 1918. U-boat UB-77 sank the *Tuscania* seven miles off-shore from France, 230 lives lost, of which 201 were American troops.

13. One "enemy" ship that visited the Columbia River was the Nazi cruiser *Emden*. The German warship was on a training cruise and made its only American port-of-call at Portland. On January 19, 1936, the *Emden* entered the mouth of the Columbia and rendered its twenty-one gun salute to the United States. Honors were returned by Fort Stevens's Third Coast Artillery. The *Emden* was beached during World War II after an aerial attack, and destroyed in July 1946.

The Great Depression punished the National Guard as much as the regular military, reducing budget allocations. But as the threat of war increased, so did the preparation by the states' National Guard. In the summer of 1937, the 41st Division joined the regular army's 3rd Division at Fort Lewis to provide army command with experience in directing a corps. Each summer, platoon, company, and battalions practiced their combat skills until 1940 saw the 41st Division combining at Fort Lewis to exercise at the regimental level.

War stood close. Axis aggression forced President Franklin Roosevelt to increase the strength of the American Army. In August 1940, Roosevelt ordered 300,000 troops of the National Guard into federal service, doubling the existing army. An additional 4,800 Air Guard units augmented the Army Air Corps.[14] Eighteen National Guard infantry divisions trained for the next fourteen months, bringing their proficiency and skills to the level needed for combat.

World War II

The first Japanese strike against the United States, undoubtedly, the most famous, was the attack on Pearl Harbor. All three elements of the Japanese Imperial Navy joined in the surprise attack: surface, air, and submarine. Most of the submarines sent with the Imperial fleet were long-range I-class submarines that had the capacity to carry additional craft. The I-class were well suited for their mission and had several variants. While some were designed to launch midget submarines, others were capable of carrying a single float plane in a deck hanger. One I-class was designed to use the extra space to carry enough fuel to have a range of 22,000 nautical miles.

14. Idaho and Wyoming did not create Air Guard units until after the end of World War II. Montana established the 7th Ferrying Group on June 22, 1941, with an initial mission to assist in flying planes to the Soviet Union. Oregon had mustered the 123rd Observation Squadron in April 1941. These two units would be ordered into federal service soon after their creation. The oldest air unit was the Washington National Guard's 116th Observation Squadron, first mustered on August 6, 1924. In turn, the 116th Observation Squadron was given that mission from its previous, active-army mission. It had flown as the U.S. Army's 116th Aero Squadron in France during World War I. The 116th was part of the original 4,800 air guardsmen ordered to federal service by FDR in August 1940.

Once the Pearl Harbor mission was completed, the Japanese Imperial Navy ordered eight I-class submarines to patrol off of the west coast of the United States. Three were assigned to stalk the Pacific Northwest: *I-9*, off Cape Blanco, Oregon; *I-25*, at the mouth of the Columbia River; and *I-26*, near the entrance to the Strait of Juan de Fuca. None of the Japanese subs were able to sink any ships on this patrol, but there were attempts. On December 18, 1941, outbound through the breakers of the mouth of the Columbia River, the Union Oil tanker *L.P. St. Clair* was unwittingly heading right toward the waiting *I-25*. Because of the shallow waters of the bar, and wishing to preserve the boat's torpedoes, Commander Meji Tagami ordered his sub to surface, and opened fire with his deck gun. As the first shells started to drop around the surprised tanker, the captain of the *L.P. St. Clair* ordered a dangerous maneuver, coming completely about right across the bar. As the oil tanker headed back into protected waters, a total of ten shell bursts cascaded water over the ship, after which the tanker ran safely back into the Great River of the West.

Later that same month, on December 27, Commander Tagami ordered the *I-25* to enter the sheltered waters of the Columbia River. Seeing another highly prized tanker, the submarine fired a torpedo at the S.S. *Connecticut*. This time, the Japanese struck home. The fish hit the tanker in the port side. The ship, riding high after discharging is cargo of fuel oil in Portland, did not sink immediately, but turned and ran for more protected waters. The *I-25* could not follow, fearing it would be trapped in shallow waters at daylight for aircraft to swoop on to it. While the sub recorded a "kill," it was not to be. The *Connecticut* ran itself aground on a sand bar in the river and was salvaged to sail again.

Part of the Japanese plan had been to shell the West Coast on Christmas Eve, but as antisubmarine patrols increased, the shelling was cancelled, and all of the subs were ordered to return to their base at Kwajalein, Marshall Islands.

Japan did, however, release hundreds of fake submarines consisting of a float and a fake periscope in an attempt to tie up Allied antisubmarine efforts. Of the 147 reported submarine sightings in 1941-42, many were these fake subs. On January 31, 1942, the Royal Canadian Army's coast artillery attacked what they believed was a sub as the "sub" started to sail past Victoria, British Columbia's harbor. Investigations found a float and realistic periscope that had been splintered by shell fire.

While Japanese submarines were attempting to menace shipping along the Pacific Northwest coast, the American civilian and military authorities began wartime mobilization. The Japanese attack on Pearl Harbor and fear of subsequent attacks on the mainland caused many reactions. Some were based solely on fear, such as the racial segregation of both foreign nationals of Japan as well as U.S. citizens of Japanese ancestry and their forced internment into concentration camps.[15] Others were based on the real threat posed by an aggressive and competent enemy. Once more, the Sunset Division sailed off to war. After December 7, 1941, the United States prepared for a two-front war. The 41st Division would first land in Australia and engage in three major campaigns: New Guinea, the Marshall Islands, and then the return to the Philippines, where the soldiers of the Pacific Northwest would be fighting with distinction under the command of another General MacArthur in the Philippine Islands.

15. Not part of the military history, but related to it is the treatment of Japanese ancestry citizens, or resident aliens from Japan. As one Japanese resident alien wrote: "We were all terror-stricken at the news. War between America, where we would live until death, and Japan, where we came from! I am a Japanese subject, but my children are Nisei and American citizens, We Issei [Japanese-born foreign nationals] were sorely troubled by this war." (Azuma, 341) Part of the problem rested with the past practice of dual citizenship. Until 1924, "Following the doctrine of *jus sanguinis*, the Japanese government claimed that all persons of Japanese descent, whatever their place of birth, were Japanese citizens." (O'Brien, 19-20) This concept fed into already existing racial prejudices. Starting in January 1942, Japanese Americans were deemed a security threat, at least in select areas. This was not wholly without some justification. Some 5,560 American citizens of Japanese ancestry renounced their citizenship and returned to fight against the Americans. This represented about five percent of the population ultimately removed in the United States. In British Columbia, another 23,000 Nisei (second generation Japanese) were removed to interior locations. The removal of the Japanese, while partially based on security concerns, was largely racial. The Western Defense Command's general officer, John DeWitt, at first proposed to treat the Japanese as the Italians and Germans were treated. However, by early 1942, he had changed his opinion largely because of political pressure. "The continued presence of a large unassimilated, tightly knit racial group, bound to an enemy nation by strong ties of race, culture, custom, and religion along a frontier vulnerable to attack, constituted a menace which had to be dealt with." (Polenberg, 63)

The Japanese Offensive, Spring 1942

On April 18, 1942, much of Japanese complacency and confidence in the invulnerability of the home islands was rudely shocked when land-based (at least by design) B-25 bombers, led by Colonel Jimmy Doolittle, dropped explosives and incendiary bombs on several Japanese cities and military targets. No substantive physical damage was done, but the psychological shock was great.

The bombers were first believed to have been staged out of the Alaskan Aleutian Islands. The closest of these islands were only 650 miles from the Kuriles, the northern most of the Japanese home islands. Later, the Japanese would learn of the Doolittle raid being staged off of the carrier *U.S.S. Hornet*. Whatever the staging source, the attack had been a great wake-up to the danger to the homeland.

The attack drove the desire of the Japanese high command to extend their defensive perimeter, keeping the Americans as far away from Japan as possible. A defensive arc was envisioned extending from the Aleutian Islands in the north, through Midway in the central Pacific, curving around to the southeast Pacific.

The principle Japanese thrust was again directed against the main United States area of strength in the Pacific: the Hawaiian Islands. The first step to neutralizing the American threat was to make the primary American bases on Oahu untenable. If Pearl Harbor and the related military installations were subject to the constant threat of land-based aerial attacks, the Americans would be forced to pull the main Pacific Fleet base back to the mainland. In order to accomplish the threat, Admiral Yamamoto designed a plan to seize Midway.

Fortunately for the United States, Naval Intelligence had partially cracked the Imperial Japanese Naval code, and was able to glean substantial information on Japanese intentions and actions. Intelligence revealed there would be a secondary Japanese target, the Aleutians. The attack on the Aleutians would have two primary objectives. First, it was hoped that it would mask the main Japanese efforts against Midway, distracting American resources away at a critical juncture. Second, the Aleutians were a valuable objective in their own right:

> The shortest route from Japan to the United States closely followed the 1,200-mile-long chain of more than 70 islands from Attu, 650 miles northeast of Japans's big naval base in the Kurile Islands, to

Umnak, just off the coast of the Alaska Peninsula. Obviously the
Aleutians could be used as steppingstones for an invasion of North
America—or for an invasion of Japan. (Rigge, 122)

While Japan did not plan to invade the United States, the desire to
prevent the Americans from attacking the home islands again was reason
enough to land troops there.

Initially, the Americans defended the only North American area to be
invaded in the war with limited, leftover resources. The primary defense
rested with the Navy. Rear Admiral Robert A. Theobold had two heavy
cruisers, three light cruisers, thirteen destroyers, and six obsolescent S-
class submarines as his primary power to repulse an enemy fleet. The
task force was supported by one squadron of PBY Catalina flying boats,
and the planes of the U.S. Army's 14th Tactical Air Force: thirty-three
inadequate P-40 fighters, and seven bombers, including obsolete B-18
bombers. Ashore on Umnak and Unalaska islands were 10,000 Army
troops.

Opposing Admiral Theobold were two fleets of the Japanese Northern
Area Force, under the command of Rear Admiral Kakuji Kakuta. His
strike force consisted of two carriers, two heavy cruisers, and three
destroyers. A follow-up fleet of transports carrying troops was protected
by light cruisers.

Originally planned for June 2, but delayed because of fog, on June 3,
the Japanese attacked Dutch Harbor with their carrier planes, ahead of
the scheduled June 4 attack on Midway. Flying back and forth, Americans
and Japanese sought out each enemy's forces, often missing the other in
the fog and low lying clouds. Several attacks were pressed home by both
aerial forces, but with little real damage inflicted by either side.

As word was received of the Japanese defeat at Midway,[16] the
Northern Area Force withdrew to the west. With Midway now outside
the grasp of Imperial power, it was uncertain if an attack of the Aleutians
was needed. Still fearing that the Americans would use the islands as a
staging point for attack on Japan itself, the invasion went forward. Far to
the west, Attu and Kiska, undefended, were invaded on June 7, 1942.

At first, American response was to harass the Japanese through air
and submarine attacks. But, beginning in January 1943, U.S. Army

---

16. The Battle of Midway was fought June 4–7, 1942.

troops started to island-hop westward. On January 12, Amchitka Island was the first seized. The reaction by the Japanese would set the stage for bitter fighting over the Japanese held Alaskan islands. The Japanese viewed the American moves with grave concern.

> The Japanese Imperial General Staff reasoned, incorrectly, that the enemy would not be pressing westward so assiduously unless they intended to use the Aleutians as a land bridge to the Kuriles and northern Japan. On February 5, orders went out from Imperial General Headquarters "to hold the western Aleutians at all costs and to carry out preparations for war" in the Kuriles. (Rigge, 133)

The Japanese reinforced their captured American islands. The "at all costs" order meant that the troops had to be gotten through, and naval ships were used to transport the reinforcements. One such reinforcement effort was ordered by Vice Admiral Boshiro Hosogaya, consisting of the heavy cruisers *Nachi* and *Maya*, light cruisers *Tama* and *Abukama*, four destroyers, and two armed merchant ships carrying troops. The United States Navy actively tried to intercept these convoys with submarines and surface ships.

On March 26, 1943, the Hosogaya convoy was detected coming out of the fog. Out-numbered but determined, a task group consisting of one heavy cruiser, *Salt Lake City*, one light cruiser, the *Richmond*, and four destroyers sallied straight toward the enemy ships. For nearly three hours, the capital ships traded salvos, with the Americans striking first, and damaging the *Nachi* when a shell penetrated her torpedo hold, exploding the Japanese weapons. The Japanese's strength of numbers started to tell, and the *Salt Lake City* eventually went dead in the water.

As Japanese victory was at hand, Admiral Hosogaya's courage faltered, as he feared American land-based aircraft were approaching. He ordered his task force to retire. The last entry in the *Salt Lake City's* log during the battle summed up the situation clearly: "This day the hand of Divine Providence lay over the ship."[17]

On May 11, 1943, the U.S. Army invaded Attu. The division selected to assault was the Army's 7th Division, nicknamed the "Sight-Seeing" Division. The 7th had been trained for amphibious assault on California shores, after having had extensive preparation for warfare in North Africa

17. Rigge, 134.

A Japanese I-class submarine (*National Archives*)

by staging maneuvers in the California desert. Wishing to preserve security, arctic equipment and clothing was not issued to the troops until after they had sailed for Alaskan waters. This lack of foresight and preparation resulted in a large number of casualties from frostbite, trench foot, and other cold-related maladies. Nevertheless, the Sight-Seers would successfully fight against the fanatical troops told to hold "at all costs."

By the end of May, Colonel Yanazaki's 2,300 troops defending Attu had been beaten. All but twenty-nine Japanese were killed. The U.S. Army suffered 549 killed, 1,148 wounded, and over 2,100 injured from cold related injuries.

The last island held by the Japanese was Kiska. On August 15, more than 34,000 ground troops invaded, only to find the Japanese had evacuated their forces three weeks earlier.

Concurrent Submarine Actions

Part of Admiral Yamamoto's 1942 offensive included submarine attacks on the American West Coast. Once more, Japanese submarines were ordered to sortie along the eastern Pacific.

Sailing directly to intercept warships sailing from Puget Sound, the *I-26* arrived off North American waters on May 30, and lurked off the entrance to the Strait of Juan de Fuca as the opening actions of Midway unfolded.

On June 7, the *I-26* observed a freighter sailing alone out of the Strait, bound for San Francisco. A quick set-up, and *I-26* launched its torpedo, sinking the S.S. *Coast Trader* with the one fish. No time was available for a distress signal to be sent. Commander Minoru Hasegawa detected a warship nearby (the HMCS *Edmondston* patrolling, but unaware of the attack), and exited the area, fearing he had been detected.

The next day, the survivors of the *Coast Trader* were rescued and search efforts were made to find the enemy submarine responsible. On June 9, a PBY search plane spotted a sub about 420 miles northwest of the tip of Washington, but no ships were in the area to prosecute the attack. But it was not the *I-26*, it was the *I-25*, which had first sailed to the Aleutians, and was then proceeded to its secondary mission of intercepting Canadian and American shipping. On June 20, near the Strait of Juan de Fuca, the *I-25* attacked the S.S. *Fort Camosun* using its 5.5.-inch deck gun. Despite repeated hits, the freighter did not sink because it was full of lumber as cargo. Calling for assistance, two Canadian Navy Corvettes responded: HMCS *Quesnel* and *Edmundston*. The *I-25*'s captain, Commander Meji Tagami, was watching to confirm his kill. But once the Canadian Navy arrived, things became hot in a hurry. The *Quesnel* started depth-charging near the *I-25* and the Japanese submarine retreated to the south.

The two Japanese submarines would remain in the area, hunting for targets. As the *I-25* was making its attack on *Fort Camosun*, the *I-26* had cruised north along the western coast of Vancouver Island. Not finding any shipping, on the night of June 20, it surfaced off the coast opposite the Estevan's Point Lighthouse, British Columbia. Wishing to strike fear into the civilian population, Captain Hasegawa ordered his deck gun to open fire. Seventeen 5.5-inch shells were fired at the lighthouse. As the captain recalled, "even out at sea we could hear the pigs squealing as shells exploded. As I watched from the *I-26*, people were quick to put out the lights in the buildings but the lighthouse was slow to respond—the last light to turn off." (Webber, 77)

While no real damage was done (not even to the pigs), this attack was historic as it was the only locale in Canada to come under direct enemy gunfire. Back on February 23, 1942, a similar attack had occurred near Santa Barbara, California, when *I-17* opened fire with its deck gun. This was the first American location shelled by an enemy since the War of 1812. Now, just as the *I-26* was firing at Canada, the American mainland would once again come under submarine shellfire. Following its attack on the *Fort Camosun*, the *I-25* neared the mouth of the Columbia River, looking for another target of opportunity. Believing there was an

A shell hole from one of I-25's rounds fired at Fort Stevens. This was the first American fort shelled by a foreign enemy since the War of 1812. (*National Archives*)

American submarine base located inside the mouth of the river, Commander Tagami decided to fire his deck guns toward the reported base. At about eleven-thirty P.M., on June 21, the *I-25* opened fire. Instead, what the Japanese fired upon was the Army's Fort Stevens, and Battery Russell. Seventeen shells landed on the fort. No damage was inflicted and the battery's two ten-inch guns did not return fire. The battery's commander, Captain Jack Woods of the 249th Coast Artillery (Harbor Defense), requested permission to fire. But, in relaying the request to the sleeping fort commander, Colonel Clifton M. Irwin, the chain of command was delayed when a communication line was cut by one of the falling shells from the sub.

After firing its salvos, *I-25* cruised northwest, looking for more ships to sink. All of the Japanese submarines would return to their base by the end of July with no more combat to their credit on this sortie.

The Last Sub Sortie and the First Aerial Attack

Up until the summer of 1942, the use of the Yokosuka E-14-Y1 floatplane[18] carried aboard an I-class submarine had been limited to scouting missions. When the *I-25* returned in July, its pilot, Flying Officer Nobuo

18. Codenamed *Glen* by the Allies.

Fujita wrote a proposal to arm the floatplane with bombs, and allow him to attack American cities.[19] The plan was received with mixed reactions.

First, the thought of one plane, or even a few planes flying together, attacking an American city with two 76-kilogram bombs (which was all the E-14-Y1 could carry) might cause a reaction other than the one of terror hoped for by the Japanese. The Americans might view the attack as pitiful, and even laughable. Certainly the damage would be negligible. But, the Japanese high command did appreciate the opportunity to strike back at the Americans. How best to gain the most advantageous response from the limited ability of the float plane?

By design, each *Glen* was carried partially assembled in an I-class submarine's deck hanger. The plane's primary purpose was for reconnaissance. Within its 900-mile range, the aircraft could carry two bombs. It was decided that the best mission for the I-class/*Glen* combination was for a submarine to catapult the plane while it carried incendiary bombs to start forest fires. The hope was that the fires would spread, cause panic, and threaten towns.

Flying Officer Fujita returned to the *I-25* and gave the new orders to Commander Tagami, captain of the submarine. Once readied, the *I-25* sailed from Yokosuka, Japan on August 15, 1942, bound for the United States Pacific Northwest.

Arriving off the coast of Oregon in early September, rough seas prevented quick deployment. On September 9, the sea was calm and the *I-25* surfaced along the Oregon-California border. Launching the *Glen*, the *I-25* submerged, and headed north to the rendezvous point. Meanwhile, Fujita and Flight Observer Choji Olcuda flew northeast toward the Cape Blanco light, and then about fifty miles into the interior of Coos County, Oregon.

19. One persistent myth of World War II in the Northwest was that the Japanese had launched a *Glen* aircraft attack on an American city, Seattle. The belief in the attack stems from an event reported by some as an enemy air raid. On January 12, 1942, the Queen Anne Hill section of Seattle first went dark, and then there were flashes of light that some thought were from an attacking plane. The actual events of that night were that a U.S. Army barrage balloon broke free and dragged its steel mooring cables across power lines, shorting out the power grid and causing sparks. Similar events would occur on February 2, 3, April 15, June 5, September 5, October 31, November 20, 1942, and January 24, 1943. The Japanese never did launch an air raid on a continental United States city.

Once over the dense forests of Oregon, aim was not critical. As they flew, the two incendiary bombs were dropped onto Wheeler Ridge and the plane tarried long enough to confirm the start of fires. The plane then headed west to return to the waiting submarines.

The bombs produced small fires that were easily put out. But more fireworks were in the works. As the *Glen* flew west, it was seen by two merchant ships. At the predicted location, the *I-25* was waiting, and the Glen landed on its float, and was quickly disassembled.

After the plane was secured, but before the submarine could submerge, a lookout cried out that a plane was coming out of the sun and an emergency dive was ordered.

The plane was from the 390th Bomb Squadron, 42nd Bombardment Group, an Army A29 Lockheed Hudson bomber, piloted by Captain Jean Daugherty; it had been on patrol out of McChord Army Air Field (now McChord Air Force Base) near Tacoma, Washington. Luck had brought Captain Daugherty upon the *I-25*, as he reported,

> I sighted something dark in the water ahead. . . . It seemed larger than the pictures of the Japanese submarines we had been briefed on. . . . My course took me into a fog bank, where I started an immediate tight left turn right down at the water level. Still in the fog bank, I headed back toward the object and opened the bomb bay doors. As we leveled out, I moved my thumb to the bomb release and peered ahead. While still in the fog, I could dimly see the object in the water slightly to the left and about 300 yards away. Suddenly we broke into the bright sunlight. I throttled back to reduce speed, lost a little more altitude, and headed straight toward the long, low object. When I felt I could get the best shots alongside the target or possibly straddle it with bombs, I pressed the release button dropping two 300-pound. . . bombs. (Webber, 138)

The bombs missed, but the *I-25* was severely rattled. The sub stayed submerged and headed for the ocean floor, settling to the bottom of Port Orford Harbor, Oregon to evade detection.

The close call with the Army bomber changed the *I-25*'s tactics when it decided to launch another bombing mission. On the evening of September 29, the submarine surfaced and launched the *Glen* for its second aerial bombardment mission. The plane flew over the woods of Oregon once again, and dropped two fire bombs onto Grassy Knob, east of Port Orford. The plane confirmed the start of fires, but like the last time the fires did not produce much damage or panic. These attacks are the only times the continental United States has ever been bombed by enemy aircraft.

The *I-25* was unable to launch its *Glen* again because of rough seas. But, it still prowled the waters looking for enemies to attack. On October 4, the sub spotted the S.S. *Camden*, a tanker carrying 76,000 barrels of gasoline from San Pedro to Puget Sound. The ship had come to a complete stop to make repairs. At 7:00 A.M., from a distance of 3,000 yards, the *I-25* fired two torpedoes, one of which missed, but the second smashed into the ship, causing an immediate fire aboard. The crew abandoned ship and the *I-25* claimed it as a kill.[20]

The next night, south of Cape Sebastian, near Gold Beach, Oregon, the *I-25* spotted another tanker. This time it was the *Larry Dohney* with 66,000 barrels of oil as cargo. The sub made one approach, fired a torpedo, but registered no hit. It maneuvered again as the unsuspecting tanker continued to steam north. At 9:20 P.M., a second torpedo run successfully put a fish into the starboard side, causing the tanker to sink, causing the loss of two crewmen out of the thirty-six aboard.

The *Larry Dohney* was the last Allied ship sunk from Japanese action along the entire American sea board. The *I-25*, now nearly two months away from home, headed west. But, the *Larry Dohney* would not be the last ship sunk on this mission.

As the *I-25* sailed for home, on October 11, it spotted two submarines on the surface about 800 miles off the Washington coastline. Believing them to be American, but having only one torpedo left, the *I-25* made a careful approach and fired its last fish. The torpedo hit the surfaced submarine near the conning tower, sinking the sub in less than twenty seconds; all hands were killed. While the two targets were submarines, they were not American.

Two Russian submarines, the *L-15* and *L-16*, were in transit from Vladivostok for the Atlantic via the Panama Canal. It was the *L-16* that was attacked by the *I-25*. Strangely enough, U.S. Navy Chief Petty Officer Sergi Andreevich Mihailoff was on-board the *L-16* because of his

---

20. Prematurely, as events turned out. A Navy boarding party put out the flames and took the ship in tow. But, the *Camden* foundered off of Grays Harbor and sank on October 10, 1942.

Russian language skills to act as a liaison officer as the submarines transited American waters. Since Japan and Russian would not be at war with one another until August 1945, the Japanese attack on a neutral ship resulted in an American death. It was the *I-25*'s last attack in the east Pacific waters.

North American Defenses

The Canadians and the Americans coordinated the defense of the Pacific Northwest. The agreement rested on the 1940 Pacific Joint Agreement on Defense.[21] As already noted, the Canadian Navy had a presence, with the main base located at Esquimalt, near Victoria, on the island of Vancouver, as His Majesty's Canadian Ships (HMCS) were at first primarily used for antisubmarine forces and coastal defense.[22] As the war expanded to Alaskan waters, the Royal Canadian Navy assumed the dominant role of convoy escort duty of supplies to the Alaskan Defense Command.

Eventually, the Canadians took other steps as well. Taking advantage of their extensive local knowledge, fishermen were organized into a fifteen-boat flotilla, a total of over 400 fishing boats, of the Royal Canadian Navy Fisherman's Reserve. The fleet was of limited value, as many of the boats lacked basic equipment, such as radios. Nevertheless, they did an important duty as the boats patrolled remote areas, and even sank Japanese submarine released floating mines.

Recognizing the vulnerability of the Strait of Juan De Fuca, both allies increased the defense of this critical waterway. The Canadian Army

21. There was considerable Canadian distrust of American command prior to the war. The Canadians were reluctant to put their forces under the command of the Americans. After the start of World War II in September 1939, Canada stripped its forces from the Pacific to concentrate on the war with Germany. Canadian distrust of American intentions continued, with some Canadians believing the June 20, 1942 attack of the Estevan's Point lighthouse was staged by an American submarine.

22. Prior to the Japanese attack on Pearl Harbor, the Royal Canadian Navy's Pacific fleet had been used to attack German shipping. In September 1940, off of Mexico, the Canadian ship *HMCS Prince Robert*, stationed in Esquimalt had intercepted and captured the Nazi freighter *Weser*. The *Prince Henry* forced the scuttling of two German freighters off of Peru. Shortly after the war broke out with Japan, the *Prince Robert* was used to transport Canadian Army troops to Hong Kong in an attempt to defend that British colony from Japanese attack.

efforts rested mostly on the placement of artillery pieces in several forts and the use of two U.S. Army eight-inch railroad cannons. One fort guarded the main base at Esquimalt, Fort Rodd Hill.[23] Many other Canadian Army bases guarded the Strait of Juan de Fuca, the inland passage, and other important ports such as Vancouver, British Columbia. The 15th Coast Brigade of the Royal Canadian Artillery manned many of these posts.

To guard against submarines, the Royal Canadian Air Force (RCAF) had several squadrons patrol British Columbian waters. Further, as part of the need to protect Alaskan-bound convoys, the RCAF moved some of their squadrons north to protect the vast Gulf of Alaska waters. The Western Air Command was placed under the command of Air Vice-Marshall Leigh Stevenson, and consisted of the 115th Squadron;[24] the 8th Bomber Reconnaissance Squadron, both flying Bristol Bolingbroke, two-engine bombers; 111th fighter Squadron; 118th Fighter Squadron, flying P-40 Kittyhawk[25] fighters; and the 120th Squadron using Stranraer flying boats.

Finally, as a defense against invasion, both countries kept troops on station through the end of 1943. For Canada, the defense rested with Victoria's 5th Infantry Regiment.

For the defense of the United States, the Army and its air forces, and the Navy, with its war time control of the Coast Guard, had numerous elements stationed throughout the Northwest. Some of them were assigned to the Northwest as their war-time stations, while others were present for training. Western Washington and Oregon provided countryside very similar to Western Europe, and several divisions were trained at Fort Lewis or temporary Army camps such as Camp Adair, near Corvallis, Oregon. Further, the generally clear skies east of the Cascade Mountains provided excellent flying weather, and many Army and Navy fliers were trained at fields throughout the region.

23. Fort Rodd Hill was originally built by the British in 1858 as part of the Empire's plans to defend against Russian aggression. The Crimean War had caused Great Britain to fear a Russian attack from Alaskan waters, and coastal defense was constructed.

24. The 115th was designated a fighter squadron, but actually flew bombers.

25. Also called the Warhawk and Tomahawk by the nations that flew the P-40.

Between 1942 and 1943, the 44th Division was assigned to act as a coast defense unit, stationed along the Pacific Ocean. The 44th was a Federalized National Guard division, drawing its units from New York and New Jersey. In addition to coast defense, and as the threat of invasion subsided, the 44th trained for combat in Europe, where it would be sent in 1944.

Assisting in coastal defense were elements of the U.S. Coast Guard. At the beginning of 1942, there were thirteen motor lifeboat stations and twenty-six coastal lookout stations already manned from prewar Coast Guard responsibilities. These stations added to their duties a Coast Guard Beach Patrol who walked, sailed, rode in vehicles and on horseback, the beaches of Oregon and Washington. Coast Guard ships and boats—many of which were private vessels used on a war-time emergency basis—also patrolled for subs, or escorted shipping through the mine fields or submarine nets used to guard port waterways. Moreover, while watching for enemy landings,[26] shipping, or aircraft, the Coast Guard still had to perform its other duties. On April 1, 1943, a Soviet freighter, the *Lamut*, ran aground near LaPush, Washington, and the Coast Guard rescued the crew.[27]

U.S. Navy ships, such as the destroyer U.S.S. *Fox*, were based out of the primary U.S. Navy base in Puget Sound (Bremerton Navy Base), and responded to submarine reports or escorted commercial shipping whenever a threat was perceived.

Army Air Forces and Naval aviation also played a role in patrol and antisubmarine duties. The Army planes used the coast as a training area, but augmented their training with antisubmarine sorties. Many Naval air stations were created as training bases and used the waters of the eastern Pacific for flights, but one base, Naval Air Station Tillamook, was established in 1943 with the sole mission of coastal defense. Navy Patrol Squadron VP-33 operated out of Tillamook and was one of only three

26. The Coast Guard was fully aware that German agents had landed in New York and Florida in June 1942, and expected similar landings from Japanese agents on the west coast.

27. Seventy-five mile an hour winds pushed the *Lamut* onto Teahwhit Head, gashing a hole it the ship's side. Several crew members, including a pregnant female, were killed, while others were rescued by various elements of the Coast Guard.

squadrons using blimps for antisubmarine patrols. The blimps provided additional security, such as detecting floating mines. While no Japanese mines had been released in the eastern Pacific since the summer of 1942, U.S. Navy mines that had broken from their moorings became a threat to allied shipping.

For the defense of harbors and waterways, the regular Army regiments given this responsibility before the war were augmented by the National Guard. The 14th Coast Artillery Regiment was assigned to the protection of the Strait of Juan de Fuca and Puget Sound. After the federalization of the National Guard in September 1940, the 248th Coast Artillery (Washington National Guard) joined the regular Army at the primary Coast Artillery bases of Forts Casey, Flagler, Lawton, and Worden. Additional forts, Hayden and Ebey, were started to increase the defensive ability in this area. But by the time the posts were finished and armed, the threat was gone; these forts were only manned with caretaker units.

The other major harbor in Washington, Grays Harbor, was manned with field artillery as harbor defense guns by the 56th Coast Artillery, also of the Washington National Guard.

The mouth of the Columbia was guarded by three Army bases: Fort Stevens in Oregon, and Forts Canby and Columbia on the Washington side of the river. The regular Army had stationed the 3rd Coastal Artillery (Harbor Defense) Regiment (renamed the 18th) before the outbreak of hostilities, and it was augmented by the 249th Coast Artillery once this Oregon National Guard unit was Federalized in September 1940. In addition to coast artillery, the Army was responsible for maintaining a mine field at the entrance to the river and used a converted ferryboat as a minelayer. After the Japanese submarine attacks in December 1941, the minefield was quickly laid, and Coast Guard boats escorted all shipping through the field.

By 1944, command authority recognized that the need for harbor defense and coast artillery had diminished as the United States continued its push west into the Japanese empire. The need for trained artillerymen overseas was only growing as battles raged in both the Pacific and European theaters of operations. By January 12, 1944, all of the coast artillery units had been pulled, and sent to Fort Monroe, Virginia, for retraining as field artillery units. Many of these men would see combat in Europe.

The remains of Battery Russell at Fort Stevens. (*Author*)

Balloon Bombs: The Last Japanese Offensive against America

By the beginning of 1944, the outlook for Japan was grim. The Imperial Armed Forces were fighting a defensive war since the last major Japanese offensive of Midway had failed. Any offensives the Japanese Imperial Forces could mount now were tactical and for limited objectives. The very nature of being forced on the defensive made the desire to lash out at America all the greater.

With the stark reality of the war's progress by 1944, both the Imperial Navy and Army were looking at ways to strike at the United States. With the Imperial Navy being forced to counter the powerful United States Navy, no longer could submarines be spared for long journeys to the American west coast. Traditional combat arms could no longer be used and imagination was needed.

The Imperial Army had tried to attack Henderson Air Field on Guadalcanal with balloons, while the Navy had tried to develop submarine launched balloon bombs. These early steps led both services, but primarily the Army, to develop long-distance bomb carrying balloons designed to use the jet stream to reach the continental United States. An early experiment in February 1944 successfully launched an unarmed balloon for 8,050 kilometers. These early experiments resulted in the perfection of a bomb-laden balloon capable of traveling for days along the jet stream.

The Japanese studied the jet stream as a means for weapons delivery for many years. Scientists had soon realized that the ideal time to launch the balloons was during the winter months, between November to March, as the jet stream flowed directly to the North American land mass. During the rest of the year, the jet stream was less dependable in its flow, and had huge swings that could send balloons far to the south, the north, or even swing them almost around to land on neutral Russia.

But, as dependable as the winter jet stream was, it was impossible to use it to deliver bombs with any precision. It was one thing to release a bomb with the intended target being North America, and something completely different and beyond the Japanese's ability to aim the weapons at specific sites, even if the sites were as large as cities. The best that could be hoped for was to strike anywhere in the United States.

With that huge limitation recognized, the weapons had to be designed to spread damage beyond the limited impact point. Two elements were used to achieve this goal. First, each balloon would carry more than one bomb designed to be released by timed dispersal; that is, after one bomb was released, there would be time delay before the next bomb dropped. Second, the best way to spread the damage was through the use of fire; so the primary weapon used was an incendiary bomb, such as had been tried earlier in *Glen/I-25* attacks on Oregon forests. If enough fire bombs were dropped, then the amount of damage could be greatly multiplied.

But, an immediate problem was recognized in Japan. The ideal time to launch the balloons was the worst possible time to hope that incendiary bombs would do damage in the United States. The bombs would fall on the wet earth of winter in North America. Nevertheless, even if little physical damage resulted, there was the hope that psychologically the weapons would prove of value beyond any physical destruction wrought.

Thousands of balloons were readied. Each carried a weapons package of six explosive charges. The primary weapons were four thermite incendiary bombs, each with about eleven pounds of thermite ignited by a flash-powder charge designed to go off on impact. The bombs would be timed, with a delay up to twenty-four hours between release, for four separate attacks. In addition to the incendiaries, one 15-kilogram (about thirty-three pounds) anti-personnel bomb was carried. The bomb had a one hundred-foot kill zone on open ground.

Finally, a two-pound self-destruct bomb was carried in the payload gondola. In addition to the destructive power of the explosive, the gondo-

The remains of a Japanese balloon bomb recovered by the U.S. Army in the Pacific Northwest. (*National Archives*)

la also carried magnesium flash powder. It was hoped that by self-destructing, the Americas would be kept in the dark about the nature of the attack, adding to the terror quality of random bombings.

The Imperial General Staff called upon a terror campaign to launch 10,000 balloons in fifty days. Three battalions of the Special Balloon Regiment were tasked with the mission and readied their assault. Choosing a site surveyed to maximize the ability to capture the jet stream, the assault started on November 3, 1944. The Japanese were confident they would know of the success of their strategy very quickly, as the civilian population would react with panic as random and deadly bomb attacks occurred.[28]

The Imperial Army launched 9,000-plus balloons carrying 45,000 bombs. The Navy, the junior service in this effort, launched thirty-four balloons. The campaign never reached the desired goal of 10,000 balloons in fifty days. Teji Takeda, a member of the development team, estimated the number of balloons launched during the terror war as follows:

November 1944	700 balloons
December 1944	1,200 balloons

28. However, as one author noted, "Toward the end of April [1945], General Kusaba was told to cease all operations. The dictum of the staff was, 'Your balloons are not reaching America. If they were, reports would be in the newspapers [as] Americans could not keep their mouths closed this long.'" Wilbur, W.H. "Those Japanese Balloons," *Readers' Digest*, August 1950, pp. 23-26.

January 1945	2,000 balloons
February 1945	2,500 balloons
March 1945	2,500 Balloons
April 1945	400 Balloons[29]

Of the 46,500 bombs launched against North America, most dropped harmlessly into the Pacific Ocean and others did such little damage in remote sections of the west as not to be noticed. Several hundred others were shot down by Army and Navy aircraft or by naval gunfire. One balloon was attacked by a P-38 Lightning fighter as it drifted over Crater Lake National Park. Leaking hydrogen gas, it eventually landed in the remote Modoc National Forest, causing no damage. But approximately 345 balloon bombs were accounted for as having been released over the continent. Eighteen states, two U.S. territories, three Mexican states, four Canadian provinces as well as two Canadian territories reported balloons or balloon bombs landing. The balloons landed as far east as Michigan, as far north as Alaska, and as far south as Mexico. Two bombs landed in Cicero, Illinois, a suburb of Chicago. In general, all of the bombs were diffused or destroyed without any effect, but there were two notable exceptions.

On March 10, 1945, near one of the country's most top secret sites, the Hanford Atomic Works, where plutonium was being prepared for one of the atomic bombs, a balloon struck a power transmission line causing a power failure. The circuit disruption forced the atomic pile to scram or shut down; this attack successfully interrupted the development of the atomic fuel for three days. Another balloon bomb was shot down by military police protecting Hanford on the same day. As the balloon descended, the soldiers opened fire with their weapons, rupturing the gas bag, causing the balloon and its bombs to land harmlessly a quarter of a mile outside the perimeter fence.

The most infamous success of the Japanese ballon bomb campaign occurred in southern Oregon on May 5, 1945. High in the Gearhart Mountains, where Colonel Crook had chased Paiute Indians nearly eighty years before, a church outing was taking place. Archie Mitchell and his wife Elsye were taking children from the Christian and Missionary Alliance Church of the small community of Bly, Oregon, into

29. Balloon construction was brought to a near standstill in May 1945, after B-29 raids had destroyed two of the three production facilities.

the mountains to fish. As the outing drove into the mountains, Elsye became carsick. Stopping the car when the road became impassable, Elsye walked out in to the woods to breathe the mountain air. There, she was heard to exclaim, "Look at what I found, dear," bringing several children to her side to examine her wondrous discovery. The next sound was the fifteen kilogram anti-personnel bomb exploding. As Mr. Mitchell and two road workers raced to see what had happened, a secondary explosion fired off as the self-destruct weapon took care of its mission.

The men found Elsye Mitchell, age 26, and five children (four boys, ages 11 to 14, and one girl, age 13) dead, torn by the shrapnel from the bomb. These were the only fatalities from enemy action anywhere in the continental United States during World War II.

With the surrender of Japan in August 1945, the Sunset Division received its final assignment of the war, occupation duty in Japan. It would not be until December 1945 that some of the troops would start the mustering out process, while others would remain in Japan into 1946.

~

This period of history, being the most recent, is the best preserved. The Spanish-American War has no sites directly associated with its history, but locations such as Vancouver Barracks were used to stage and/or support the war effort. Many locales have monuments, or cemeteries of the era. In downtown Portland, Oregon, there is a monument to the 2nd Oregon Volunteer Regiment. Not too far from downtown, near Lewis and Clark College, is a cemetery, white headstones neatly arranged, with the dead from the Philippines.

Similarly, World War I has left nothing but monuments and headstones directly associated with the history of the Pacific Northwest. Many of the sites used during the "War to End all Wars" were used again in World War II, and very little is left to distinguish that which was used in The Great War.

Many sites remain to be explored. The coastal defense forts, created even before the Spanish-American War, still stand including Fort Worden,[30] near Port Townsend, Washington, and three forts guarding the

---

30. Fort Worden gained some additional glamour as it was used as the locale for filming the movie, *An Officer and a Gentleman*. It still looks very much like a military base.

mouth of the Columbia River, Forts Columbia and Canby, on the Washington shore, and Fort Stevens. The forts are state parks and have museums. A history seeker can still walk the ramparts of Battery Russell, and see where *I-25*'s shells landed.

Today, Fort Lewis is the primary military post in the Pacific Northwest. Starting off as Camp Lewis in World War I, and named for Meriwether Lewis, it is a large and active Army base. In World War I, the 91st Division trained here, and during World War II, the 3rd, 33rd, 40th, 41st, 44th, and 96th Infantry Divisions were readied for combat at Fort Lewis. Starting in 1943, the fort also housed a prisoner of war camp.

Also located at Fort Lewis, just off the Interstate freeway, I-5, is the Fort Lewis Military Museum, an excellent place to obtain a perspective on the region's military past and present. Situated nearby is an air museum at McChord Air Force Base.

The Oregon National Guard base, Camp Wythecombe, located in the suburbs of Portland, Oregon, is the home of the Oregon Military Museum. A similar themed museum, the Idaho Military History Museum, is located at the Boise Airport, known as Gowen Field, from its days as an Army Air Corps field.

The site of the fatal balloon bomb attack can be visited in the remote Gearhart Mountains of Lake County, Oregon. A picnic area and a plaque are a memorial to the six victims.

Many other sites note the history of the Pacific Northwest as it struggled to contribute its share of the home front effort to win the war. A roadside historical marker notes the site of Camp Adair, near Corvallis, Oregon. Now nothing more than a memory and a marker, Camp Adair was the World War II training site for the 70th, 91st, 96th, and 104th Infantry Divisions, for both the Pacific and European Theaters of Operation. To prepare the divisions, full-scale European villages were built to school men for urban fighting. All of the base's infrastructure including the village, have been razed. Camp Adair was later used as a prisoner of war camp for Italian and German soldiers.

Many former World War II air fields have been converted to civilian fields. Little remains to mark the former military presence once so prominent throughout the country. An exception is the Tillamook Naval Air Station. One of the huge hangers that housed six blimps at once still stands and is used as an air museum. The former air station is near the ocean, about ninety miles west of Portland. Other air fields have museums dedicated to the history of flight, which includes the history of military flight. Boeing Field in Seattle has the Seattle Museum of Flight; Olympia, Washington has the Olympic Flight Museum, while the Washington city of Vancouver has the historic Pearson Air Museum, located on the site of the Pearson Army Air Field, one of the oldest air fields in the west. About fifty miles southwest of Portland is the Evergreen Air Museum, located in McMinnville. Its most famous display item is the huge "Spruce Goose" amphibious aircraft, developed by Howard Hughes' aircraft company during World War II to move troops above the threat of submarines.

Even as recent as these events are, their history is fading as development takes over many of the sites. But still, the traveler seeking history has but to drive the roads of the Pacific Northwest to go back into time.

Conclusion

With the official close of the Indian Wars in 1905, the U.S. Army established the Indian Wars Medal for "any action against hostile Indians in which U.S. troops were killed or wounded" between 1865-1891. It cited several specific campaigns of which the following took place within the Oregon Country:

1865-68   Northern California and Nevada, Southern Oregon and Idaho

1872-73   The Modoc War

1877   The Nez Perce War

1878   The Bannock War

1879   Against the Sheepeaters, Piutes (or Paiute), and Bannocks

Of the fourteen battle streamers issued to the Army's regiments, three of the streamers were for the campaigns that were fought in the Oregon Country: Modocs, Nez Perces, and Bannocks.[1]

The issuance of a medal conferred a greater status on veterans, but that was only half the story. The American Indians' continual loss of territory through the elimination or reduction of their reservations had been devastating to the remnants of their traditional lifestyles. The world the American Indians knew no longer existed and could not be recovered. Chief Joseph never did regain his beloved Wallowa Valley; he died in

1. The fourteen campaign streamers issued for the Indian Wars are Miami, Tippecanoe, Creeks, Seminoles, Black Hawk, Comanches, Modocs, Apaches, Little Big Horn, Nez Perces, Bannocks, Cheyennes, Utes, and Pine Ridge.

1904, on the Colville Indian Reservation. Some Indian nations ceased to exist altogether.

Despite the loss and the atrocities committed by both sides, and despite the desire to forget and move on, both sides had some things to be proud of as a people. For the American Indians, they can look back on heroes, and leaders of extraordinary vision and courage. Kamiakin's call for greater Indian unity against white encroachment ranks alongside those of Pontiac, Tecumseh, Sitting Bull, and Geronimo. In some ways, the Pacific Northwest Indian struggle of the 1850s was the greatest epic of Indian resistance in American history; an entire region rose up in arms through coordination or simultaneous recognition of the need to fight back. Indian efforts failed, not because of a lack of will or strategy, but because by the time they acted, white forces were simply too large to be overcome.

Chief Joseph, another great American Indian leader (and never really the "war chief" attributed to him by the white press), expressed a desire for peace that still resonates to this day: "I will fight no more, forever." The war against the Nez Perce, clearly seen as an injustice, helped turn public opinion away from the destruction of the Indians toward one of a more just and fair treatment of the Indian. The Nez Perce War was larger than the Oregon Country were it began, as were its consequences.

There were prominent whites who also stood out as notable heroes. As a man of peace and justice, Joel Palmer was without equal. He fought for Indian rights and the preservation of Indian nations, not perfectly, but as a man of his time. Few others of his stature easily come to mind as peacemakers.

As for white men of war, there were several remarkable men. Prior to the Civil War, Colonel George Wright, in his actions against the Spokane coalition, waged one of the most successful Indian war campaigns ever fought within the Oregon Country, decisively defeating his enemy.

Eventually credited with being the most able of the Indian fighters, George Crook first developed his ideas for fighting Indians in Oregon Country before the Civil War. He returned to Oregon after the war to take command and to perfect his strategy for defeating American Indian forces. He would go on to successfully fight on the plains against the Sioux and Cheyenne nations and then again in the Southwest against the Apaches.

If George Crook represents the acme of strategic command, tactical command was rarely wielded better than it was by Captain Reuben F. Bernard. The U.S. 1st Cavalry earned its reputation for mediocrity in actions against Indians. However, an exception came to be recognized in the captain from Boise Barracks. Personally fearless, he was able to lead his men against superior forces with success by doggedly pursuing the Indians through some of the harshest country imaginable.

The military history of the area after the Indian wars was one of training on the homeland, then shipping out to fight elsewhere. There were heroes from the Pacific Northwest, but they fought in fields far from the paradise of their homes. Many men who served in the Pacific Northwest would go on to serve with distinction and would add their names to the roll call of the past military leaders. Men such as Thomas Anderson and George Marshall were commanders of Vancouver Barracks, and both would reach high rank, serving their nation well.

The Oregon Country has a rich military history. Countless actions and battles were fought, innumerable patrols led, and dozens of remote posts garrisoned. It is a military history long overlooked and almost forgotten, but that does not diminish the respect that all of those who fought for paradise deserve.

∼

This book started as trail of discovery for me. Always a seeker of history, I would frequently slam on the brakes as I motored on a highway whenever I saw a sign, "Historical Marker Ahead." What so often frustrated me was the lack of the "big picture." I can recall one vacation in the Northwest when I read a road side sign in Washington, near the Canadian border, on the North West Company's Fort Okanogan; another in Idaho near Craters of the Moon National Monument on the Bannock War; and two signs in the far southeastern corner of Oregon, one on the Bannock War, and another about Peter Skene Ogden's 1825 stay on the Malheur River. I walked away wondering how all of these events contributed to the Northwest's creation.

As I continued my studies, I kept finding more about the people who were here before my ancestors arrived. I knew that for me, the Northwest is paradise, and I found that the American Indians shared the same love of the land. I came to realize that if I had been them, at that time, I, too, may have fought the white encroachment.

Another realization that came to me was how brutal the wars were for this paradise. Neither side had an exclusive claim to moral conduct, but both acted as was the custom and norms of the time. It is wrong to sit back hundreds of years later, and condemn one side or another for their actions.

The two strongest impressions I came away with both involve preservation. Perhaps preservation is the wrong idea for the problem I encountered; I wanted to bring perspective to the narrative by giving an Indian account of the events, but few exist. The histories that have been written, just as this one, have a distinct European point of view. Several older histories were racist, casting the Indians as demonic savages, fighting against the march of progress. Clearly none of the American Indian peoples were that, and the march of progress was foot fall on their way of life. The Indians were as justified to resist the white invasion as any other people have been when their country has been attacked. It is more a statement of how civilized they were, at least in attitude, that their initial inclination was to live in accommodation with their new neighbors. What I longed to read was a book on the Indian viewpoint.

The other piece I found missing was the preservation of historical sites. Not merely the ground that the events occurred on, but a historical interpretation of the site. In each period covered by this book, I found a place particularly needing restoration or preservation (at least in my eyes). I would love to see Fort Astoria returned to its original configuration. In addition, built next to it in a historical park should be a Clatsop village. It would be a wonderful addition to bringing history alive to show how the trappers and the natives interacted, and even the history of the British and American competition for paradise.

I can remember the thrill I had as I tracked down the site of a battle. As I stood on a hill overlooking a location where a camp of two thousand Indians had lived, I could recall reading the participants' description of the land as they readied their cavalry charge. It had changed little. I would love to see the spot preserved to tell the story of the Indians, the settlers, and the troopers who fought for the small piece of Eden I looked at that morning, at about the same time as the attack.

I would hope that at the very least we might erect a few more signs and a few more historical markers so as others drive the roads of the Northwest, they might understand how paradise was fought over, how each side won and lost, and why we are now standing looking at the future together.

Appendix

Military and Civilian Forts, Camps, and Blockhouses in the Pacific Northwest, 1809–1879

IDAHO

BONNEVILLE'S POST ON THE SALMON RIVER, Lemhi County, 1832. Captain Benjamin Bonneville's first effort to build a wintering fort.

CAMP CONNER, Caribou County, 1863-1865. Built by 3rd California Volunteer Infantry near Soda Springs to protect the Oregon Trail in May 1863.

CAMP HOWARD, south of Grangeville, Idaho County, 1878-79. A temporary U.S. Army camp established during the Bannock Indian War and also used in the Sheepeater War.

CAMP LANDER, Bingham County, 1865-1866. A temporary camp used in the Snake Indian Wars.

CAMP LYON, Jordan Valley, Owyhee County, 1865-1878. A camp established during the Snake Indian War and used up to the time of the Bannock Indian War.

CAMP REED, Custer County, 1865-1866. Used during the Snake Indian Wars.

CAMP THREE FORKS, the Jordan Valley, Owyhee County, 1878. A temporary camp established during the Bannock Indian War.

CANTONMENT LORING, Bingham County, 1849-50. A wintering camp for the Mounted Rifles located near the old Fort Hall. Named for the Mounted Rifles' colonel, William W. Loring.

FORT BOISE, Canyon County, 1834-1854. A Hudson's Bay trading post built near Parma. A museum marks the site today.

FORT BOISE/BOISE BARRACKS, Ada County, 1863-1913. U.S. Army post first built by Oregon Volunteers to protect the Oregon Trail. Renamed Bosie Barracks in 1879.

FORT COEUR D'ALENE, the first name for Fort Sherman; see below.

FORT HALL, Bingham County, 1834-1853. Originally built by Nathaniel Wyeth, it was purchased by the Hudson's Bay Company, and in turn sold to the U.S. Army. Abandoned by 1853, it became the center of the Fort Hall Indian Reservation. A replica has been built in the town of Pocatello, Idaho.

FORT HENRY, Fremont County, 1811. In 1810, trappers under Andrew Henry and his St. Louis Missouri Fur Company erected cabins on the North Fork of the Snake River. Abandoned, the cabins were occupied the next year by Wilson Price Hunt's Astorian party, who had been led to the spot by former Henry trappers. They christened the location Fort Henry.

FORT LAPWAI, Nez Perce County, 1862-1882. Built by Oregon Volunteers to guard the friendly Nez Perce during the Snake Indian War.

FORT SHERMAN, near Coeur d'Alene, Kootenai County, 1878-1901. Originally called Fort Coeur d'Alene. A museum marks the site today.

FORT SIMON, Near Waha, Nez Perce County. Uncertain date or use.

FORT WILSON, near Payette, Payette County. Uncertain date or use.

MCKENZIE'S POST, near Lewiston, Nez Perce County, 1812-1813. Built by Astor's Pacific Fur Company as a trading post. Abandoned when news of the War of 1812 reached the post and Donald Mckenzie defected to the Northwest Company.

OLD FORT, on the Payette River, south of McCall, Valley County. Uncertain date or use.

OREGON

ADOBE CAMP, Harney County, 1865. Used for about one month prior to the establishment of Camp Wright (see below). Built by Captain L. L. Williams and Company H, 1st Oregon Infantry.

CAMP ALDEN, Jackson County, 1853. Used for a brief time during the Rogue Indian War. Named for Captain Bradford Ripley Alden, 4th U.S. Infantry.

CAMP ALVORD, Malheur County, 1864-1866. Used sporadically in the Snake Indian War. Used by 1st Oregon Cavalry, under Lt. J. A. Waymire, and, later, by Captain George B. Currey. Named for Brigadier General Benjamin Alvord.

CAMP BAKER, Jackson County, 1862-1865. Established by the First Oregon Volunteer Cavalry and named for Major General E. D. Baker (of Oregon) who died at the Battle of Balls Bluff in the Civil War.

CAMP BARLOW, Clackamas County, 1862-? Used as a recruit depot for the 1st Oregon Volunteer Cavalry.

CAMP CASTAWAY, Coos County, 1852. The transport ship *Captain Lincoln* sailed from San Francisco on December 28, 1851 with C Troop, 1st [U.S.] Dragoons, Lieutenant H.W. Stanton commanding. The ship was wrecked on January 3, 1852 while en route to Port Orford. The survivors established a camp which was maintained for about four months.

CAMP C.F. SMITH, Harney County, 1866-1869. Constructed after Camp Alvord was abandoned during the Snake Indian War.

CAMP COLFAX, Malheur County, 1865. Established by F Company, 1st Oregon Volunteer Infantry during the Snake Indian War.

CAMP CURREY, Harney County, 1865-1866. Used in the Snake Indian Wars by elements of 4th California Infantry, 1st Washington Territorial Infantry, 1st Oregon Infantry, and the 14th U.S. Infantry.

CAMP DAHLGREN, Crook County, 1864. A temporary post used by the 1st Oregon Cavalry during the Snake Indian War.

CAMP DAY, Klamath County, 1860. Established by Company L, 3rd U.S. Artillery as a camp to protect the emigrant trail from Yreka to the Klamath country.

CAMP DRUM, Wasco County, 1850. First name given to the U.S. Army post that became Fort Dalles. Established by the Mounted Rifles Regiment.

CAMP ELLIFF, Douglas County, 1855-1856. Company B, 2nd Oregon Mounted Volunteers, established a post to protect the road along Cow Creek during the Rogue Indian War.

CAMP GIBBS, Crook County, 1864. During the Snake Indian War, Camp Maury was established (see below) but was abandoned as forage was poor. The renewed camp was called Gibbs. When forage again ran low, Camp Gibbs was abandoned, too, and a new post, Camp Dahlgren, was established (see above).

CAMP HENDERSON, Malheur County, 1864. A temporary post established during the Snake Indian War.

CAMP LINCOLN, Grant County, 1864. A temporary post of about three months used during the Snake Indian War.

CAMP LOGAN, Grant County, 1865-1867. A post established for use in the Snake Indian War.

CAMP MAURY, Crook County, 1864. A temporary post used in the Snake Indian War. See Camps Dahlgren and Gibbs, above. Named for Colonel R.F. Maury, commander of the First Oregon Volunteer Cavalry.

CAMP MCDOWELL, Umatilla County, 1865. A temporary post for use in the Snake Indian War. Named for Major General Irwin McDowell, commander of the Division of the Pacific.

CAMP POLK, Deschutes County, 1865-1866. Winter camp for Company A, 1st Oregon Volunteer Infantry during the Snake Indian War.

CAMP RUSSELL, Marion County, 1864-1865. Used as a recruit depot for the 1st Oregon Volunteer Infantry.

CAMP STUART, Jackson County, 1851-1853. James Stuart was a member of Philip's command and was killed as a result of wounds received on June 17, 1851. The camp was named for the fallen soldier by George B. McClellan, also a member of Kearny's command.

CAMP WARNER, Lake County, 1866-1873. Used during the Modoc Indian War, the first camp named Warner was established on the east side of the valley. In 1867, George Crook had the camp moved to the west side of the valley as being more desirous.

CAMP WATSON, Wheeler County, 1864-1868. Used during the Snake Indian Wars.

CAMP WRIGHT, Harney County, 1865. Used during the Snake Indian War and named for Brigadier General George Wright, Commander of the Department of the Columbia, who drowned while en route to his command from San Francisco.

FORT ASTORIA, Clatsop County, 1811-1824. Built by the Astor party for the Pacific Fur Company. See Fort George, below. One blockhouse has been reconstructed and is located in downtown Astoria.

FORT BAILEY, Josephine County, 1855-1856. Established during the Rogue Indian War.

FORT BIRDSEYE, Jackson County, 1855-1856. Used during the Rogue Indian War.

FORT BRIGGS, Josephine County, 1855-1856. Used by settlers as a defensive redoubt during the Rogue Indian War.

FORT CLATSOP, Clatsop County, 1805-1806. Lewis and Clark's Pacific wintering post; now a unit of the National Park Service.

FORT DALLES, Wasco County, 1850-1866. Established by Colonel Loring of the Mounted Rifles and was the principle fort along the Columbia River. One original building still remains and is located within the City of The Dalles as a city park.

FORT FLOURNEY, Douglas County, 1855. Built as a defensive rallying point for settlers during the Rogue Indian War, it was never used.

FORT GEORGE, Clatsop County, 1813-1818. The name given to Fort Astoria by the British after it had been sold to the Northwest Fur Company and then "seized" by Captain William Black of the *H.M.S. Racoon*.

FORT HARNEY, Harney County, 1867-1880. Intended to be the major American military post of southeastern Oregon, it was used during the Bannock Indian War.

FORT HAYES, Josephine County, 1855-1856. Used as a settlers' defensive position in the Rogue Indian War.

FORT HENRIETTA, Umatilla County, 1855-1856. Built by elements of the 1st Oregon Mounted Rifles during their winter campaign during the Yakima War. A blockhouse has been reconstructed and is located in Echo.

FORT HILL, Polk County, 1855-1856. Used by settlers as a defensive position. Taken over by the U.S. Army. See Fort Yamhill below.

FORT HOSKINS, Benton County, 1856-1865. As a result of the Rogue Indian War, a reservation was established for the Indians and three forts were created to protect the Siletz Agency as it was called. Fort Hoskins was one of the three posts. Benton County (OR) maintains a county park to commemorate the site.

FORT KITCHEN, Coos County, 1855. A defensive location for settlers during the Rogue Indian War.

FORT KLAMATH, Klamath County, 1863-1889. The principle fort of south-central Oregon and used extensively during the Snake Indian, Modoc, and Bannock Indian Wars. A museum marks the location of the old post.

At the park are the graves of the Modoc hung at the fort in October 1873, including Captain Jack.

FORT LAMERICK, Curry County, 1856. A fort built at the site of the Battle of Big Meadows and named after the Brigadier General in charge of Oregon troops during the Rogue Indian War.

FORT LANE, Jackson County, 1853-1856. Established September 28, 1853. Originally manned with three companies of 2nd U.S. Infantry. Fort Lane was the principle U.S. Army post during the Rogue Indian War.

FORT LEE, Wasco County, 1847. A temporary fort used by Oregon troops during the Cayuse Indian War.

FORT LELAND, 1855-1856. Josephine County. Used by Oregon Volunteers during the Rogue Indian War.

FORT MINER, Curry County, 1855-1856. Used by settlers and miners as a defensive position during the Rogue Indian War.

FORT ORFORD, 1851-1856. A civilian stockade was built earlier in 1851 (see Fort Point, below) but was abandoned when the U.S. Army established the post to help with protecting the southern coast from the hostile Indians.

FORT POINT, Curry County, 1851. Two blockhouses were built as defensive fall-back positions for local settlers.

FORT ROWLAND, Coos County, 1855. A defensive position for local settlers during the Rogue Indian War.

FORT SMITH, Douglas County, 1855-1856. Used by Oregon troops during the Rogue Indian War.

FORT STEVENS, Clatsop County, 1864-1947. Principle coast artillery fort protecting the mouth of the Columbia River. Authorized by the Northwest Coastal Defense Act of 1862. Named for Isaac Stevens, Washington's territorial governor until the Civil War. A state park preserves its history but emphasizes its role in the twentieth century.

FORT UMPQUA (I), Douglas County, 1832-1848. A Hudson's Bay Company fur trading post. Attacked by Indians in the summer of 1840.

FORT UMPQUA (II), Douglas County, 1856. One of the three U.S. Army forts built to protect the Siletz Agency.

FORT VANNOY, Josephine County, 1855-1856. The main headquarters of Oregon Volunteers during the Rogue Indian War.

FORT WILLIAM, Columbia and Multnomah Counties, 1834-1836. A trading post established by Nathaniel Wyeth.

FORT YAMHILL, Yamhill County, 1855-1865. Established as one of three forts to protect the Siletz Agency after the Rogue Indian War. An original blockhouse has been moved to a city park in nearby Dayton. The State of Oregon opened a park to commemorate the site in 2006.

WAGNER'S FORT, Jackson County, 1853-1854(?). A strong-point at the Wagner's farm (on what is now called Wagner's Creek, near Talent, Oregon) used for defense against Indian attack.

WILLAMETTE POST, Clackamas County, 1812-1814. A trading post established by the Pacific Fur company. Taken over by the Northwest fur Company and renamed Henry House.

WASHINGTON

CAMP STEELE, San Juan County, 1859-1873. A temporary camp established in the Pig War to assert American interests in the San Juan islands.

COLUMBIA BARRACKS, Clark County, 1849. Name first given to the First U.S. Artillery establishment which became Vancouver Barracks/Fort Vancouver.

FORT ALDEN (ALDEN BLOCKHOUSE), King County, 1856. Built for defense by the Washington Territorial Volunteers during The Great Outbreak.

FORT ARKANSAS (ARKANSAS BLOCKHOUSE), Cowlitz County, 1856. Built by settlers as a defensive position.

FORT BELLINGHAM, Whatcom County, 1856-1860. A U.S. Army post for protecting the north boundary. Established by Captain George E. Pickett, 9th U.S. Infantry.

FORT BENNET, Walla Walla County, 1855-1856. During the winter campaign in the Yakima War, Oregon Mounted Volunteers erected Fort Bennet.

FORT BORST, Lewis County, 1856. Built by settlers to protect against Indian attacks.

FORT CANBY, Pacific County, 1864-1950. Originally built as Fort Cape Disappointment (see below) as part of the coast artillery defense network for the Columbia River, its name was changed on January 28, 1875 to honor General Canby, killed during the Modoc Indian War. World War II revetments remain accessible.

Fort Cape Disappointment, see Fort Canby.

Fort Cascades, Skamania County, 1855-1861. Erected by the U.S. Army (Captain [Brevet Major] Granville Haller's 4th U.S. Infantry) as a consequence of the Indian attacks at the Cascades of the Columbia. It is now a U.S. Army Corps of Engineers' historical site.

Fort Chehalis (Camp Chehalis), Grays County, 1860-1861. Company A, 4th U.S. Infantry, under Captain Maloney, occupied this post until recalled for service in the Civil War.

Fort Colvile, Okanogan County, 1825-1871. Built as a fur trading post for the Hudson's Bay Company.

Fort Colville, Ferry County, 1859-1882. Major Lougenbeel brought four companies of the 9th Infantry to protect miners from Indians.

Fort at Cowlitz Landing, Lewis County, 1856. Washington Territorial Volunteers built the fort to protect an important passage from Oregon to the Puget Sound.

Fort Decatur (Seattle Blockhouse), King County, 1855-1856. Built by the U.S. Marines from the *U.S.S. Decatur* to protect the city of Seattle against Indian attack.

Fort Dent, King County, 1856. Built by Territorial Volunteers to protect against Indian attack.

Fort Duwamish, King County, 1855. Erected by settlers in the area to protect themselves.

Fort Eaton, Thurston County, 1856. Erected by settlers to protect themselves.

Fort Ebey (Ebey Blockhouse), Snohomish County, 1855. Built by Northern Rangers, Washington Territorial Volunteers, to prevent the successful link-up of coastal Indians with those of the interior.

Fort Gilliam, Skaminia County, 1848. Built by the Oregon Mounted Rifles during the Cayuse War as a supply base.

Fort Hays (Hays Blockhouse), Thurston County, 1856. A Washington Territorial Volunteers' post built during the Indian wars.

Fort Henderson, King County, 1856. Built to help guard the Cascade passes.

Fort Henness (Hennes Blockhouse), Pierce County, 1856. Built by settlers for protection. A historical marker notes the site of this fort, off of U.S. Highway 12, between the town of Rochester, and west of Interstate 5.

FORT HICKS (HICKS BLOCKHOUSE), Pierce County, 1856-1857. Built by Washington Territory to protect against Indian attack.

FORT LANDER (LANDER BLOCKHOUSE), King County, 1856. Built by Washington Territory to protect against Indian attack.

FORT MALONEY (MALONEY BLOCKHOUSE), Pierce County, 1856. Built by the U.S. Army, under the command of Captain Maurice Maloney, 4th U.S. Infantry, it was designed to protect the town of Puyallup.

FORT MASON, 1856-1857. Walla Walla County. Built by Colonel Shaw as a temporary establishment.

FORT MASON (MASON BLOCKHOUSE), Jefferson County, 1857. Built by Washington Volunteers.

FORT MCALLISTER (MCALLISTER BLOCKHOUSE), Pierce County, 1856. Built by the Central Battalion, Washington Territorial Volunteers to protect against Indian attack.

FORT MILLER (MILLER BLOCKHOUSE), Thurston County, 1856. Built by the Washington Territorial Volunteers as a quartermaster depot.

FORT NA-CHESS (CAMP NACHES), Kittitas County, 1856. Built by the 9th Infantry as a depot and a blocking fort during The Great Outbreak.

FORT NESQUALLY, Pierce County, 1833-1843. A Hudson's Bay Company trading post.

FORT NEZ PERCE, Walla Walla County, 1818-1860. North West Company fur post, later called Fort Walla Walla (see below) after being taken over by the Hudson's Bay Company.

FORT NISQUALLY, Pierce County, 1843-1860. A continuation of Fort Nesqually, it was a relocation of the fort two miles north with a slightly different spelling. A City of Tacoma park has recreated the old fur trading post.

FORT OKANOGAN, Okanogan County, 1811-1816. A Pacific Fur Company trading post taken over by the North West Company in 1813.

FORT OKANOGAN, Okanogan County, 1816-1859. A North West Company post. The previous post was abandoned and reestablished about a half mile to the northwest.

FORT PIKE (PIKE BLOCKHOUSE), Pierce County, 1856. Built by Washington Territorial Volunteers to guard a crossing of the White River.

FORT POSEY (POSEY BLOCKHOUSE), Pierce County, 1856. Also built by Washington Territorial Volunteers to guard another crossing of the White River.

FORT PRESTON (PRESTON BLOCKHOUSE), Pierce County, 1856. A Washington Territorial Volunteer post to protect a crossing on the Nisqually River.

FORT RAINS, Skamania County, 1856. A U.S. Army blockhouse built to protect the crossing of the Columbia. Built and named by Major Gabriel Rains, Fourth U.S. Infantry.

FORT RAGLAN (RAGLAN BLOCKHOUSE), Lewis County, 1856. A Washington Territorial Volunteer post built to protect Packwood's Ferry on the Nisqually River.

FORT RIGGS, Clark County, 1856. Built by the Clark County Rangers during the The Great Outbreak threat.

FORT SIMCOE, Yakima County, 1856-1859. Built in the heart of the Yakima Indian nation by elements of the 9th U.S. Infantry. The State of Washington has established a park with some of the original buildings still standing.

FORT SKOOKUM, Mason County, 1856. Built by Washington Territorial Volunteers.

FORT SLAUGHTER (SLAUGHTER BLOCKHOUSE), Pierce County, 1856-1857. Built by the 3rd U.S. Artillery, under First Lieutenant Erasmus Darwin Keyes, to protect against Indians on the Muckleshoot Prairie.

FORT SPOKANE, Spokane County, 1812-1826. Built by the Pacific Fur Company but purchased by the North West Company in 1813. Note: The U.S. Army post called Fort Spokane was built after the Indian wars period.

FORT STEILACOOM, Pierce County, 1849-1868. This was the main U.S. Army post on the Puget Sound during the majority of the Indian wars. Built by Captain Bennett H. Hill, 1st U.S. Artillery.

FORT STEVENS (STEVENS BLOCKHOUSE), Pierce County, 1856. Built by Washington Territorial Volunteers.

FORT TAYLOR (CAMP TAYLOR), Columbia County, 1858. Built to protect a major river (Tucannon River) crossing during the build up of Wright's campaign against the Spokane Indians. Named for First Lieutenant Oliver Hazard Perry Taylor, 1st U.S. Dragoons, killed at Steptoe's Battle.

FORT THOMAS (THOMAS BLOCKHOUSE), King County, 1856. Built by the U.S. Army to protect against Indians.

Fort Tilton (Tilton Blockhouse), King County, 1856. Used as the main headquarters of the Northern battalion, Washington Territorial Volunteers during the Indian Wars.

Fort Townsend, Kitsap County, 1856-1893. Established by the 4th U.S. Infantry as protection from northern Indian attacks.

Fort Vancouver, Clark County, 1825-1860. The premier Hudson's Bay Company post in the entire Oregon Country. A National Park Service Historical Site has recreated the fur trading post.

Fort Vancouver (Vancouver Barracks), 1849-present. Originally called Columbia Barracks when it was established by the U.S. Army. It was the headquarters for the Department of the Columbia throughout the major Indian wars. It remains an army facility for the National Guard. The regular U.S. Army ended its 151 years of service at the post in July 2000. A national historical reserve helps to maintain some of the original buildings from the era covered in this history.

Fort Walla Walla, Walla Walla County, 1818-1855. A North West Company post (first called Fort Nez Perce; see above) assumed by the merger by the Hudson's Bay Company.

Fort Walla Walla (I), Walla Walla County, 1856. Built by Colonel Steptoe's 9th Infantry but abandoned for a new Fort Walla Walla (below).

Fort Walla Walla (II), Walla Walla County, 1856. The post above was moved a short distance for better advantage.

Fort Walla Walla (III), Walla Walla County, 1857-1917. The final location of the primary fort for the area was established in 1857. A park and museum preserve the history of the fort and the region.

Fort Waters (Camp Waters), Walla Walla County, 1848. Built by the Oregon Mounted Rifles at the site of the Whitman Massacre as protection from Indian attack during the Cayuse Indian War.

Fort White (White Blockhouse), Pierce County, 1856. Built by the Washington Territorial Volunteers to protect a Puyallup River crossing.

Fort Yakima Valley (Yakima Station Blockhouse), Yakima County, 1856. Washington Territorial Volunteers built a post to protect a stage station.

Kullispell House, Pend Orielle County, 1809-1810. Established by David Thompson as a temporary fur trading post.

SEATTLE BLOCKHOUSE, King County, 1855-1856. Another name for Fort Decatur (see above).

MONTANA

FLATHEAD POST, Lincoln County, 1809-1810. Northwest Fur Company post built by David Thompson for wintering over.

FORT CONNAH, Sanders County, 1846-1871. A Hudson's Bay Company post and the last established below the 49th Parallel, allowed under the treaty of 1846.

FORT FIZZLE, Mineral County, 1877. Captain Charles C. Rawn, 7th U.S. Infantry, established the defensive position, with Montana Volunteers, to stop the Nez Perce Indians. When the Montana Volunteers reached an independent agreement with the Nez Perce, the Indians were able to avoid a fight with the few Regular Army troops. The fort was called Fort Fizzle in ridicule. Now a State Historical Site (and Park), on U.S. Highway 12.

FORT HOWSE, Lake County, 1810-1811. A Hudson's Bay Company establishment built for wintering over.

FORT MISSOULA, Missoula County, 1877-1898. Established by Lt. Col. Charles C. Gilbert, 7th U.S. Infantry.

FORT OWEN, Ravali County, 1841-1872. First a Catholic mission under Father DeSmet, it was sold to private hands in 1850 for a trading post.

KOOTENAI HOUSE, Lincoln County, 1808. Several posts were named Kootenai House by Nor'Wester David Thompson. This post was abandoned and supplies moved to Kullispell House, in Washington.

THOMPSON'S TRADING POST, Bonner County, 1808-1809. Northwest Fur Company post built by David Thompson.

WYOMING

FORT BONNEVILLE, Sublette County, 1832-1835. The only fort located in Wyoming in the Oregon Country. Build by Captain Benjamin Bonneville for a base of operations. Because of the poor location for wintering over in the harsh conditions of Wyoming, it was also called Fort Nonsense and Bonneville's Folly.

Bibliography

Aderkas, Elizabeth von. *American Indians of the Pacific Northwest*. University Park: Osprey Publishing, 2005.

Alfred, B. et al, editors. *Great Western Indian Fights*. Lincoln: University of Nebraska Press, 1960.

Ambrose, Stephen E. *Undaunted Courage*. New York: Touchstone/Simon and Shuster, 1966.

Azuma, Eiichiro. "A History of Oregon's Issei, 1880-1952," *Oregon Historical Quarterly*, December 1993.

Bakeless, John, ed. *The Journals of Lewis and Clark*. New York: Signet, 2002.

Barry, J. Neilson. "Early Oregon Country Forts: A Chronological List," *Oregon Historical Quarterly*, June 1945.

Beckham, Stephen Dow. *Requiem for a People*. Corvallis: Oregon State University Press, 1998.

Beeson, John. *A Plea for the Indians*. Fairfield: Ye Galleon Press, 1998.

Binns, Archie. *Peter Skene Ogden: Fur Trader*. Portland: Binfords and Mort, 1967.

Bonney, William P. "The Death of Lieutenant Slaughter," *History of Pierce County*, Volume 1.

Boylan, Bernard L. "Camp Lewis: Promotion and Construction," *Pacific Northwest Quarterly*, Volume 58, number 4, October 1967.

Braly, David. Juniper Empire: *Early Days in Eastern and Central Oregon*. Prineville: American Media, 1976.

Brown, William Carey. "Two Cavalrymen's Diaries of the Bannock War, 1878," *Oregon Historical Quarterly*, September 1967.

Calloway, Colin G. *One Vast Winter Count. The American Indian West before Lewis and Clark*. Lincoln: University of Nebraska Press, 2003.

Carey, Charles H. *General History of Oregon*. Portland: Binfords and Mort, 1971.

Clark, Robert Carlton. "Military History of Oregon, 1849-1859," *Oregon Historical Quarterly*, March 1935.

Cline, Gloria Griffen. *Peter Skene Ogden and the Hudson's Bay Company*. Norman: University of Oklahoma Press, 1974.

Coyle, Brendan. *War on our Doorstep: The Unknown Campaign on North America's West Coast*. Surrey: Heritage House, 2002.

Converse, George L. *A Military History of the Columbia Valley*. Walla Walla: Pioneer Press Books, 1988.

Cornwall, Robert. "Oliver Cromwell Applegate, Paternalistic Friend of the Indians," *The Journal of the Shaw Library*, 1992.

Coulter, C. Brewster (senior editor). *The Pig War: The Journal of William A. Peck, Jr.* Medford: Webb Research Group, 1993.

Cozzens, Peter. *Eyewitness to the Indian Wars, 1865-1890: Wars for the Pacific Northwest*. Mechanicsburg: Stackpole Books, 2002.

Cresap, Bernarr. "Captain Edward O.C. Ord in the Rogue River Indian War," *Oregon Historical Quarterly*, June 1953.

Deac, Wilfred C. "Indian Fortress Assailed," *Wild West Magazine*, February, 1991.

Dean, Jonathan R. "The Hudson's Bay Company and Its use of Force, 1828-1829." *The Oregon Historical Society Quarterly*, Fall 1997.

Dennon, Jim. "Columbia River Exploration." *CUMTOX Clatsop County Historical Society Quarterly*, Spring 1992.

De Voto, Bernard, ed., *The Journals of Lewis and Clark*. Boston: Houghton Mifflin, 1953.

Douthit, Nathan. "Between Indian and White Worlds on the Oregon-California Border, 1851-1857," *Oregon Historical Quarterly*. Winter, 1999.

———. "The Hudson's Bay Company and the Indians of Southern Oregon," *Oregon Historical Society Quarterly*, Spring 1992.

———. *Uncertain Encounters: Indians and Whites at Peace and War in Southern Oregon, 1820s to 1860s*, Corvallis: Oregon State University Press, 2002.

Drake, John M. "The Oregon Cavalry," *Oregon Historical Quarterly*. December 1964.

Droker, Howard A. "Seattle Race Relations During the Second World War," *Pacific Northwest Quarterly*, Volume 67, number 4, October 1976.

Drew, Charles S. *An Account of the Origin and Early Prosecution of the Indian War in Oregon*. Fairfield: Ye Galleon Press, 1973 (reprint of the 1860 report).

Dryden, Cecil. *Up the Columbia for Furs*. Caldwell: Caxton Press, 1949.

Dunn, J. P. *Massacres of the Mountains: A History of the Indian Wars of the Far West*. Mechanicsburg: Stackpole Books, 2002.

Edwards, G. Thomas. "Six Oregon Leaders and the Far-reaching Impact of America's Civil War," *Oregon Historical Quarterly*. Spring 1999.

Elliott, T.C. "The Murder of Peu-Peu-Mox-Mox," *Oregon Historical Quarterly*. June 1934.

Ermantinger, C.O. "The Columbia River under Hudson's Bay Company Rule," *The Washington Historical Quarterly*. July 1914.

Ermantinger, Frank. "Earliest Expedition Against Puget Sound Indians," *The Washington Historical Quarterly*. January 1903.

Frazier, Robert W. *Forts of the West*. Norman: University of Oklahoma Press, 1965.

Friedheim, Robert L. "The Seattle General Strike of 1919," *Pacific Northwest Quarterly*, Volume 52, number 3, July 1961.

Glassley, Ray H. *Indian Wars of the Pacific Northwest*. Portland: Binfords and Mort, 1972.

Gough, Barry M.. "H.M.S. America on the North Pacific Coast," *Oregon Historical Quarterly*. December 1969.

——. *The Royal Navy and the Northwest Coast of North America, 1810-1914*. Vancouver: University of British Columbia Press, 1971.

——. "Send A Gunboat! Checking Slavery and Controlling Liquor Traffic Among Coast Indians of British Columbia in the 1860s," *Pacific Northwest Quarterly*, volume 69, Number 4, October 1978.

Guie, H. Dean. *Bugles in the Valley: Garnett's Fort Simcoe*. Portland: Oregon Historical Society Press, 1977.

Haines, Aubrey L. *An Elusive Victory: The Battle of the Big Hole*. Helena: Falcon Publishing, 1999.

Haines, Francis. *The Nez Perces: Tribesmen of the Columbia Plateau*. Norman: University of Oklahoma Press, 1955.

Hanft, Marshall. *The Cape Forts: Guardians of the Columbia*. Portland: Oregon Historical Society Press, 1973.

Hathaway, Edward E. *The War Nobody Won: The Modoc War from the Army's Point of View*. Show Low: American Eagle Publications, 1995.

Hatheway, John S., edited by Ted Van Arsdol. *Frontier Soldier: The Letters of Major John S. Hatheway, 1833-1853*. Vancouver: Vancouver National Historic Reserve Trust, 1999.

Hayes, Derek. *Historical Atlas of the Pacific Northwest*. Seattle: Sasquatch Books, 1999.

Howerton, Norman A. "The U.S. Schooner Shark," *Oregon Historical Quarterly*. September 1939.

Hussey, John A. "Fort Casey-Garrison for Puget Sound," *Pacific Northwest Quarterly*, Volume 47, number 2, April 1956.

Jackson, John C. *A Little War of Destiny: The First Regiment of Oregon Mounted Volunteers and the Yakima Indian War of 1855-56*. Olympia: Ye Galleon Press, 1996.

Jackson, Royal, and Jennifer Lee. *Harney County: An Historical Inventory*. Burns: Gail Graphics, 1978.

Jessett, Thomas E. *The Indian Side of the Whitman Massacre.* Fairfield: Ye Galleon Press, 1985.

Josephy, Jr., Alvin M. *Chief Joseph's People and Their War.* Yellowstone National Park: The Yellowstone Association, 1964.

Karamanski, Theodore J. Fur *Trade and Exploration.* Norman: University of Oklahoma Press, 1983.

Karlin, Jules Alexander. "The Anti-Chinese Outbreaks in Seattle, 1885-1886," *Pacific Northwest Quarterly*, Volume 39, 1948.

Kenny, Judith Keyes. "The Founding of Camp Watson," *Oregon Historical Quarterly*. March 1957.

Kip, Lawrence. *Indian War in the Pacific Northwest.* Lincoln: University of Nebraska Press, 1999.

Knoles, George H. "American Intellectuals and World War I," *Pacific Northwest Quarterly*, Volume 59, Number 4, October 1968.

Knuth, Priscilla, editor. "Cavalry in the Indian Country, 1864," *Oregon Historical Quarterly*. March 1964.

——. "HMS Modeste on the Pacific Coast 1843-47: Log and Letters," *Oregon Historical Quarterly*. September 1960.

——. "Picturesque Frontier," *The Army's Fort Dalles.* Portland: Oregon Historical Society Press, 1987.

Kone, W.W. "The Peacock Wrecked: An Eyewitness Account from 1841," *CUMTUX Clatsop County Historical Society Quarterly*. Summer 1994.

Laidlaw, Lansing S. "Aleutian Experience of the 'Mad M,'" *Oregon Historical Quarterly*. March 1979.

LaLande, Jeff. "'Dixie' of the Pacific Northwest: Southern Oregon's Civil War," *Oregon Historical Quarterly*. Spring 1999.

Lambert, Carol Carruthers. "The Great Fishermen's Strike of 1896," *CUMTUX Clatsop County Historical Society Quarterly*. Summer 2006.

Laurie, Clayton D. "The Chinese Must Go," *Pacific Northwest Quarterly*, Volume 81, Number 1, January 1990.

Leader, Herman A. "Douglas Expedition, 1840-41," *Oregon Historical Quarterly*. June 1931.

Loy, Edward H. "Editorial Opinion and American Imperialism: Two Northwest Newspapers," *Oregon Historical Quarterly*, September 1971.

Madsen, Brigham D. *The Bannock of Idaho.* Moscow: University of Idaho Press, 1996.

Marshall, Don. "The Peacock, Sloop-of-War," *CUMTUX Clatsop County Historical Society Quarterly*. Fall 1981.

Mayer, Frederick W. "Two Cavalrymen's Diaries of the Bannock War, 1878," *Oregon Historical Quarterly*. December 1967.

McArthur, Lewis L. *Oregon Geographic Names*. Portland: Oregon Historical Society Press, 1982.

McEnroe, Sean. "Painting the Philippines with an American Brush," *Oregon Historical Quarterly*. Spring 2003.

McKelvie, B.A. Fort Langley. *Victoria: Porcepic Book*, 1991.

McWhorter, L.V. *Hear Me, My Chiefs! Nez Perce Legend and History*. Caldwell: Caxton Press, 2001.

_____. *Yellow Wolf: His Own Story*. Caldwell: Caxton Printers, 1995.

Michino, Gregory F. *Encyclopedia of Indian Wars: Western Battles and Skirmishes, 1850-1890*. Missoula: Mountain Press Publishing Company, 2003.

Morgan, Dale L. *Jedediah Smith and the Opening of the West*. Lincoln: University of Nebraska Press, 1953.

Morgan, Murray C. *Skid Road*. Seattle: University of Washington Press, 1982.

Morrison, Dorothy Nafus. *Outpost: John McLoughlin and the Far Northwest*. Portland: Oregon Historical Society Press, 1999.

Movius, James Gilbert. "White-Paiute Conflicts, 1825-1868," *The Journal of the Shaw Historical Library*, 1992.

Murray, Keith A. *The Modocs and Their War*. Norman: University of Oklahoma Press, 1959.

Neils, Selma. *The Klickitat Indians*. Portland: Binfords and Mort, 1985.

Nesmith, James W. "A Reminiscence of the Indian War, 1853," *Oregon Historical Quarterly*. June 1906.

Newell, Gordon. *Totem Tales of Old Seattle*. Seattle: Superior Press, 1956.

Newman, Peter C. *Caesars of the Wilderness*. Ontario: Viking Press, 1987.

Nisbet, Jack. *Sources of the River*. Seattle: Sasquatch Books, 1994.

Noble, Dennis L, and Truman R. Stonebridge. "Early Cutterman in Alaskan Waters," *Pacific Northwest Quarterly*, Volume 78, Number 3, July 1981.

O'Brien, Robert W. "Reaction of the College Nisei to Japan and Japanese Foreign Policy from the Invasion of Manchuria to Pearl Harbor," *Pacific Northwest Quarterly*, Volume 36, 1945.

O'Donnell, Terence. *An Arrow in the Earth*. Portland: Oregon Historical Society Press, 1991.

Parnell, William R. "Operations Against Hostile Indians with General George Crook, 1867-68." *The Journal of the Modoc County Historical Society*. No. 1, 1979.

Perras, Galen Roger. "Who Will Defend British Columbia? Unity of Command on the West Coast, 1934-1942," *Pacific Northwest Quarterly*, Volume 88, Number 2, Spring 1997.

Polenberg, Richard. *War and Society: The United States, 1941-1945*. Philadelphia: J. B. Lippencott, 1972.

Prosch, Thomas W. "The Indian War in Washington Territory," *Oregon Historical Society Quarterly*, March 1915.

Reese, J.W. "OMV's Fort Henrietta: On Winter Duty, 1855-56," *Oregon Historical Quarterly*. June 1965.

Richards, Kent D. Isaac I. *Stevens: Young Man in a Hurry*. Pullman: Washington State University Press, 1993.

Richardson, David. "The Old Ship's Log Reveals the Story Behind the Port Gamble Incident," *Seattle Times*, April 2, 1967.

Rickey, Don Jr. *Forty Miles a Day on Beans and Hay*. Norman: University of Oklahoma Press, 1963.

Riddle, Jeff C. *The Indian History of the Modoc War*. San Jose: Urion Press, 1998.

Rigge, Simon. *War in the Outposts*. Morristown: Time-Life Books, 1981.

Ronda, James P. *Astoria & Empire*. Lincoln: University of Nebraska Press, 1990.

Robertson, R. G. Competitive Struggle. *America's Western Fur Trading Posts, 1745-1865*. Boise: Tamarack Books, 1999.

Ross, Alexander. *The Fur Hunters of the Far West*. London: Smith, Elder, and Co., 1855.

——. *Adventures of the First Settlers on the Oregon or Columbia River*. London: Smith, Elder, and Co., 1849.

Rowe, Mary Ellen. "The Early History of Fort George Wright: Black Infantrymen and Theodore Roosevelt in Spokane," *Pacific Northwest Quarterly*, Volume 80, Number 3, July 1985.

Ruby, Robert H., and John A. Brown. *The Cayuse Indians, Imperial Tribesmen of Old Oregon*. Norman: University of Oklahoma Press, 1972.

——. *A Guide to the Indian Tribes of the Pacific Northwest*. Norman: University of Oklahoma Press, 1986

——. *Indians of the Pacific Northwest*. Norman: University of Oklahoma Press, 1981.

Russell, Don. *One Hundred and Three Fights and Scrimmages: The Story of General Reuben F. Bernard*. Washington: United States Cavalry Association, 1936.

Sanford, George B. *Fighting Rebels and Redskins*. Norman: University of Oklahoma Press, 1969.

Santee, J.F. "Pio-Pio-Mox-Mox," *Oregon Historical Quarterly*, June 1933.

Saum, Lewis O. "The Western Volunteer and the new Empire," *Pacific Northwest Quarterly*, Volume 57, Number 1, January 1966.

——. "The Schooner Shark's Cannon," *CUMTUX Clatsop County Historical Society Quarterly*. Summer 1989.

Schlesser, Norman Dennis. *Bastion of Empire: Fort Umpqua*. Oakland: Oakland Printing Co., 1973.

Schlicke, Carl P. General George Wright: Guardian of the Pacific. Norman: University of Oklahoma Press, 1988.

Schwantes, Carlos Arnaldo. *The Pacific Northwest: An Interpretive History.* Lincoln: University of Nebraska Press, 1989.

Schwartz, E.A. *The Rogue River Indian Wars and its Aftermath, 1850-1980.* Norman: University of Oklahoma Press, 1997.

Scott, Leslie M. "Indian Diseases as Aids to Pacific Northwest Settlements," *Oregon Historical Quarterly*, 1928.

Shannon, Donald H. *The Utter Disaster on the Oregon Trail.* Caldwell: Snake Country Publishing, 1993.

Sheridan, Philip H. *Indian Fighting in the Fifties in Oregon and Washington Territories.* Fairfield: Ye Galleon Press, 1987.

Shine, Gregory Paynter. "Respite from War. Buffalo Soldiers at Vancouver Barracks, 1899-1900," *Oregon Historical Quarterly.* Summer 2006.

Sims, Robert C. "A Fearless Patriotic, Clean-cut Stand," *Pacific Northwest Quarterly*, Volume 70, Number 2, April 1979.

Sinclair, Donna L. "Our Manifest Destiny Bids Fair for Fulfillment: An Historical Overview of Vancouver Barracks, 1846-1898, with suggestions for further research," Unpublished document, National Park Service, 1999.

Smith, Jean Edwards. *Grant.* New York: Simon and Schuster, 2001.

Smith, Robert Barr. "Battle of Pierre's Hole," *Wild West Magazine.* April, 1999.

Splawn, A J. *Ka-Mi-Akin: The Last Hero of the Yakimas.* Portland: Binfords and Mort, 1944.

Stern, Theodore. *The Klamath Tribe.* Seattle: University of Washington Press, 1965.

Stevens, Isaac Ingalls. *A True Copy of the Record of the Official Proceedings at the Council in the Walla Walla Valley 1855.* Fairfield: Ye Galleon Press, 1996.

Stone, Buena Cobb. *Old Fort Klamath.* Medford: Pacific Northwest Book Company, 1990.

Symonds, Craig L. *Historical Atlas of the U.S. Navy.* Annapolis: The Naval Institute, 1995.

Thompson, H. C. "Oregon Volunteer Reminiscences of the War with Spain." *Oregon Historical Quarterly*, September 1948.

——. "War Without Medals," *Oregon Historical Quarterly*, December 1958.

Trenholm, Virginia Cole, and Maurine Carley. *The Shoshonis: Sentinels of the Rockies.* Norman: University of Oklahoma Press, 1964.

Underwood, Amos. "Reminiscences of the Cayuse War," *Skamania County Heritage.* June 1986.

United States National Park Service. Nez Perce National Historical Park: *Guide to Sites.*

Utley, Robert M. *A Life Wild and Perilous*. New York: Henry Holt and Company, 1997.

———. *Frontier Regulars: The United States Army and the Indian, 1866-1891*. Lincoln: University of Nebraska Press, 1973.

———. *Frontiersmen in Blue*. Lincoln: University of Nebraska Press, 1967.

———, and Washburn, W. *American Heritage Library of Indian Battles*. Boston: Houghton Mifflin, 1977.

Victor, Frances Fuller. "The First Oregon Cavalry," *Oregon Historical Quarterly*. June 1902.

Walsh, Frank K. *Indian Battles Along the Rogue River, 1855-56*. North Bend: Te-Cum-Tom Publications, 1986.

Warren, James R. *The War Years: A Chronicle of Washington State in World War II*. Seattle: University of Washington Press, 2000.

Webber, Bert. *Silent Siege-III*. Medford: Webb Research Group, 2001.

Whiting, J.S. *Forts of the State of Washington*. Seattle: Kelly Printing, 1951.

Wiegand, Wayne A. "Oregon Public Libraries during the First World War," *Oregon Historical Quarterly*. March 1989.

Wilcox, W.P. "Anti-Chinese Riots in Washington," *Washington Historical Quarterly*, Volume XX, Number 3, July 1929.

Wilson, Nancy. *Dr. John McLoughlin: Master of Fort Vancouver, Father of Oregon*. Medford: Webb Research Group, 1994.

Yenne, Bill. *Indian Wars: The Campaign for the American West*. Yardley: Westholme Publishing, 2006.

Web Sites

"A Place Called Oregon-Cayuse Indian War 1848." http://gesswhoto.com/cayuse.html (June 1, 2002).

"The Applegate Trail." www.webtrail.com/applegate/ (December 10, 2006).

"First to respond to their country's call': The First Montana Infantry and the Spanish-American War and Philippine Insurrection, 1898-1899." www.findarticles.com/p/articles/mi_qa3951/is_200210/ ai_n9085574 (September 30, 2006).

"John Jacob Astor." http://en.wikipedia.org/wiki/John_Jacob_Astor. (December 9, 2006).

"The Oregon Trail." www.endoftheoregontrail.org/road2oregon/ (December 10, 2006).

"Pacific memories: Montana National guardsmen recall the fighting on New Guinea in World War II." Montana: The Magazine of Western History, Summer 2002, by O'Neil, Carle F. www.findarticles.com/p/articles/mi_qa3951/is_200207/ai_n9146548 (September 30, 2006).

"The Sinking of the Tuscania." www.worldwar1.com/dbc/tuscania. htm (November 12, 2006).

www.historylink.org "Army and National Guard Troops Hold American Lake Maneuvers Beginning on July 1, 1904," *The Online Encyclopedia of Washington State History*. October 30, 2006.

www.historylink.org "Battleship U.S.S. Arizona rams and sinks purse seiner off Cape Flattery, killing two on July 26, 1934," *The Online Encyclopedia of Washington State History*. October 30, 2006.

www.historylink.org "Buffalo Soldiers are stationed at Fort Lawton beginning on October 5, 1909," *The Online Encyclopedia of Washington State History*. October 30, 2006.

www.historylink.org "Construction of massive plutonium production complex at Hanford begins in March 1943," *The Online Encyclopedia of Washington State History*. October 30, 2006.

www.historylink.org "1st Washington Volunteer Infantry Regiment musters for the Spanish-American War on May 1, 1898," *The Online Encyclopedia of Washington State History*. October 30, 2006.

www.historylink.org "Fort Lawton is established on February 9, 1900," *The Online Encyclopedia of Washington State History*. October 30, 2006.

www.historylink.org "Japanese incendiary balloons land in Washington beginning on February 12, 1945," *The Online Encyclopedia of Washington State History*. October 30, 2006.

www.historylink.org "Japanese submarine shells Fort Stevens at the mouth of the Columbia River on June 21, 1942," The Online Encyclopedia of Washington State History. October 30, 2006.

www.historylink.org "Japanese submarine torpedoes and shells the freighter Fort Camosun off Cape Flattery on June 20, 1942," *The Online Encyclopedia of Washington State History*. October 30, 2006.

www.historylink.org "Japanese submarine sinks the SS Coast Trader on June 7, 1942," *The Online Encyclopedia of Washington State History*. October 30, 2006.

www.historylink.org "Kaiser shipyard in Vancouver launches its first escort air-craft carrier on April 5, 1943," The Online Encyclopedia of Washington State History. October 30, 2006.

www.historylink.org "Navy planes torpedo and sink the U.S.S. Crow in Puget Sound on August 23, 1943," *The Online Encyclopedia of Washington State History*. October 30, 2006.

www.historylink.org "Riot involving African-Americans soldiers occurs at Fort Lawton and an Italian POW is lynched on August 14, 1944," *The Online Encyclopedia of Washington State History*. October 30, 2006.

www.historylink.org "Seattle mob rounds up Chinese residents and immigrant workers on February 7, 1886," *The Online Encyclopedia of Washington State History*. October 30, 2006.

www.historylink.org "Spanish American War volunteers return to Seattle on November 6, 1899." *The Online Encyclopedia of Washington State History*. October 30, 2006.

www.historylink.org "U.S. Army flyers depart Sand Point Airfield for first aerial circumnavigation of the globe on April 6, 1924," *The Online Encyclopedia of Washington State History*. October 30, 2006.

www.historylink.org "U.S.S. *Lexington* provides electricity to Tacoma beginning about December 17, 1929," *The Online Encyclopedia of Washington State History*. October 30, 2006.

www.historylink.org "U.S.S. *Oregon* is first battleship to dock at Puget Sound Naval Shipyard in Bremerton on April 11, 1897," *The Online Encyclopedia of Washington State History*. October 30, 2006.

www.washingtonarmyguard.com?96TC/248th/sponsor/history.htm   Untitled. September 30, 2006.

www.spanamwar.com/2ndoregon.htm Untitled. September 30, 2006.

spanishamericanwar.com/2ndOregonVolunteers.htm Untitled. September 30, 2006.

www.globalsecurity.org/military/agency/army/arng-or.htm Untitled. September 30, 2006.

Index

Acknowledgements

The list of individuals to acknowledge is always great, and I am sure incomplete. Yet, some names easily come to mind. As a friend, an educator, and an editor, Larry LaBeck made my writing better. I am deeply appreciative of his patience, his efforts, and his time. Mel Ivey helped with some proof-reading, and as a friend, he helped with encouragement. For unwavering support and encouragement, Al Cardwell is without peer, and I count myself rich indeed to have such a friend as Al. I also want to acknowledge a great teacher, Professor Jim Heath, retired from Portland State University. If I have success with history, it was from his teaching. If I have any failures, it is my failure as a student, and not his as a teacher. Bruce H. Franklin's enthusiasm for this project has made it a pleasure, as well as an adventure, and I thank him and his staff at Westholme Publishing as well.

My biggest supporter, first proof-reader, patient friend, and best cheerleader is my wife, Sandi, and without her, nothing would ever have gotten done.

To the others I have failed to mention, thank you.